DEVELOPING EUROPEAN REGIONS?

For Neil

Developing European Regions?

Comparative governance, policy networks and European integration

MAURA ADSHEAD
University of Limerick

Ashgate

Published by
Ashgate Publishing Limited
Gower House
Croft Road
Aldershot
Hants GU11 3HR
England

Ashgate Publishing Company
131 Main Street
Burlington, VT 05401-5600 USA

Ashgate website: http://www.ashgate.com

British Library Cataloguing in Publication Data
Adshead, Maura
Developing European regions? : comparative governance, policy networks and European integration
1. Regional planning - Germany 2. Regional planning - Ireland 3. Regional planning - England 4. Germany - Politics and government - 1990- 5. Ireland - Politics and government - 1949- 6. Great Britain - Politics and government - 1997- 7. Europe - Economic integration
I. Title
321'.023'094

Library of Congress Control Number: 2001099225

ISBN 0 7546 1965 6

Printed and bound by Athenaeum Press, Ltd.,
Gateshead, Tyne & Wear.

Contents

List of Tables

Acknowledgements

The best thing about writing a book is the opportunity it affords to publicly acknowledge the help and support of all the people who contributed to its completion. At the outset, Brigid Laffan provided practical support and encouragement towards the doctoral work that forms the basis of this book. Thereafter, I worked up a series of debts in Britain, Ireland and Germany. A generous studentship from the University of Liverpool, together with grants from the Royal Irish Academy, the British Council and the German Academic Exchange Service (DAAD) ensured that none of these debts were financial. In Ireland, Nick Rees and Brid Quinn from the University of Limerick shared information, interviews and obscure references. Eddie Glacken of the Irish Trade Union Trust was extremely helpful in setting up interviews with the 'great and the good' in Dublin - and all for no reward. Especial thanks to Joe and Joan O'Kelly who helped me out no end by securing my Irish accommodation and to John Logan, who bent over backwards to secure me time to finish this book. In Germany, Susan Morrissey and Hubertas Jahn, on nothing but the most tenuous of connections, fed and found me, helped with tricky translations, gave of their fax, email and time (and most important of all, their cheese). Rainer Heck and Claudia Rauschen offered more technical support and a refreshing *Kur* whenever it was needed. Andrea Terstappen helped to arrange interviews and gave me the secret for the best *Frikadellen*. Herr and Frau Karl Heinz-Fabig made me so welcome, so often, in their guest house, that it began to feel like a second home. In Britain, Sahra Ryklief showed me all the good places to eat and drink in Liverpool (which is much harder than you might think). David and Antonia Phinnemore shared their home, a passion for 'funny beer' and fresh bagels with the newspapers every Sunday. Helen and Jim Leslie looked after me in Dundee and Daniel O'Kelly was especially helpful in organizing the transport for all of my interviews. Finally, as is the tradition with these things, I leave the biggest 'thank-you's and the greatest debts of gratitude to the last. Thank-you to mum and dad for enthusiastic support throughout this study. Thank-you to Stephen Padgett (and Maria too) for offering me a scholarship in Liverpool and for putting up with me thereafter. Last, but by no means least, thank-you to Neil Robinson for all good stuff. It's hard to know what to give to a man to whom you've given more or less everything already - but surely a book on European regions will make your life complete.

Chapter 1

The Re-ordering of Governance and European Integration: A Framework for Analysis

Introduction

Across Europe, the process of policy change has been beset by developments along two dimensions. The first, or vertical dimension, refers to the shifting levels of policy authority and influence between international, national, regional and even local levels of government or administration. The second, or horizontal dimension, refers to the shifting competencies of policy actors and agencies arising as a consequence of new interpretations of government's role in the organization and administration of public policy. The so-called 'Europeanization' of state policy processes, associated with the increasing involvement of the EU in domestic policy is central to both dimensions of policy change. The transnational policy cooperation encouraged and facilitated by the European Union policy making framework, combined with EU initiatives to increase its accountability and legitimacy through direct cooperation with policy partners at national, regional and local levels not only raises important questions about the shifting levels of policy authority, but also about the changing configuration of key policy making actors and agencies at each level.

Whilst the significance of European integration to the process of policy change is widely accepted, there is still no commonly accepted methodology with which to approach empirical study. Cross-national differences in the policy environment are reflected in variations in the way European integration impacts on policy at domestic level, creating problems for comparative analysis. This research employs a distinctive methodology designed to overcome some of the problems associated with cross-national comparison. Using policy network analysis as a neutral heuristic device to provide comparative characterizations of cross-national policy making processes, the methodology provides a framework to evaluate propositions from the literature on multi-level governance about the shifting levels of policy authority and changing configuration of policy actors assumed to be part of the integration process.

Since the multi-level governance literature provides no concrete expectations about the precise working out of its generalized propositions about the process of European integration, this research methodology applies neofunctionalist expectations about the effects of European integration on the networks of actors involved in the policy process. Assuming that the presence of multi-level governance correlates with the process of European integration, it uses Lindberg's (1963:6) definition of integration to outline the process by which multi-level governance emerges in different policy networks. It hypothesises Lindberg's four integration propositions as evidence of positive integration in policy networks and assumes that the higher the incidence of positive integration indicators, the higher the level of integration (or, more precisely, the extent of multi-level governance) between policy actors and institutions in the network.

The capacity of Lindberg's neofunctionalist integration theory to explain change in policy networks *occurring as a consequence of EU involvement in policy* lies in the clarity with which it defines the integration process. For Lindberg, the process of European integration has four main dimensions. First, it concerns the institutional development that accompanies EU involvement in the policy process. A second dimension is the re-orientation of elite behaviour and attitudes towards the EU. A third expectation is that national governments should demonstrate increasing support for EU involvement in policy. Finally, Lindberg's main legacy is the concept of functional and political spillover. These propositions are modified for use with policy network analysis in order to determine the extent of European integration in selected regional policy networks.

This study focuses on the constellation of interests that gather around EU regional policy programmes in Objective One areas in Germany, Ireland and Britain.[1] It shows how the configuration of alternative policy networks are determined by the specific institutional and political policy environments pertaining in each state and how the impact of European integration is both determined by and helps determine alternative network configurations. In doing so, it provides a comparative evaluation of the impact of European integration in one policy area across different EU states.

Objective One regions are significant in that they have been prioritized by the European Commission for EU Structural Funds assistance, subject to certain conditions relating to policy implementation. They thus make particularly good case studies since they are able to embrace both horizontal and vertical aspects of policy change. At national level, they illustrate relations between the state and sub-national government. At sub-national level, they allow an examination of relations between traditional local government and a range of new actors and agencies introduced into the policy process as a consequence of changing patterns in governance. Finally, given the extensive role of EU Structural Funding in Objective One regions, they facilitate an evaluation of relations between each of the above actors and the European Union.

The remainder of this chapter outlines how new patterns of governance described above have been characterized in European integration and comparative politics literatures and illustrates how the development of EU regional policy is a striking exemplar of alleged shifts in governance. It explores the different approaches used to characterize the influence of the European Union over policy making processes in different states and argues that traditional approaches to the study of European integration are limited by their tendency to concentrate their efforts on a single level of analysis. As a consequence little attention is given to the relationship between international, national and sub-national levels of the policy process. Although the concept of multi-level governance addresses this shortcoming, this approach is also flawed since it provides no clear methodology for analysis. This chapter addresses the methodological problems of comparative analysis and evaluates the utility of network analysis as a means of providing neutral concepts for the comparison of different policy making processes. Finally, it provides an outline of the research design that underpins this study.

European integration theory and the 'governance turn'

The apparent revival in European integration begun in the mid to late 1980s - signalled by the substantive economic, political and institutional changes in the SEA, the resolution of significant EC budgetary difficulties, the appointment of Jacques Delors as Commission President and moves towards economic and political union in the Maastricht Treaty - brought about a revival of academic interest in the process of European integration (Rosamund, 2000:98-128). Most significantly, the 1990s witnessed an increasing trend amongst EU scholars to incorporate analytic tools and concepts from other mainstream branches of political science and policy analysis into European integration studies (Hix, 1994, 1996). One consequence of this development was that, generally speaking, EU studies became less concerned with the grandiose questions about the future direction of European integration and more focused upon pertinent questions in political science *as applied to the EU*. Perhaps chief amongst these was the widespread and substantive interrogation of the newly emerging 'governance' concept.

Although 'governance' has become a 'popular if not trendy concept in much of the contemporary political and academic debate' (Pierre and

Peters, 2000:12), still a uniform definition remains illusive. In the field of public policy, Rhodes (1996) uses the term 'governance' to refer to a change in the meaning of government. Central to this depiction of change is the idea of policy networks. Rhodes argues that changes in government have led to the development of 'governance as self-organizing networks' whereby 'the state becomes a collection of inter-organizational networks made up of governmental and societal actors with no sovereign actor able to steer or regulate' (Rhodes, 1996:666). He argues that 'as British government creates agencies, bypasses local government, uses special purpose bodies to deliver services, and encourages public-private partnerships, so networks become increasingly prominent among British government structures' (Rhodes, 1996:658). The decreasing role of government in public service provision and the increasing involvement of alternative actors and agencies has been characterized by Rhodes as 'the new governance'.

Many of the trends Rhodes' identifies in the UK are apparent, to greater or lesser degrees, in other west European states. Wallace notes that 'although the UK may be an extreme case, the reduction of public functions and of the citizen's dependence on the state has become a common theme of political debates and public policy in many west European countries' (Wallace, 1993:294). In the fields of international relations and comparative politics, Eising and Kohler-Koch (1999:03) argue that governance has become a central focus of research because 'authoritative allocation takes place without or outside government' (see also: Rosenau and Czempiel, 1992). Increasing and more widespread use of the term governance to characterize these developments suggests that it is a useful metaphor in reference to a range of common trends occurring within and throughout EU states.

In European integration studies, Stone Sweet and Sandholtz's (1997; Sandholtz and Stone Sweet, 1998) theory of supranational governance pays close attention to the role of transnational exchange in creating demand for European level regulation and governance capacity. They argue that the institutionalization of transnational exchange feeds into both supply and demand side pressures for integration (see also Wessels, 1992). In this interpretation of European integration, the emphasis is on the development of *supranational* elements to European governance. Eising and Kohler-Koch's (1999; also: Kohler-Koch, 1996, 1997) theory of network governance in the European Union proposes that the development of the EU is best understood as an exercise in *system building*, involving the transformation of European governance from a 'compound of member states, into an overarching transnational political space' (Kohler-Koch, 1999:19). Here, emphasis is given to the segmented and differentiated aspects of the European polity at national and sub-national levels and their capacity for congruent development.

Finally, perhaps the most widely known deployment of the governance concept in European integration studies is in Marks and Hooghe's development of Multi-Level Governance theory (Marks, Hooghe and Blank, 1996; Marks, Nielsen, Ray and Salk, 1996). Multi-Level governance analysis is based on three main assumptions. First, decision-making competencies are *shared* by actors at different levels rather than monopolized by state executives. Second, collective decision-making between member states implies some loss of control by individual state executives. And third, political arenas are interconnected rather than nested. The multi-level governance literature seeks to avoid two traps: state centrism and the treatment of the EU as only operating at the European level in the institutional arena of Brussels and Strasbourg (Rosamund, 2000:110). Thus, whilst multi level governance theorists do not reject the notion that state executives and state arenas are 'the most important pieces of the European puzzle', they nevertheless assert that states have lost their monopoly - both over European policy-making and over the aggregation of domestic interests (Marks, Hooghe and Blank, 1996:346). Essentially then, multi-level governance theory presents a means of acknowledging the multi-layered and complex nature of the EU system, whilst synthesizing intergovernmentalist and institutionalist approaches.

Rosamund (2000:105) argues that this shift in attention, away from the traditional 'theoretical joust between neofunctionalists and intergovernmentalists' has facilitated the exploration of a wider range of issues in European studies, suggesting that one clear outcome of so-called 'governance turn' in EU studies has been the widespread disposal of 'grand theory' and the migration of theoretical work to the 'middle range' (Rosamund, 2000:126). Where once European studies were focused more or less exclusively on the cause, direction and pace of 'the integration project', attention is now focused much more clearly on the shape and substance of *new processes of governing* associated with the 'transformation of governance'. This changed nuance in integration studies still recognises the central questions: what is the EU? and how does it impact on member states? but the teleological dimension to change is largely absent. Instead, the EU is increasingly viewed as a complex polity - a mass of parts that must all be understood. Evidence of this trend can be found in a rash of studies attempting to explain the foundations of the EU polity at the sectoral and/or state level of analysis. Analysis of the evolution of the European Single Market is a notable case in point, but there are plenty of others.

Perhaps more than any other area, the Single Market and more specifically its foundations in the Single European Act, has been subject to analysis from a variety of alternative standpoints - laying emphasis on the roles of supranational and transnational actors (Sandholtz and Zysman, 1989; Cameron, 1995), interstate bargaining (Putnam, 1988; Moravcsik, 1991, 1998) and institutions (Armstrong and Bulmer, 1998; Pierson, 1996) respectively. In other areas, *network analysis* has become increasingly popular as a means of characterizing the EU policy process (Heritier, 1993) and has been used to interpret EU involvement in agriculture (Adshead, 1996; Collins, 1995; Daugbjerg, 1997, 1999), the environment (Bomberg, 1994, 1998), regional policy (Bache, 1998; Hooghe, 1996; Marks, Hooghe *et al*, 1996; Marks, Nielsen *et al*, 1996), research and development (Peterson, 1994), social policy (Falkner, 1999) and telecommunications (Fuchs, 1994).

The rising tide of network analysis in EU studies points to the obvious heuristic utility of policy network models for studies of EU policy-making. By their nature, policy network models are able to portray the intricacy of newly emerging governance systems in the EU. They are able to highlight the interactions and 'networking' between different types of policy interests at supranational, national and increasingly sub-national levels of government; within the public and private spheres; and at the interface between traditional government institutions and actors, and increasingly significant new governance institutions and actors (such as quangos, para-public bodies and various associations from civil society). In doing so, studies of the EU using network analysis are able to contribute to and help support interpretations of the EU polity as multi-level governance. Indeed, the proliferation of these studies supports 'a growing convergence among international relations and comparative scholars conceptualizing the EU as a multi-level structure of governance where private, governmental, transnational and supranational actors deal with each other in highly complex networks of varying density, as well as horizontal and vertical depth' (Risse-Kappen, 1996:62).

The governance idea is particularly apposite to EU policy studies because it captures both vertical and horizontal dimensions of change: the former referring to shifting levels of policy authority and influence between international, national, regional and even local levels of government and administration; and the latter referring to the shifting competencies of policy actors and agencies arising as a consequence of new interpretations of government's role in the organization and administration of public policy. The so-called 'Europeanization' of state policy processes associated with increasing involvement of the EU in domestic policy processes is central to both dimensions of policy change.

This research seeks to marry the vertical and horizontal aspects of policy change described in the governance literatures with the analytical tools provided by policy networks. It presents a comparative evaluation of the precise working out of alleged shifts in governance with a view to understanding the nature and extent of the European Union's involvement in these processes. In order to illustrate these developments, this study is concerned with a comparative examination of regional development strategies in European Union Objective One regions in Britain, Ireland and Germany. Through a cross-national comparison of regional development strategies and the types of policy networks with which they are associated, this study examines the relationship between alternative network types and differing levels of European integration. The remainder of this chapter is centred around a discussion of the difficulties encountered comparing policy making processes in different states and attempting to account for the influence of the European Union in these processes. Before embarking on this discussion, however, it is worth outlining the re-ordering of governance structures in EU regional policy, which form the backdrop to this research.

The re-ordering of governance structures in EU regional policy

The increasing involvement of the European Union in the development of European regions is one of the clearest examples of transnational policy cooperation outlined above. Since the first substantive reform of EU regional policy in 1988, there has been a steady and significant increase in the resources of the Structural Funds. In 1987 they comprised approximately Ecu7,000 million and represented about 19% of the Community budget (CEC, 1992). In February 1988, the European Council agreed to double the funding for priority regions by 1992 (in real terms taking account of inflation) and it was anticipated that the Structural Funds would account for one quarter of the EU budget by the end of 1993 (CEC, 1992). In fact (largely due to reductions in Common Agricultural policy expenditure) during the period 1987-1992 Structural Funds expenditure increased from 17% of the Community budget to 27%, with the absolute amount doubling in real terms from ECU6.3 billion in 1987 to ECU14.1 billion in 1993 (Michie and Fitzgerald, 1997:19).

Following the European Council meeting in Maastricht in December 1991, it was agreed that EU regional policy should be further developed. This led ultimately to the addition of a protocol to the Maastricht Treaty reaffirming states' commitment to economic and social cohesion and confirming the development of EU Structural Funds. It also resulted in the creation of an additional Structural Fund (the Financial Instrument for Fisheries Guidance or FIFG) to support the fisheries sector plus a further increase in the budgetary commitment. Structural Funds assistance (including the FIFG and excluding the new Scandinavian member states) for the period 1994-99 amounted to ECU141, 471 billion, with approximately 68% of this allocation given over to Objective One regions. The total budget for Structural Funds assistance during the period 2000-06 amounts to €195 billion with a similar percentage devoted to Objective One regions (*Europa*, 29/02/00). In addition to the increasing financial significance of EU Structural Funds, successive reforms have developed their administrative impact as well.

In the 1988 reform, five Structural Funds objectives were set in order of priority: Objective One promoting the development and structural adjustment of the regions lagging behind (ERDF); Objective two, tackling those regions (frontier regions or parts of regions) seriously affected by industrial decline (ERDF, ESF); Objective three, combating long-term unemployment (ESF); Objective four, facilitating the occupational integration of young people (ESF); Objective five, contributing to the reform of the Common Agricultural policy by speeding up the restructuring of agricultural production and promoting the development of rural areas (EAGGF, ERDF, and ESF). These objectives sought to add a new coherence to the distribution of Structural Funds. Instead of each fund having its own set of rules and priorities, the deployment of Structural Funds was combined to concentrate their efforts on the achievement of the five overall objectives. This system of coordination was intended to prevent either the overlapping of resources by different funds being deployed independently in the same area, or the waste of resources that might occur if the funds were spread too thinly, attempting too many objectives, in too large an area.

In addition to establishing and prioritizing development objectives, six new guidelines governing the administration of Structural Funds were also introduced (CEC, 1988):

1. The submission of plans by member states in accordance with the priority objectives set out by the Community.
2. The implementation of *partnerships* between competent authorities at national, regional and local levels.
3. The need to demonstrate the *additionality* of Community support and policy measures to those pertaining nationally.
4. The *compatibility* of structural policy with other Community policies.
5. The *concentration* of resources, with particular emphasis on the least prosperous regions.
6. The *coordination* and combination of different Community instruments.

Throughout this period, in order to avoid unnecessary problems of administration and implementation, the Commission attempted to move further towards the financing of *programmes* in preference to individual projects. Under the reformed procedures, each assisted region has to submit an overall development plan, prioritizing areas for action and detailing the specific plans to combat regional disadvantage through use of Union funding. Within six months of the plan's submission, the Commission adopts a Community Support Framework (CSF), giving the official EU response to the submission and commenting on its aims and objectives. The CSF enables the EU to establish an agreed framework for assistance over a four year period, with built-in provision for monitoring and evaluation of the programmes at the end of each project. Under the CSF, each region is required to submit more detailed information in the form of 'operational programmes'. The final stage in this process entails interaction and exchange of views between the Commission and national agencies.

The adoption of a programmatic approach to allocating the funds has enabled the Commission to operate its *partnership principle* more effectively, whilst facilitating its role in managing the deployment of Structural Funds for the attainment of Union objectives. 'Partnership' is defined as 'close consultations between the Commission, the member states concerned and the competent authorities designated by the latter at national, regional or local level, with each party acting as a partner in pursuit of a common goal' (CEC, 1988). Under the partnership principle, national authorities are given delegated discretion to select appropriate members of partnerships. It is assumed that the best chance of development will occur if the impetus comes from within the regions themselves. Those based at local level are judged to be in a better position to define the needs of their region and to mobilize its resources through the interaction of private and public funding. The Commission acts as the partner on behalf of the Union, ensuring that the Union's resources are spent in accordance with Union priorities and policies.

The principle of *additionality* states that EU funds should not be used as a substitute for funding from national sources. The desire for *compatibility* refers to the need to ensure that all Union policies and initiatives should be working towards the same overall goals. For example, projects seeking financial support for rural development must also be consistent with efforts to adapt the CAP to avoid over-production. The principles of *concentration* and *coordination* refer to the desire to achieve integrated, long-term and strategic planning. Efforts to help weaker regions should be made with a view to understanding their situation as a whole and with particular emphasis on the concentration of Structural Funds resources in disadvantaged areas in order to achieve maximum impact. Thus, for example, there would be little point in supporting the building of a new factory in an area where there is no ready supply of locally skilled and trained personnel to work in it. In order to prevent this, Structural Funds instruments must be both concentrated and coordinated in target regions. Taken together, the new procedures offer a more coordinated approach to the allocation of funding, together with significantly increased opportunities for interaction between national and Union agencies.

During the negotiations over the Draft Treaty on European Union (the Maastricht Treaty), the Spanish government argued for a new compensatory mechanism in addition to the Structural Funds (Bache, 1998:88). With Irish, Greek and Portuguese support, the Spanish argued for additional resources to tackle ongoing regional disparities across the Community. Their chief success was the establishment of the Cohesion Fund. At the Edinburgh European Council in 1992, it was agreed to set aside Ecu 15.15 billion for the Cohesion Fund to be allocated during the period 1993-99. The additional Structural Funds assistance, together with the new Cohesion Fund, amounted to a doubling of EU aid in real terms for the four Cohesion member states of Greece, Ireland, Portugal and Spain. The administrative amendments made to the operation of the Structural Funds during the 1993 reform were, however, fairly minimal and concerned the establishment of new eligibility criteria, programming periods and EU administrative procedures (Michie and Fitzgerald, 1997:20). Regulations regarding Structural Funds implementation continued to be based on the principle guidelines - of planning, partnership, additionality, compatibility, concentration and coordination - set out by the 1988 reforms (Bache, 1998: 83-92).

In June 1999, the General Affairs Council formally adopted the new structural fund regulations. The same meeting also adopted the regulations for the Cohesion Fund and the Pre-accession structural instrument (ISPA). Financial allocations to the structural funds were set at €195 billion over the period 2000-2006, with a further €18 billion provided for the Cohesion Fund (CEC, 1999). In addition, €7.28 billion was set aside for pre-accession structural assistance to applicant states. Total funding under these measures remained at 0.46 of EU GNP over the period (CEC, 1999).

The guiding principles proposed by the Commission were accepted. On *concentration*, this meant that the number of structural fund Objectives would be reduced from six to three. In addition, the number of *Community Initiatives* would be substantially reduced from the existing thirteen.[2] The Commission had proposed three Initiatives: Interreg (cross border, transnational and inter-regional cooperation); Leader (rural development); and Equal (tackling discrimination in the labour market). However, at the insistence of the European Parliament, a fourth programme (Urban) was retained to regenerate inner cities. The *programming* process was retained, with the Commission adopting a more strategic role by delegating more responsibility to domestic actors for the day-to-day implementation and monitoring of programmes. The re-worded *partnership* principle required the involvement of organizations that reflected the 'need to promote equality between men and women and sustainable development through the integration of environmental protection and improvement requirements' (OJ L161, 26/6/99: 12). The principle of *additionality* was maintained, although its verification would depend on baseline figures of domestic spending that member state governments would be play a key role in determining. Finally, in line with the principle of *efficiency*, a performance reserve was agreed by member states. This was limited, however, to four per cent of each member state's share of funding, rather than the ten per cent the Commission had proposed (Bache, 1998: 120-133).

In agreeing to these reforms, European states have tacitly shifted some policy authority to the European level of government. Moreover, implementation of the Structural Funds reform principles further contributes to shifting patterns of governance within states: relating to changing relations between central and sub-national levels of government; and also between the variety of new actors and agencies involved in public/private partnerships as a consequence of changing trends in government. In this respect, the European Union itself represents yet one more actor in an increasingly complex policy arena. The multi-layered process of EU regional policy, involving policy actors at European, national and sub-national levels of government has been characterized by some as the advent of *multi-level governance* (Hooghe, 1996; Marks, Nielsen *et al*, 1996).

Referring to the shifting patterns of policy making authority and competencies between different levels of government and administration, the propositions of multi-level governance literature tend, however, to focus more on vertical - as opposed to horizontal - dimensions of policy change. This is because the multi-level governance literature provides no clear expectations about how the changes they identify in the policy process are worked out in detail at respective levels of analysis. The difficulty of embracing different levels of analysis in accounts of EU influence over policy is dealt with more substantively in the following section, which evaluates alternative approaches to the study of the EU and European integration.

Accounting for the role of the European Union in state policy making

Until recently, there were two main schools of thought regarding the influence of the European Union on national policy making: those whose accounts emphasized the importance of intergovernmentalism in their explanations (Bulmer, 1983; Lange, 1992; Moravcsik, 1991, 1993; Putnam, 1988) and those whose accounts placed more emphasis on institutionalism. Proponents of this latter group of approaches, which includes historical institutionalism (Pierson, 1996), new institutionalism (Armstrong and Bulmer, 1995; Bulmer, 1994a, 1994b), functionalism and neo-functionalism (Deutsch, 1954, 1957; Haas, 1958a, 1958b; Lindberg, 1963, 1965, 1966; Lindberg and Scheingold, 1970; 1966; North, Koch *et al*, 1960), are distinguished by their willingness to depict the European Union as a much more complex and pluralistic political structure, less firmly under member state control than is suggested by inter-governmentalist accounts of the EU.

In fact, there is nothing to suggest that these processes are mutually exclusive, though a greater emphasis on one over another is the traditional distinction between competing approaches to the study of European integration. These approaches may be differentiated by their assumptions about where the origins of influence lie when policy changes as a consequence of EU involvement. Intergovernmentalist approaches typically attempt to assess the extent to which different states or state policy actors avail of opportunities to change policy processes that arise as a consequence of EU involvement in the policy area. In this case, the chief cause of policy change and hence the predominant source of influence over policy is the state. Intergovernmentalist approaches, because of their assumptions about the sovereignty and importance of states, tend to view the occurrence of integration between EU and state actors as a *consequence of state action*. However, since European integration is regarded as a consequence of more important 'games' being observed (ie. state strategies and policy intention both towards other states and the EU), it is not rigorously defined. State-centred or intergovernmentalist approaches to the study of the EU identify a cause of European integration, but because it is not their primary focus of attention, they provide no adequate account of it.

Institutionalist approaches, on the other hand, tend to assess the extent of the impact that European Union institutions, decision-making procedures and rules have upon different state policy making processes. In this case, the chief cause of policy change and hence the predominant source of influence over policy is the European Union. Institutionalist approaches to the study of the EU, such as historical and new institutionalism, offer more comprehensive accounts of the influence of the European Union and its effects on national policy making. Neo-functionalism even posits the desire for further European integration as the primary *cause of change*. However, because of their central assumptions about the importance of institutions, decision-making procedures and rules, many institutionalist studies of the EU are vulnerable to the criticism that they overlook alternative determinants of European integration lying outside their own institutional framework for analysis, such as the strategic behaviour and intentions of key policy actors. Whilst institutionalist approaches to the study of the EU explain certain aspects of policy integration, because of the highly specific focus of their analysis, they often give only a limited explanation of the causes of European integration.

These conflicting approaches to the analysis of European integration reflect the difficulties associated with linking together different levels of analysis within a single explanatory framework. The problem over levels of analysis has long been recognized as a central difficulty in studies of international relations and relates to the choice confronting social scientists over whether to focus their studies upon certain component parts of a system, or upon the system in its entirety (Singer, 1961:89; Peters, 1998:109-135). In relation to the studies of European integration it represents the choice between studying the European Union as a system in its own right or the component parts that go up to make up that system. Focusing on one part of a system generally leads to greater descriptive detail, though often at the cost of distorting the significance of that part in relation to the whole. Focusing on the system as a whole might give a better overall picture of the wider contours of the subject of study, but often relies on a simplification of detail.

Outside of international relations (IR) literature, policy-making studies are often referred to as middle-range or meso-level analysis, falling mid-way between macro (or systemic) and micro (or actor oriented) levels of policy analysis. For example, a macro-level study of European integration might seek to characterize the collection of entities that together make up the European Union as a 'governance regime' in its own right, whereby the sum (the European Union as a polity) is bigger than the parts (the constituent states, interests and institutions). This approach is developed by Bulmer's (1994) adaptation of new institutionalism as a way of characterizing the revival of European integration in the mid-1980s. Micro-level studies of the European integration seek to examine particular developments occurring within states or institutions, or amongst interests in the (see for example: Fitzmaurice, 1988; Nicoll, 1984; Teasdale, 1993). Meso-level analysis, by contrast, concentrates on sectoral studies. The intention of this level of analysis is to characterize broader patterns of change than would be possible in single micro-level studies and to give greater explanatory detail than is possible with macro-level studies. Thus meso-level analysis is designed to give explanatory depth by simplifying a complex political system and focusing on one part of that whole without losing sight of the 'bigger picture' (see for example: Adshead, 1996; Bomberg, 1994; Ford and Lake, 1991; Geyer, 1996; Peterson, 1991). In order to develop the clearest picture of what the process of European integration might mean in different states, this research focuses on the sub-systemic or meso level of analysis.

An evaluation of the policy impact of the European Union needs to embrace international, national and sub-national levels of government (or in IR terminology, systemic, sub-systemic and actor-oriented levels of analysis). Failing to provide this broad embrace, traditional approaches to the study of the European Union have often led to an atomized and less than coherent picture of the process of European integration. On the one hand, state-centred approaches to the study of the European Union tend to focus on intergovernmental parts of European Union policy process such as the European Council and the Council of Ministers, emphasising the different approaches of member state governments in this intergovernmental environment. On the other, institutionalist approaches to the study of the European Union tend to focus on institutions, especially the Commission and European Parliament decision-making processes and rules, or the effects of EU directives and regulations in common policy areas (Alter, 1996; Cameron, 1992; Cawson, 1992; Wincott, 1993). Consequently there has been little work that links together different levels of analysis within a coherent theoretical framework.[3]

More recently, the concept of *multi-level governance* (MLG) has been offered as a means of acknowledging the multi-layered and complex nature of the EU system, through its emphasis on the *shared*, *collective* and *interconnected* roles of different states, policy arenas and policy actors in the EU policy process. In this respect, the notion of multi-level governance represents the first attempt in studies of EU influence over policy to accommodate different levels of analysis in its account of the role of the European Union in national policy making. Although multi-level governance is conceptually very useful in this regard, it is nevertheless methodologically limited. First, because it provides no clearly defined expectations that can be used to evaluate integration and second, because it does not make clear how changes at different levels of analysis relate to each other and why. These problems have been acknowledged by the MLG theorists themselves:

> If ... competencies have slipped away from central states both up to the supranational level and down to the sub-national level, then, *ceteris paribus*, one would expect greater interaction among actors at these levels. But the details remain murky and apart from a generalized presumption of increasing mobilization across levels, they provide no systematic set of expectations about which actors should mobilize and why (Marks, Nielsen *et al*, 1996:41).

Whilst multi-level governance postulates a ‘set of overarching, multi-level policy networks', in which 'political control is variable, not constant, across policy areas' (Marks, Nielsen *et al*,1996:42), it fails to identify the origins of these networks. Nor does it explain the connection between the formation of these new policy networks and the decline of national government control over policy. This raises a third limitation with multi-level governance. In the absence of organizing concepts that can be used for comparison between different states, and without a set of hypotheses about change, multi-level governance is only a statement of belief that is not susceptible to verification or falsification.

If, however, multi-level governance propositions are underpinned by a theory of European integration setting out clear expectations about the impact of this alleged 'polity creating process' on domestic policy making arrangements, and if these expectations are set against a policy making model that allows for cross-national comparisons of policy change and political integration, these shortcomings are remedied. Modified in this way, multi-level governance provides a valuable framework for policy analysis and constitutes the methodological structure of this research. Before providing a detailed overview of the research design, it is necessary first to explain the proposed application of integration theory, which will be made possible by developing policy network analysis as an instrument for cross-national comparison. The deployment of policy networks and integration theory are both discussed below.

Using policy networks for cross-national comparison

In order to compare the influence of the European Union on policy-making processes in different states, it is necessary to overcome the central difficulty associated with all comparative studies: that is, how to find a neutral way of describing policy processes in differently constituted states. Even where it is possible to select similar policy areas for examination, cross-national differences in policy making institutions, actor communities and policy preferences make comparison difficult. It is therefore necessary to find a way of characterizing cross-national policy-making processes that does not rely on idiosyncratic descriptions of specific national institutions or actors. For example, though it is clear that the federal system of government is of central importance to any discussion of German policy making processes, in order to develop a comparative analysis with the UK and Ireland, it is necessary to find a way of setting out the structural relations between different German policy institutions and actors in a way that facilitates comparison with other non-federal states. In this research, we shall attempt to overcome this problem through the use of policy network analysis.

Policy network analysis represents the relations between different policy actors in a given policy area, without resorting to descriptions of unique country-specific institutions and agents. It can be used to characterize the policy process along a number of dimensions: the number of participants and the type of interests they represent; the relations between policy actors in terms of the frequency, quality and continuity of their interactions; the distribution of resources amongst them, in terms of the finances, status, access to information or authority; and finally, the distribution of power or policy authority between key policy actors and institutions. Empirical studies offer different definitions of policy networks, clustering around two divergent interpretations of how policy is organized.

The first group, associated primarily with Rhodes (1981a, 1981b), deploys the notion of policy networks emphasising inter-organizational relations and structural - as opposed to personal - relationships between political institutions. Rhodes defines a policy network as a cluster or complex of organizations connected to one another by resource dependencies where members of a policy network behave in such a manner that 'each deploys its resources, whether constitutional/ legal, organizational, financial, political or informational to maximize influence over outcomes whilst trying to avoid becoming dependent on the other players' (Marsh and Rhodes, 1992:11). Networks are rooted in resource exchange and the distribution of resources between actors is thus central to the distribution of power in networks. Rhodes distinguishes between different types of networks along two dimensions: first, according to the pre-eminence of the interests that constitute the network; and second, according to the cohesiveness within the group. On one hand, large atomized networks, with no close professional, producer or governmental relations, he termed 'issue networks'. On the other hand, closely knit networks, characterized by stable relations and restrictive memberships, he termed 'policy communities'. The term policy community was not, however, a new one. It was already being deployed by the second major group of network analysts, associated primarily with Richardson and Jordan (1979).

This second group of network analysts, laid emphasis on the inter-personal nature of relations between policy actors, stressing the existence of disaggregated governmental sub-systems, which together with certain recognized interests form separate policy communities in their own field or interest. Policy communities are characterized by three key features. First, a disintegration of central policy-making authority, whereby policy-making is divided into sub-systems within which the government, or government agencies, and pressure groups negotiate:

> The central point is that policy-making is fragmented into sub-systems and the main boundaries are between sub-systems rather than between component

> units of government, agencies and pressure groups, and inter-penetration of department and client group, an osmosis in personnel terms with ex-civil servants appearing in groups (and less so, vice versa) (Richardson and Jordan, 1979:44).

Second, this organization of the policy-making process results in highly personalized relations between policy actors - it is increasingly difficult to differentiate groups, agencies and departments because they are players in the same game: 'Boundaries are unclear; "government" and "governed" is difficult to maintain as a distinction. Matching this complex network of organizations is a complex network of personnel. In effect, policy is now made between an internal and an external bureaucracy. So similar are both sides that transfer is relatively easy' (Richardson and Jordan, 1979:61). Third, a policy community represents a negotiated order, achieved through a process of pragmatic improvisation and accommodation that must be continually 'worked at' (Richardson and Jordan, 1979:101). In this conception, policy networks develop through 'pragmatic improvisation' whereby new structures are created to ensure that policy authority is shared between government and private and semi-private institutions (Richardson and Jordan, 1979:59).

In order to impose order on a proliferating variety of network definitions, Rhodes and Marsh (1992) constructed a typology based on the distinction between policy communities and networks using 'policy network' as a generic term. The typology proposes a continuum, marked at each end by an ideal-type - at one end, the policy community and at the other, the issue network - and it is designed so that individual empirical studies will be located somewhere in between the two (see Table 1). According to the Rhodes and Marsh typology, an ideal-type policy community has the following characteristics: a limited number of participants *with some groups consciously excluded*; frequent and high quality interaction between all members of the community on all matters of common interest; consistency in values and membership plus policy outcomes that persist; consensus, with the ideology, values and broad policy preferences shared by all participants; all members of the policy community have resources so the links between them are exchange relationships. As a result of this last criterion, the basic interaction in the policy community is one involving bargaining between members with resources. Marsh and Rhodes argue that in the ideal type policy community there is a balance of power that is a positive-sum arrangement, even if all members do not benefit equally. They suggest that the structures of the participating groups are hierarchical, so that leaders can guarantee compliant members. Marsh and Rhodes' characterization of an ideal-type issue network is in many instances the extreme opposite of the policy community: many participants; fluctuating interaction and access for the various

Table 1: Marsh and Rhodes typology of networks

Dimension	**Policy Community**	**Issue Network**
Membership		
No. of participants	Very limited number, some groups consciously excluded	Large
Type of interest	Economic and/or professional interests dominate	Encompasses range of affected interests
Integration		
Frequency of interaction	Frequent, high quality, interaction of all groups on all matters related to policy issue	Contacts fluctuate in frequency and intensity
Continuity	Membership, values and outcomes persistent over time	Access fluctuates significantly
Consensus	All participants share basic values and accept the legitimacy of the outcome	A measure of agreement exists, but conflict is ever present
Resources		
Distribution of resources within network	All participants have resources; basic relationship is an exchange relationship.	Some participants may have resources, but they are limited, and basic relationship is consultative
Distribution of resources within participating organizations	Hierarchical; leaders can deliver members	Varied and variable distribution and capacity to regulate members
Power	There is a balance of power among members. Although one group may dominate, it must be a positive-sum game if the community is to persist	Unequal powers, reflecting unequal resources and unequal access. It is a zero-sum game

Source: Rhodes (1997:44)

members; limited consensus and ever-present conflict; interaction based on consultation rather than negotiation or bargaining; and finally, an unequal power relationship in which many participants may have few resources, little access and no alternative.

The Marsh and Rhodes typology presents a useful set of organizing concepts for cross-national comparison between European states with different policy making institutions, organizations and actors. Using this typology not only facilitates uniform characterizations of policy processes in different states, but also allows a range of comparisons along the five suggested dimensions of network analysis. There remains, however, the problem of how to relate the differences found between alternative networks to the common external influence of the European Union.

Critics argue that the difficulty with networks is that once they have been used to characterize the policy process, their explanatory utility is exhausted. Dowding argues that they are 'merely a set of metaphors' created for the study of British and European politics (Dowding, 1994; see also, Keohane and Hoffman, 1990). Networks, he argues, can add nothing new to characterizations of the policy process because all that they offer are models of policy processes that still resort to standard macro-economic or political theories in order to explain their existence:

> The network protagonists have tried to answer empirical questions by definitional dogma rather than constructing theories - which often already exist - to explain their empirical observations. Conversely, they try to resolve theoretical disputes by reference to evidence compatible with both theories. Essentially the conflict between Jordan and the Rhodes-Marsh acolytes is over the nature of the state. Both sides use their versions of network theory to try to secure their position, but the empirical evidence they cite is exactly the same (Dowding, 1994:66).

This criticism of network analysis raises important points in relation to this study, suggesting that if network concepts are to be employed successfully for policy analysis, they must be underpinned by an appropriate explanatory theory. An appropriate theory should be constructed in such a way that the evidence collected cannot be claimed by opposing theoretical viewpoints and if it is to be of use in cross-national comparison, it must also be one that does not resort to macro-level explanations of the state in its construction.

This research uses early neofunctionalist definitions of integration to develop a set of 'integration indicators', which may be used to account for and explain differentiation between policy networks in different states *in relation to the impact of the EU upon the policy process*. Neo-functionalism has been chosen because it provides a clear-cut definition of integration and because its hypotheses cannot be used to support any alternative propositions about the policy making process that are unrelated to the process of European integration. They thus avoid any explanation of difference centred around the nature of the state in which policy networks are located, since to do so would prevent a comparative evaluation of the impact of EU involvement in the policy processes of policy networks in different states.

Neofunctionalist propositions as indicators of change in policy networks

Neofunctionalism is centred around two main concepts: functional spillover and political spillover. Functional spillover refers to the belief that when states integrate one sector of their economies, technical pressures will push for similar levels of integration in other sectors. This belief is based on the assumption that modern industrial economies are made up of interdependent parts so that it is not possible to isolate one sector from another. In addition to the technical logic of functional spillover, political spillover refers to the political pressure for continued integration, which neofunctionalists assumed would be exerted upon government from sectional interests envious of the benefits of integration achieved by other more integrated sectors of the economy.

From the late 1950s to the mid-1970s, neofunctionalism dominated European Community literature and found favour not only in academic circles, but also amongst policy practitioners seeking to deploy its insights to affect change. The widespread acceptance of neofunctionalism as a means of explaining the origins and development of the European Community led many to believe that it could also predict the future. The attitude, prevalent amongst many Europeanists, was summed up by Groom (1994:113) who stated that 'European experience suggests a further aspect of neo-functionalism, that it is both a conceptual framework and a plan of action. In the former guise it purported to describe what was happening, while in the latter role it pointed to what should be done to further that process'. Initially convincing, the neo-functionalist paradigm was soon to fail in this respect.

The failure of neo-functionalism as a predictive theory points to its limited utility as it has been traditionally employed. As a non-predictive indicative theory of change, however, it retains its analytical utility. In particular it can be used to develop hypotheses about changes in policy networks occurring as a consequence of European Union involvement in policy. In deploying a neofunctionalist framework for analyzing changes in the composition and dynamics of policy networks, this research avoids the predictive failings of the genre by adopting Lindberg's (1963) definition of integration. This is because Lindberg distinguishes between the notion of political integration as a *condition* and as a *process*; and having adopted the latter perspective, he stops short of identifying an end-point in the process.[4] Lindberg defines integration as:

> First, the process whereby nations forgo the desire and ability to conduct foreign and key domestic policies independently of each other, seeking instead to make joint decisions or to delegate the decision-making process to new central organs; and second, the process whereby political actors in several distinct settings are persuaded to shift their expectations and political activities to a new centre (Lindberg, 1963:6).

In presenting this dual definition, Lindberg suggests that although it lacks the analytical clarity and precision of model analysis, it is appropriate to the problem since it presents a set of inter-related indicators by which to judge the experience of the European Community. The first part of the definition refers to modes of decision-making where, as a consequence of developing integration between states, the processes of sharing and of delegating decision-making are likely to affect the governmental structures in each state involved, leading to new internal problems of coordination and policy direction. The second part of the definition refers to patterns of behaviour shown by high policy-makers, civil servants, parliamentarians, interest-group leaders, and other elites. Suggesting that the relationship between these two sets of indicators is very close, Lindberg argues that attention should be focused upon the perceptions and resulting behaviour of the actors in each of the states involved.

In contrast to other neofunctionalist work, Lindberg's definition of political integration does not prejudice his analysis to any one aspect of inquiry. Instead, it leads him to examine a variety of factors such as governmental structure, decision-making, high policy makers, civil servants, parliamentarians, interest group leaders and other elites. Furthermore, although Lindberg does not explicitly state his basic assumptions about the political process, it is evident from his definition of integration that his assumptions are not linked irretrievably to notions of either structure or agency - but possibly a mixture of the two. It is for this reason that Lindberg's definition of political integration is more value neutral than those found elsewhere and thus more easily adapted to the analysis of cross-national differentiation in policy networks in this research.

Lindberg (1963:1-11) suggested that if the process of integration were taking place, it would be manifest in four main ways: first, there would be some form of institutional development of a kind that facilitated the European Community's direct involvement in policy; second, there would be what Lindberg termed 'elite activation', referring to the changing behaviour of key policy makers in favour of integration; third, the government would provide continuing support for integrationist measures; and fourth, functional and political spillover would lead to the creation of 'inherently expansive tasks', that would further advance the integration process. These propositions provide a good basis from which to derive a set of integration hypotheses or indicators that are able to relate the differences found between policy networks to different levels of European integration.

The difficulties associated with examining the influence of the European Union have already been discussed in detail: because states have both proactive and reactive relations with the European Union, a full evaluation of EU influence needs to embrace developments at European, national and sub-national levels of government. Given that policy developments at one level of analysis do not preclude developments at another level, and that changes in different levels may or may not be inter-linked, this raises the difficulty of finding a way to characterize change in the policy process that embraces different levels of analysis in the study. So far, this difficulty has been addressed only by the multi-level governance literature. Proponents of the *multi-level governance* thesis argue that:

> European integration is a polity creating process in which authority and policy-making influence are shared across multiple levels of government - sub-national, national, and supranational. While national governments are formidable participants in EU policy-making, control has slipped away from them to supra-national institutions. States have lost some of their former authoritative control over individuals in their respective territories. In short, the locus of political control has changed (Marks *et al*, 1996:342).

If the 'polity creating process' known as multi-level governance is at work in member states, then we can expect to see evidence of central government control over policy-making slipping away - both downwards and upwards - towards sub-national and supranational levels of government respectively. The difficulty, however, arises in finding ways to characterize this slippage.

One way, might be to look at institutional and organizational developments in the European Union and to examine the extent to which central government control over policy has slipped upwards to the European level. Generally, this is the line of enquiry most favoured by European integration scholars and it is used extensively by advocates of the multi-level governance thesis. If, however, multi-level governance is about slippage of central government control downwards as well as upwards to supranational levels of government, then we should also expect to see some indication of this 'polity-creating process' in developments occurring in sub-national government. Unfortunately, MLG theorists have not framed clear expectations about the dynamics of this polity creating process. The problem then, is that whilst multi-level governance posits a 'set of overarching, multi-level policy networks', where 'political control is variable, not constant, across policy areas', it does not tell us how these networks come into existence or explain the connection between their existence and the alleged decreasing central government control over policy (Marks, Hooghe *et al*, 1996:41).

In this respect, Rhodes' (1988) work on the development of policy networks in the UK has much to offer. Using the term *governance* to depict both the decreasing government role in public service provision and the increasing involvement of alternative actors and agencies including the European Union, Rhodes (1996) argues that these changes have led to the development of *governance as self-organizing policy networks*. The fact that networks are self-organizing is related to central government's loss of its 'control capacity':

> The control capacity of government is limited for a number of reasons: lack of legitimacy, complexity of policy processes, complexity and multitude of institutions concerned etc. Government is only one of many actors that influence the course of events in a societal system (Kickert, 1993:275).

If the multi-level governance thesis is correct, we might expect to see the emergence of self-organizing networks, or at least trends in that direction, evidenced in those UK policy areas where there is the strongest concentration of European Union activity. In order to test this proposition, this research examines the regional policy networks that have developed in the British Objective One region of Merseyside and compares it with other policy networks in Objective One regions of Germany and Ireland. Instead, however, of attempting to imbue policy networks with any explanatory capacity of their own - other than their obvious heuristic utility - and to facilitate cross-national comparisons of the impact of EU involvement in the regional policy process, this research uses propositions from neofunctionalist integration to evaluate the development of regional policy networks. In doing so, it avoids the usual criticisms about the explanatory capacity and utility of policy network analysis.

The suitability of neofunctionalist theory as an indicator of change in policy networks arises for three reasons. First, although the integration hypotheses may be positively or negatively proven in different networks, they cannot be used to support alternative propositions about policy making processes that are unrelated to the process of integration. Because of this the deployment of network analysis does not fall prey to the major criticisms over its explanatory utility. Second, the use of neofunctionalist integration hypotheses enables us to make comments about cross-national differences between networks in relation to integration instead of (or at least in addition to) differences between state systems within which the policy networks are located. In other words, it facilitates an evaluation of policy making processes that does not concentrate solely on how state policy making processes differ, but why that might be so in relation to integration. Third, because neofunctionalist hypotheses may refer to changes in individual policy networks at sub-national level, or to policy relations between sub-national and central government levels, or to policy developments taking place between sub-national, national and EU levels in the policy process, they are able to embrace different levels of analysis in the study of policy influences and outcomes. Used in this way neofunctionalist hypotheses provide a framework to examine the extent and nature of multi-level governance (or more simply - the level of integration) in policy networks.

This work will hypothesize the existence of each of Lindberg's four integration propositions as evidence of positive integration in policy networks. It is assumed that the higher the incidence of positive integration indicators (as suggested above), the higher the level of integration between policy actors and institutions in the network. Since, however, Lindberg's hypotheses were designed to account for changes at state level arising as a consequence of European Community involvement in policy-making, it is necessary first to clarify their use as a set of integration indicators for policy networks at sub-national level.

Hypothesis One proposes that if integration is taking place, there will be some form of institutional development that facilitates the European Union's direct involvement in policy. This hypothesis has two dimensions. On the one hand, policy networks may already have some institutional mechanism for incorporating the European Union into the policy process. If this is the case then it is a positive sign of integration between EU, national and sub-national level actors in the policy network. On the other hand, if this is not the case we may see evidence of moves towards new institutional frameworks that do incorporate European Union representation into regional policy networks. If so, then we may take it as a positive sign of *moves towards* integration between alternative levels of government in the policy process.

Hypothesis two concerning 'elite activation' proposes that if integration is taking place it will be manifest in the changing attitudes and behaviour of key network members *in favour of further integration*. These may be reflected in their own positive opinions about EU involvement in the policy process, or in the strategic development of either their own or their organization's interaction with the EU. If integration is occurring, then an increase in both of these developments can be expected to lead to a positive consensus regarding EU involvement in regional policy.

Hypothesis three proposes that if integration is taking place, it will be manifest in government support for continuing integrationist measures. The level of government 'enthusiasm' for policy integration may be gauged by examining not only whether the government enables EU involvement in policy or not, but also the degree to which they attempt to facilitate and support it. If governments are non-enthusiastic, they may give only minimal support in order to avoid the charge of obstruction or presiding over policy failure. If governments are enthusiastic, they may wish to develop the organization of policy in such a way that it actively supports further integration.

Hypothesis four proposes that if integration is taking place, it should - as a consequence of both functional and political spillover - lead to the creation of 'inherently expansive tasks', which will both cement the level of integration achieved and push for further integration where possible. Spillover refers to the idea that for the process of integration to move forward 'a given action, related to a specific goal, creates a situation in which the original goal can be assured only by taking further actions, which in turn create a further condition and a need for more action, and so forth' (Lindberg, 1963:11). In many ways, this hypothesis represents a composite of the previous three. For example, the logic of functional spillover suggests that if an initial form of institutional development that facilitates the involvement of the EU in the policy process proves successful, it should create greater pressure for similar developments in other aspects of the policy process. Alternatively, according to the logic of political spillover, if there is a convergence of elite attitudes in favour of integration and government support for it, this should lead to an increase in political activities that support policy integration.

Research design and organization of the book

The four neofunctionalist 'integration indicators' may be related to aspects of network structure (hypothesis one regarding institutional development); network management (hypotheses two and three regarding 'elite activation' and government policy); and finally, network members behaviour (hypothesis four relating to the incidence of functional and political spillover). Accordingly, the organization of empirical material in subsequent chapters is correspondingly divided. Chapter two deals with the structuring of the policy environment by providing a comparative analysis of the organizational and institutional environment within which each of the networks are located. Chapter three deals with the management of policy environments in each of the states through a comparative treatment of regional policy approaches.

The primary research is found in chapters four, five and six, which provide policy network analysis of the regional development policy process in selected case studies in Germany, Ireland and Britain. This analysis is based on the Marsh and Rhodes typology of networks (outlined already in table 1).

'Network formation' looks at the geographical, economic, political and institutional boundaries that determine the effective operational space for the conduct of regional policy. 'Network membership' examines the range of policy actors and interests involved in regional development. 'Network resources' details the distribution of information, skills and experience as well as finances between network members. 'Network dynamics' evaluates how network members interact with each other and the impact this has upon policy outcomes. Finally, each chapter concludes with a characterization of the network type according to the Marsh and Rhodes' typology, plus an evaluation of the impact this has upon the policy process. Deploying policy network concepts in this way provides a *uniform* way to describe the variety of policy making arrangements in policy networks in different states.

Germany, Ireland and Britain were selected for comparison in order to compare the impact of EU involvement in policy and associated developments in governance upon both federal and unitary systems of governance. There is a strong case for comparing Irish and British systems of sub-national governance on the basis of most similar systems design. With the exception of a couple of County Management Acts, the entire body of legislation pertaining to local government in Ireland is the same as that in Britain. The two cases do diverge in the mid-1980s with the coming to power of the Conservative party in Britain and the experience of 'Thatcherite' reforms to local government. Still, however, many of the reforms that were ideologically driven in Britain (contracting out of local government service provision, the contraction of government involvement in public administration, the creation of numerous boards, bodies and quangos to carry out public policy) were also carried out in Ireland. In Ireland, however, these changes were more *ad hoc* and carried out incrementally be a variety of different government coalitions. As a consequence, they garnered consensus around them and were introduced with much less controversy. The fact that broadly similar state systems can witness broadly similar developments and yet sustain divergent outcomes makes these two states interesting cases for comparison. In opposition to these two unitary states, Germany has been chosen as a contrasting case study because of its system of cooperative federalism. Still, however, the recent introduction of devolution in Britain and regionalization in Ireland gives this study added salience, since it enables a more generalized comparison of the impact of EU involvement in regional policy on patterns of regionalization in each of the states.

Within these states, each of the three case studies represents an area defined by the European Union as an Objective One priority for Structural Funds assistance. The varying sizes of Objective One regions determined by the EU, however, means that policy networks may differ significantly in size (some may be relatively large and others quite small) and that often in the absence of a single large policy network, multiple smaller ones may exist. Such differences may also be determined by alternate sub-national arrangements in different states, or by the attitudes and values of policy actors themselves. The cross-national element to this comparison makes it impossible to choose similar sized case studies, however the neutral descriptive value of network concepts enables us to 'factor in' the size of the network as another element in the comparison. The final arbiters in determining network borders were the individuals and institutions involved in the regional policy process themselves. In each case study area, having selected a number of 'obvious candidates' for interview, the extent of the network was subsequently determined by reputational analysis.

All interviewees (listed at the back of the book) were guaranteed anonymity. Overall, seventy six interviews, lasting between one and a half and three hours, were carried out with policy actors: twenty seven in Thüringen, twenty five in Merseyside, and twenty four in Limerick and Dublin. Interviews were designed to find out who were the 'main players' in regional policy and it was not long before a consensus emerged in each case study about who were the most important policy actors: these constituted the network's membership (questions 1 & 7). Network resources and dynamics were investigated by asking each interviewee a series of questions about the operation of regional policy within the network: what function they performed (question 1); what they believed to be the most significant developments in the operation of regional policy and how they were affected by them (question 2); whether or not they could determine the functional responsibilities of other network members (question 3); what links they had with other network members and what was the nature of these associations - formal/informal, personal/institutional, strong/weak *etc*. (questions 4 & 5); which network members were best at promoting their aims and objectives (question 6). These questions formed the basic interview structure but the questions were open-ended and interviewees were encouraged to contribute their own views and opinions about the conduct of regional development strategies. Interviews were also designed to ascertain what were the trends in regional policy formulation and implementation and which actors played the most significant role in policy change.

Profile of case study areas

Thüringen, Limerick and Merseyside were chosen because they represent areas targeted by the European Union for Objective One support and can therefore be expected to exhibit the most pronounced effects of EU involvement in policy. In addition, each of these areas is also strategically important as an engine for broader regional development. Thüringen is located in the south-west corner of the former DDR, bordering the old *Bundesländer* of Niedersachsen, Hessen and Bayern to its west, and the new *Bundesländer* of Sachsen-Anhalt and Sachsen to the east. Placed in the centre of Germany, mid-way between east and west it is seeking to develop as a central hub for European and German trade between the east and west. Limerick is situated on the river Shannon in the centre of a 100km arc that forms the mid-west region and includes Shannon Airport and the Shannon Free Zone as well as the National Technological Park. Limerick forms the central urban hub to this region mid-way between the smaller regional conurbations of Ennis and Shannon, accounting for almost a quarter of the region's population and acting as its economic, administrative and educational centre. Limerick is therefore important because of its strategic significance for development throughout the rest of the mid-west region. Merseyside is an important region in its own right, but also as an integral part of the wider north-west region of England, that stretches from north Wales up to the Lake District. The north-west comprises a significant part of the traditional industrial heartland of England, including not only Liverpool and the Merseyside area, but the large conurbation around Manchester. As such, development of Merseyside is strategically important as an engine for wider regional regeneration across the north-west.

Before unification, Thüringen was a region of the DDR mostly dependent on manufacturing industry. In attempting to rebuild the economy, there have been a number of difficulties associated with trying to introduce alternative large-scale industry into the region: relocating large firms from other parts of Germany is not always practically or politically feasible, and economies of scale often prevent the creation of new large-scale industries.[5] The problem of high dependency on a few key industries has affected Merseyside too. In common with other areas in the north-west of England, Merseyside was once part of Britain's industrial heartland renowned for its traditional heavy industries centred around shipbuilding, the docks and vehicle manufacture. These industries provided the major source of growth and employment in the region and when - as a consequence of industrial decline - they began to suffer, the whole region was affected. In Ireland, the problem of manufacturing decline has been less significant because of the predominance of agriculture. Still, however, the city of Limerick suffered badly in the 1970s and 80s through the closure of many major traditional industries.

In attempting to restructure local economies all of the cases have been affected by high or long-term unemployment and other associated social problems. In Thüringen, unification resulted the collapse of most large industrial combines, many bankruptcies and massive rationalisations, leaving the *Land* with many well-qualified but unemployed workers. In Limerick, significant growth and investment in the 1990s created a boom in technological and service-related industries but this masks a significant amount of long-term unemployment concentrated in inner city areas. In Limerick city and suburbs, whilst the overall population remained stable throughout the last two decades, the suburban population doubled, leaving behind a declining inner city population, where a few large public housing estates are characterized by high unemployment, welfare dependency and associated social problems.

In Merseyside between 1971 and the mid-1980s, around 20,000 people employed in dock work and sea transport lost their jobs, leaving only a quarter of the original workforce employed (Meegan, 1990:87). In the same period, more than half the region's manufacturing jobs were lost, hitting the outer areas of Merseyside heavily (CEC, 1994c:87). Registered unemployment is on average double the national rate and in some estates more than treble (CEC, 1994c:88). By the early 1990s, unemployment had increased to 70% above the EU average and 40% of all unemployed (around 30,000) had either never had a permanent job or had not worked in the previous ten years (CEC, 1994c).

Adding to these difficulties each area suffers a tendency towards outwards migration, further contributing to regional decline. In Thüringen, this problem is reflected in the threat of a 'brain-drain' from the new German *Lander* to the more prosperous west. The same is true for Merseyside and, combined with industrial decline, this has left widespread areas of concentrated dereliction - over ten times the national average (CEC, 1994c:6). In Merseyside, however, the problem is further exacerbated by low levels of educational attainment and professional qualifications (CEC, 1994c:6). In Limerick, outwards migration is manifest not only in increasing disparities between suburban and inner city areas, but also between rural and urban areas of the county. Southern rural parts have long suffered the effects of emigration and more recently further trends in outwards national migration. In these areas, maintaining a stable population upon which to base any attempts at development activity and stemming the rise of de-populated and derelict villages in the area is a critical task.

Taken together then, these cases are comparable in terms of their strategic importance as engines of wider regional development and because of the problems they face as a consequence of economic restructuring, high and/or long-term unemployment and associated social problems, plus a tendency towards outwards migration from the region. In each case, the policy responses have centred around the desire to achieve economic diversification through the development of small and medium sized enterprises. This research examines the regional development policy process in each of these areas. It attempts to evaluate the form and substance of policy change in established regional policy processes and to assess the impact of European Union involvement in the policy process according to the research design set out above.

Notes

1. Objective One regions are areas designated by the EU as priority targets for EU assistance because they are regions which are lagging behind the EU average. Under Objective One, support is available from the European Regional Development Fund (ERDF), the European Social Fund (ESF) and the Guidance section of the European Agricultural Guidance and Guarantee Fund (EAGGF) to those areas whose GDP per capita is less than 75% of the EU average, or regions included as special cases.
2. Since 1979, the Commission has reserved a small portion of the European Regional Development Fund for the financing of specific Community actions, provided that they are based on the principles of integration, partnership and programming. Although the finance available for these initiatives is extremely small - some 5% of ERDF money - they have played an important role in determining the effectiveness of programmatic initiatives. It is also likely that the Commission's early experience in these initiatives was a precursor to later structural reform and the further development of the use of Community initiatives (Hooghe, 1996; Bache, 1998).
3. Some Marxist approaches to world politics provide the exception to this rule, though they seldom single out the progress of European integration for treatment, see for example: Grahl and Teague, 1989; Holland, 1980.
4. Deutsch (1954, 1957) and later writers, such as North, Koch and Zinnes (1960), conceptualised political integration as a *condition*, using the central concept of a 'security community' to denote 'a group of people which has become integrated'. Haas (1958b, 1964), on the other hand, argued that political integration should be conceived of as a *process* of change - one which would lead inevitably to the creation of a European federal polity.
5. For a detailed examination of the problems associated with restructuring the east German economy after unification, see Grabher, 1997

Chapter 2

Structuring Policy Networks: Sub-national Government in Germany, Ireland and Britain

Introduction

This chapter contextualizes the primary research presented in later chapters by examining the institutional environments that shape policy networks in each of the three states. It looks at the origins of sub-national government and illustrates how early institutional configurations influenced subsequent development. In doing so, it identifies the critical junctures and key trends that have shaped institutional structures. Emphasis is placed upon the administrative organization and financial arrangements for sub-national government in each of the states. The chapter concludes with a summary view of the relationship between institutional environment and network potential in each of the states, highlighting the significance for the rest of the research.

The origins of sub-national government in Britain, Ireland and Germany

In each of the states, the origins of modern sub-national government partially conditioned their future development. In Germany, for example, as a consequence of allied occupation after the second world war, regional government effectively pre-dated central government. As a result regional politicians were in a strong position to shape the development of the post-war German state and asserted their influence by creating constitutional guarantees for regional government structures, organizations and influence. By contrast, the creation of the Irish state was marked by an equally strong desire for centralized power. After a long struggle for independence, which resulted in a bitter civil war over its conclusion, the newly established government of Ireland sought to exercise as much control over the machinery of government as possible. As a result the Irish constitution made no provision for sub-national government and Irish governments quickly established a clear preference for functional efficiency in the structures and organizations of sub-national institutions, often at the cost of democratic accountability. In Britain, contrary to both Germany and Ireland, there is no definitive point in history that marks the birth of sub-national government. The British system of local government was not created but developed gradually and incrementally over time, its evolution shaped and controlled at all stages by the primacy of central government. The remainder of this section examines the different origins of sub-national government in each of the states and their importance for subsequent institutional development.

Germany

After Germany's defeat in 1945, the occupying allied powers sought to encourage local responsibility by both restoring old and creating new *Länder*. In the course of the reorganization of public authority, the occupation powers transferred their supervisory functions on a step by step basis to local German administrative authorities. In June 1945, the Russians set up five state or *Land* administrations in their zone. By the end of 1945, the Americans had also divided their zone into *Länder* and established German authorities at *Land* level. By 1947, the British and French followed suit. However, as a consequence of the French veto and also the widening gulf between the Russian and other allies, no over-arching national administrative structure was developed until the Germans themselves regained control in 1949 (Balfour, 1992:98-99). By this time, the *Land* governments had benefitted unexpectedly from their post-war experience and emerged as strong, central players in the construction of the *Grundgesetz*, or Basic Law, which was to underpin the new Federal Republic of Germany.[1]

The original intention of the Parliamentary Council that drafted the Basic Law, was that the *Länder* should have precedence in the federal system (Bulmer, 1989:45). As it turned out, the German federal system became an 'unusual hybrid': the federation was endowed with a clearly defined set of exclusive powers; but was also empowered to enact laws in the fields covered by categories of concurrent and framework legislation set out in the Basic Law, but *only* when a specific need for overarching federal legislation could be identified and justified (Jeffery, 1994). In all other fields, the power of legislation was invested in the *Länder*. Throughout the post-war years, the increasing interdependence of alternative levels of government in the exercise of joint policy-making led the system to be characterized as 'Cooperative Federalism'(Scharpf *et al*, 1976; Hesse, 1978, 1987; Schmidt, 1987; Paterson and Southern, 1991). Smith (1992:44) suggests that the 'intertwining of policy formation and implementation' between Federal and *Land* authorities 'promotes a form of intergovernmentalism and a bargaining relationship that is quite different from traditional models of federalism'. Over the years a close network of intergovernmental relationships, reflected in numerous permanent committees, has developed to help ensure that the two sets of authorities work well together.

As the demands upon government have increased, so has the need for central coordination of important government functions, particularly in relation to the economy and economic growth. This has often been cited as an example of increasing centralization in the federal system (Bulmer, 1989:44). The increased prominence of the Federal government in areas of policy responsibility that are shared with the *Länder* should not, however, be viewed as a straight-forward 'zero-sum' equation. In many cases, the *Länder* have viewed this limited loss of sovereignty as the price that must be paid in order to ensure the effective provision of public goods (Bulmer, 1989:45).

This particularistic approach to federalism was not without consequences for the process of unification. Immediately after unification in October 1990, 144 MPs from the former Democratic Republic were delegated to join the *Bundestag*. After elections in December 1990, 123 (out of total of 662) were elected to represent areas of the former Democratic Republic and were thereby immediately subsumed into the federal system. The decision over whether or not to adapt central government structures was left to the Bonn political parties. Convinced of the superiority of their own system and with representatives of eastern Germany in the minority, the majority of representatives opted for complete integration of the former Democratic Republic into the political and institutional network of the Federal government. As a consequence, they choose *not* to set up any specialist working groups or Parliamentary committees to represent the unique interests of the former Democratic Republic (Sturm, 1992:104).

The Federal Republic's enthusiasm for complete and immediate integration with east Germany was matched in the former Democratic Republic and this was reflected in both the functional and territorial organization of sub-national government. The former Federal Republic of Germany had been established on the territory of the three western occupation zones and consisted of eleven federal states or *Länder*. The German Democratic Republic (GDR) was created on the territory of the Russian occupation zone and when in 1952 the Democratic Republic became a centralist one-party state, the original five *Länder* were replaced by fourteen administrative districts. In 1990, during the course of the German unification process, the people of the former Democratic Republic were keen to see the 'original' German states reintroduced and it is thus one of the ironies of the German unification process that despite extraordinary political change, the principle organizational features of German sub-national government remained largely unaffected.

Ireland

When the Irish state was established, it inherited the British system of local government, which pre-dated the state's birth. When the local government reform acts, which were carried out in Britain and paralleled in Ireland under British rule, the local franchise was extended to such an extent that local government soon became the basis for a developing national struggle for independence.[2] Between 1898 and independence, local government was dominated by national political issues and movements. It is even argued that the Local government of Ireland Act of 1898 was - unintentionally - 'the legislative father of the Irish Free State' (Horgan, 1926:535). County councils in particular became centres of nationalism (Chubb, 1992:269). This intermeshing of national politics with local politics created the first instance of an unusual paradox in Irish sub-national government - the existence of strong local influence in a highly centralized state (Farrell, 1983; Komito, 1989, 1992).

After independence, despite the drafting of an extremely prescriptive constitution (see: Farrell, 1988), no constitutional provision was made for local government. The Irish state developed a highly centralized system of government not only because the majority of its political institutions and administrative bureaucracy were inherited from Britain - an unequivocally unitary state, but also because the manner in which they were placed under Irish control was the ultimate act of political consolidation. Barrington (1987:136) argues that the state established in 1922 was consciously and deliberately a centralized one:

> The revolutionary government that took over was determined to show itself fully in control of the system of government and to establish its willingness and capacity to rule, faced as it was with: a bitter civil war with former comrades; well developed public institutions fully staffed by public servants transferred from British rule whose loyalty to the new order they naturally, if wrongly, distrusted; a major post-war slump; the general consciousness of the smallness and poverty of the whole; a 'business-like' determination to keep things simple, solvent and, so far as possible, depoliticized.

The Irish government's desire for centralized power was, however, concerned less with political principle and more with finding immediate and pragmatic solutions to the problems of government in the aftermath of war. The preference for functional efficiency, even at the expense of democratic accountability is a trait that has characterized government in Ireland since its foundation.

Britain

Whereas in both Ireland and Germany the origins of sub-national government can be traced to their establishment as modern states in 1922 and 1949 respectively, the origins of British sub-national government go back much further. Some shire counties date back to Anglo Saxon times and other historic cities, such as Bristol, Oxford, Newcastle, Aberdeen and Dundee were centres of genuine self-government as early as the 12th century when they were granted Royal Charters guaranteeing local autonomy (Wilson and Game, 1998:41). Still, there was no systemized administrative organization of local government in Britain until the end of the 19th century, when a series of local government reform acts established the key areas of local government responsibility.[3] Based on the principle of parliamentary sovereignty, the status of British local government is determined by the doctrine of *ultra vires,* which is understood to mean that 'local authorities have no powers, save those defined by statute' (Goldsmith and Page, 1987:11). In what has since become known as the 'dual polity' convention, British central government kept control over issues of 'high politics' such as foreign affairs, defence and the economy, leaving the provision of local services and 'low politics' to the local authorities (Bulpitt, 1983).

Wilson and Game (1998:41) have suggested that the British system of local government 'like most other institutions, has evolved gradually and piecemeal over the centuries, uninterrupted by an invasion or violent revolution that might have prompted a formal constitutional settlement'. Without a written constitution, British government is based upon an inheritance of conventions relating to political procedures and practice premised upon the principle of parliamentary sovereignty. Some commentators have referred to this as Britain's 'unwritten constitution'. If this is so, then it is one that is continually evolving and if we are to understand the basis of British sub-national government, we must look to the most recent government reforms and legislative acts. The most significant of these changes, together with other key developments in German and Irish sub-national government are detailed in the next section.

The shaping of contemporary sub-national government: critical junctures

In each of the three states, the different origins of sub-national government influenced the trajectory of subsequent institutional change. The relative autonomy of German sub-national government, for example, arises to a large extent as a consequence of its position being guaranteed in the federal constitution. German constitutional provisions safe-guarding the role and responsibilities of sub-national government ensured that the new federal states incorporated into Germany following unification were free - within specified legal parameters - to adopt whichever institutional arrangements they deemed appropriate. This level of autonomy contrasts sharply with the position of sub-national government in Britain and Ireland. Without equivalent guarantees, both British and Irish systems of sub-national government are far more susceptible to institutional re-organization at the hands of central government. An examination of the most significant developments in British and Irish sub-national government reveals that the impetus for change is linked very definitely to changes in the policy preferences of central government.

Although both the British and Irish cases point to the important role played by central government in setting the conditions for sub-national government, there are differences between the two. In Britain, the fact that a change of government can also herald sweeping changes in government organization is related to the British system of governance. In the first past the post electoral system, a government with a strong parliamentary majority has the authority to effect whatever changes they like. The capacity of Irish governments to introduce significant or sweeping reforms is, by contrast, practically limited by the nature of Irish politics. The propensity both for coalition governments and frequent changes in government has led to a greater degree of consensus-building in Irish politics than is usually found in Britain. The remainder of this section looks at the evolution of sub-national government in each of the states, highlighting the key developments that have helped determine the current institutional arrangements.

Germany

As might be expected in a highly prescriptive system of government, guaranteed by provisions in the federal constitution, the institutional arrangement of German sub-national government cannot be modified without a major structural overhaul of the federal system of government. In 1989, the fall of the Berlin wall presented just such an opportunity. In what later came to be known as the 'big bang' approach to German unification (OECD, 1996:127), the constitutional and legal framework of the Federal Republic was up for review. The restructuring of government and administrative systems in the Federal and Democratic Republics as a result of unification was, however, an asymmetrical process. For the former Democratic Republic, unification meant the wholesale disappearance of many of its institutions including its own elected parliament, the *Volkskammer*, and a step by step dismantling of the administrative and constitutional framework that it had developed throughout the preceding four decades. For the Federal Republic, unification was more like an acquisition and merger deal: a smaller less viable system was formally incorporated, lock, stock and barrel, into a larger, more successful and democratic system (Lehmbruch, 1994; Sturm, 1992).

In circumstances that are ironically similar to the Federal Republic's first creation of sub-national government, regional actors from the former Democratic Republic maintained a significant degree of influence over the organization of sub-national government in the 'new' German *Länder*. Although the new *Länder* did not come into being until the 14th October 1990, the creation of sub-national administration under the federal system had already begun in the former Democratic Republic when it introduced the Law on the Establishment of *Länder* in the GDR, adopted by the *Volkskammer* on 22 July 1990. Under this law, spokespersons were appointed for each of the new *Länder*. These positions were retained despite the election of the Minister-Presidents in each of the new *Länder* on the 14th October 1990 and ensured the presence of sustained local influence throughout the period of institutional development (Osterland, 1993).

In the former Democratic Republic, historically at least, federalism was also familiar. Initially, the GDR constitution gave recognition to the original five *Länder* created by the Russians. Gradually, however, the process of communist democratic centralism (see: Goetz, 1993:448-9) led to the abandonment of federalism and in 1952 the GDR was reorganized into administrative districts, leaving the former *Land* boundaries as historical appendages only (*RWI-Mitteilungen*, 1990:120). As a consequence, the restructuring of *Land* level administration in the former Democratic Republic was by no means straightforward. Goetz has characterized the process as involving three major developments: first, the dissolution of former GDR institutions; second, the transfer of their responsibilities to institutions of the Federal Republic; and third, the establishment of new *Land* administrations (Goetz, 1993:447-69). Further details of the functional organization of sub-national government in the new *Länder* are found in the following section.

Ireland

Ireland is almost unique among her European neighbours in not having implemented any major reform of local government throughout the post-war period (Coyle, 1994:25). Whilst there have been several proposals for reform, such changes as have occurred have been *ad hoc*, functionally expedient and minimalist. The Cork City Management Act in 1929 - the consequence of lobbying by businesses and professionals for a more accountable system of local government - marked the introduction of the 'managerial system' (discussed in the following section). It was followed by a series of local Acts for various cities, culminating in the County Management Act of 1940, which extended the system and operationalized it throughout the state by 1942.[4] Under this system, the provision of all local services fell under the direction of a single individual - the city or county manager - answerable to the council but with a statutory position and statutory powers. The consequence of this was virtually a single administration in each county area (Chubb, 1992:271).

Over time, sub-county districts faced the problem of how to provide an increasing range of public services with a relative scarcity of technical, administrative and financial resources when compared to larger county units. As a result, many gave up some of their functions to county level. Counties and county boroughs (the major cities that have county status) increasingly began to dominate sub-national government and 'local government in Ireland became and is now primarily county council government' (Chubb, 1992:271). Added to this, the small number of elected authorities at sub-county level (represented by Boroughs, Urban Districts and Town Commissioners) means that by the standards of comparable small states there are very few locally elected councils (1980:43). Over the years, despite numerous reports and policy studies instigated by central government (IPA, 1971, Government of Ireland, 1971, 1973, 1985, 1991), no major changes occurred. With the exception of a little tinkering to the system here and there, it could reasonably be argued that Irish local government has changed very little since the foundation of the state.[5]

Despite the lack of any formal institutional reorganization of sub-national government, over time the need to develop policy delivery mechanisms led to the creation of several types of organization operating at sub-national level (Chubb, 1992:262). On the one hand, there are a number of authorities responsible for the administration of some service, whose governing bodies consist both of members of the local authority and interested associations or groups in the region, such as the eight Area Health Boards, or the eight Regional Tourism Organizations. On the other hand, some central authorities have themselves decentralized their business to regional level for administrative, managerial or customer convenience. These include state-sponsored bodies such as the Electricity Supply Board (ESB), the Industrial Development Authority (IDA) and certain government departments. The authorities with devolved powers and those with decentralized administrations all operate boundaries to suit themselves and so the regional areas thus far created do not coincide. Chubb (1992:263) notes that since there is also an underlying network of local authorities, 'the result is a jungle of administrative areas that is both impenetrable to the ordinary citizen and frequently inconvenient for any kind of business that involves more than one authority or regional organization'. It was not until the early 1990s that the first steps towards long-awaited reform were introduced.

In 1991, the area covered by Dublin county council and Dun Laoghaire corporation was re-divided into four county authorities: Dublin County Council was reduced and three new county boundaries were created in Fingal, South Dublin and Dun Laoghaire/Rathdown. The 1991 Local Government Act 'substantially relaxed' the *ultra vires* restriction upon local government by introducing broad powers of general competence for local authorities to act in the interests of local communities (Government of Ireland, 1996a:8). Although local authorities' continued dependence upon central government for financial and technical resources meant that in practice this freedom was limited, it was taken as a sign of the government's commitment to local government reform. As part of a review of public sector management, the government commissioned a report on the financing of local government (KMPG, 1991).

In 1993, following provisions made in the 1991 Local Government Act, eight Regional Authorities were set up in order to co-ordinate public service provision and to act as a review bodies to advise on the deployment of EU Structural and Cohesion Funds in their regions. This might have been another *ad hoc* response to demands for more efficient policy delivery, but in 1994 a new 'Rainbow Coalition' took over government and pledged to 'build on the reforms of recent years by the adoption of a strategic approach to the renewal of local government' (Government of Ireland, 1996a:10).[6] In July 1995, the 'Rainbow' government established the Devolution Commission charged with investigating all aspects of decentralization. In 1996, the Interim Report of the Devolution Commission noted that 'Irish local government is in a particularly weak position as regards its status and role in society and in the overall framework of government'. In 1997, the 'Rainbow Coalition' lost office following a general election. The incoming government agreed to review plans for local government re-organization but promised to change nothing.

Britain

In Britain, after the consolidation of local government in the 1920s, the system experienced no significant change for a number of decades (Wilson and Game, 1998:42-57). In 1963, London County Council was replaced by a two-tier structure, with a Greater London Council and 32 London Boroughs.[7] The two-tier system was later expanded by the Local Government Act of 1972, which abolished all county boroughs and reduced the number of county councils from 58 to 47. Within these counties, 1,250 municipal boroughs, urban districts and rural districts were replaced by 333 district councils (Wilson and Game, 1998:50). In the major conurbations, six metropolitan county councils were established (Greater Manchester, Merseyside, West Midlands, Tyne and Wear, South Yorkshire and West Yorkshire) and 36 metropolitan districts. Outside the metropolitan areas, the old county boroughs were absorbed as district councils into the newly created counties. Although the extent of the reforms illustrated the obvious tip in the balance of power towards the central executive and parliament, the 'dual polity' convention ensured that local government retained a substantial degree of autonomy and discretion. It presided over a wide range of local services that constituted the bulk of public-sector resources and employment - excluding the armed forces, central government ministries employed only 15% of all public workers (Goldsmith and Page, 1987:71).

In 1979, however, the election of the Conservative party to government resulted in almost fifty separate parliamentary acts affecting local authorities (King, 1993:194). Amongst these, the Education Reform Act and the Housing Act - both in 1988 - together with the NHS and Community Care Act in 1990, were significant in that they all but removed the traditional mainstay of local government responsibility for these areas. Added to these legislative acts, three further changes took place that held considerable consequences for the structure of local government: the abolition of the GLC, the ILEA and the metropolitan counties in 1986; the advancing of the idea of the 'enabling authority'; and the altered pattern of party control in local government (R. Leach, 1994:348-50).

The abolition of the GLC and metropolitan counties was promoted by the government as a one-off exercise designed to rid local government of unnecessary levels of bureaucracy (HMSO, 1983a). The metropolitan counties had never enjoyed whole-hearted acceptance when they were first introduced in 1972 and whilst it was acknowledged that these authorities were predominantly controlled by the opposition Labour party, their abolition did not seem to hold any implications for the older traditional shire counties. This was not the case. Abolishing the metropolitan counties provided a clear precedent for further changes and indeed many of the arguments used to justify the elimination of one tier of government were later commanded to justify major changes in other aspects of local government (*Financial Times*, 4/9/85:11).

The promotion of the notion of the 'enabling authority' - as opposed to the traditional idea of local government acting as a service provider - transformed the nature of local government. Compulsory competitive tendering (CCT), introduced first in the 1980 Planning and Land Act, and later reformed in 1988, revolutionized the functions of local authorities (see: Shaw, Fenwich and Foreman, 1994). Under CCT over 200 authorities, constituting almost one half of the local authorities in England and Wales, contracted out at least one service to a private contractor (Williams, 1993:96). Whilst the bulk of these contracts were won by local government's own Direct Service Organizations (DSOs), a growing number went to the private sector. As a consequence, the relationships between local authority contracting departments and DSOs are being gradually transformed: the traditional notion of 'public service' has been replaced by the orthodoxies of stringent contract specification, contract management and monitoring. The acceptance of public/private partnerships is now widespread in all local authorities.

The erosion of Conservative support at local government level was perhaps an unintended consequence of increasing powers to central government. Following the 1993 local elections, only one county remained with an overall Conservative majority (R. Leach, 1994:350). This is significant since the Conservative party, which was always traditionally strong in county areas, could be counted upon to defend their existence. The commitment of both the Liberal Democrats and more recently the Labour party to regional government suggests that the present organization of British sub-national government is not the last.

Administrative organization

Paradoxically the least change has occurred in Germany, where the process of unification has resulted in the simple addition of five new federal states, or *Länder*, to the existing system of Federal government. In Ireland the formal system of local government has changed very little: county councils (and county borough councils in the four main Irish cities) remain the primary unit of sub-national government. Beneath them borough corporations and urban district councils provide another layer of representation in areas of significant urban populations. By far the most significant changes to sub-national government have taken place in Britain, where county boundaries have been re-drawn, old counties have been abolished and new authorities have been created.

Still, an overview of the administrative organization of sub-national government is more straight-forward for some states than for others. For example, in Germany the *Rechtsstaat* concept (state based on the rule of law) ensures the allocation of functional responsibility between the Federal government and the federal states, and between the different constituent parts of sub-national government, is comprehensively provided for in the federal and state-level constitutions. By contrast, in both Ireland and Britain the roles and functions of sub-national government are determined entirely by central government policy and statutes. In both states the desire of central governments to create a more efficient system of local service delivery has resulted in a redefinition of the functions of local government. In Britain central government has sought to deliberately replace local government with alternative governance structures. In Ireland, central governments reluctance to delegate authority directly to local government has been matched by its sponsorship of numerous state-sponsored bodies and agencies at sub-national level, plus a wide range of community development groups. As a result, although the organization of Irish sub-national government seems similar to that in Britain (with minimal powers delegated to local councils and a growing number of alternative local actors), the trends in sub-national institutions are quite different. In Britain they are undoubtedly evidence of more central control, whilst in Ireland they may be evidence of moves towards a more devolved system of local governance.

Germany

Article 79.3 of the *Grundgesetz* guarantees constitutional protection to all German *Länder*. Each *Land* is allowed its own constitution (provided it conforms to the *Grundgesetz*) and a constitutional presumption of *Land* competence is maintained throughout the *Grundgesetz*. Article 30 states that 'the exercise of state powers and the fulfilment of state tasks is the concern of the *Länder*, in so far as the Basic Law does not otherwise prescribe or permit. Article 70.1 states that 'the *Länder* shall have the right to legislate, in so far as this Basic Law does not confer legislative power on the Federation. Article 83 states that 'the *Länder* shall execute federal law autonomously, in so far as this Basic Law does not otherwise prescribe or permit'.

Generally speaking, matters pertaining to the whole area of Germany are regulated by the Federal government. Otherwise, law-making is effected by the democratically elected *Land* parliaments that also provide the respective *Land* governments. These have both governmental and administrative responsibilities and are each headed up by a Minister President. The following areas are the exclusive legal domain of the *Länder*: culture (this brief includes educational institutions and radio communications); municipal laws; building codes; water rights; police regulations; internal revenue sharing; and the organization of state administration. In practice all constitutions of the sixteen German states are almost identical (EURES, 1995). Small variations do occur in relation to the number and allocation of ministerial briefs (Goetz, 1993:451). The real potential for differences between *Länder*, lies in their arrangements for regional administrative districts, or *Regierungsbezirke*, which carry out the functional and administrative tasks delegated to them by *Länder* governments.

The *Regierungsbezirk* acts as the administrative arm of the *Land* executive. Heading up the *Regierungsbezirk*, the *Regierungspräsident* and her staff are known as the *Bezirksregierung*; they are appointed as civil servants and responsible to the *Land* ministries, in particular the Ministry of the Interior. With the exception of a few dedicated *Land* agencies that operate at this level - such as the school, police, forest and finance authorities - the majority of administrative tasks in each *Land* are co-ordinated by the Regierungsbezirke (often referred to as *Mittelstanz*, or middle-level administration). Under the supervision of the *Regierungspräsident*, the *Regierungsbezirke* further ensure that each of the *Land* counties (*Kreise*) - the next level down - carry out a large number of remaining delegated tasks according to the *Land* law.[8]

For the new *Länder* then, following unification, the most pressing question was whether to create a *Mittelstanz* such as the *Regierungsbezirke*, or whether to leave the ministries and central *Land* offices as the upper tier, with the *Kreise*, or counties, as the sole lower tier. In the former Democratic Republic there had existed fourteen districts, which acted as the territorial representatives of the central state with extensive powers to control lower level administrations. Few wanted to reinstate these districts and this made the task of re-organizing district authorities less straightforward. The dilemma was clearly more than a question of administrative efficacy: the newly established *Kriese* were reluctant to cede any authority upward to *Land* level, fearing it might diminish their new-found independence. This resulted in various solutions across the new *Länder*.

Mecklenburg West Pomerania decided early on not to re-instate district authorities, and replaced them with several specialized agencies (Goetz, 1993:453). Brandenburg chose a similar path, replacing their old districts with twenty one central non-ministerial offices (*Landesoberbehörden*), with the existing *Kreis* chief officers and twelve individual *Kreis*-level agencies underneath (*untere Landesbehörden*) (Lörler, 1993:244-48). Both Saxony and Saxony-Anhalt created *Regierungsbezirke* (Hoffman, 1992:689-96). Saxony's decision was made soon after unification. Saxony-Anhalt waited a little longer to decide, established three *bezirke* on a temporary basis and subsequently decided to keep them (Hoffman, 1993:6-9). In Thüringen, the government sought compromise with the creation of a hybrid organization, the State Administrative Office, or *Landesverwaltungsamt* (Müller, 1992). The intention was to limit the number of *Land* agencies and central offices, yet still provide for administrative co-ordination. The *Landesverwaltungsamt* comprises three regional offices and is intended to relieve the ministries from administrative burdens whilst at the same time securing effective territorial implementation (Goetz, 1993:453).

All *Länder* are sub-divided into *Kreise*, or counties, which represent an association of small to medium-sized *Kommunalen*, or municipal corporations. Cities deemed to be large or important enough (usually with a minimum of 100,000 inhabitants) may become county-free (*Kreis-frei*) and function as a city-county (*Stadtkreis*). *Landkreis* and *Stadtkreis* are general purpose institutions with both co-ordinating and implementing functions, serving as the 'lowest level' of the *Land* administration. According to the constitution, *Kreise* are the 'direct expression of the peoples' sovereignty' and have the authority to administrate within their territorial jurisdiction on all 'local issues'.

The chief administrative officer of a *Kreis* or *Stadtkreis* has the dual responsibility of carrying out self-government functions and those delegated by the *Regierungsbezirk*: she is responsible to the *Regierungspräsident* for the legal quality of *Kreis* administration (*Rechtsaufsicht* - legal supervision). Typical areas of *Kreis* responsibility are: the local road network, refuse disposal, administration of local welfare office or rescue service, and supervision of local education. Kreise are financed through allocations from the Federal government and so-called 'municipal cost-sharing' whereby the *Kommunalen* (districts) pay the *Kreise* for local services under their responsibility. Although the functions of the *Kreise* and the *Kommunalen* may seem similar, the difference is that *Kommunalen* are automatically delegated responsibility for their local area, whereas the *Kreise* are delegated their responsibilities by the legislature.

Most *Kommunalen* are small villages, many are medium-sized towns and a small number are cities with over 100,000 inhabitants: if this is the case, *Stadtkreis* status may have been denied because of the problems it could create for the surrounding rural area. In principle, there is no state bureaucracy at this level of administration, with the exception of national postal and *Land* police services. The municipalities are thus free to administer all their activities under the principle of *Allzuständigkeit* (local jurisdiction). Some small municipalities, however, find that their size prevents them from carrying out required or desirable public services. In such cases, the *Kreis* may often act as a co-ordinator for joint *Kommunalen* initiatives.

In Baden-Württemberg, Bavaria, Lower Saxony, Rhineland-Palatinate and Schleswig-Holstein, small municipalities are permitted to form associations of villages, in a kind of municipal federation (called in various *Länder*: *Verbandsgemeinde, Verwaltungsgemeinschaft, Samtgemeinde* or *Amt*). In some *Länder*, such as North-Rhine Westphalia, large villages or towns have annexed small surrounding villages in order to create an enlarged unitary municipality (*Einheitsgemeinde*). These operate on the same basis as the voluntary co-operative arrangements of other *Gemeinde* but are formally constituted by law. Where this is the case, the unitary municipality will often create local districts (*Ortschaften*) based on the old boundaries of annexed villages, delegating tasks downwards where feasible to areas that were previously independent municipalities. Such areas often have their own elected councils, with powers limited to those granted by the 'parent council'.

With the exception of Saxony, the new *Länder* each rejected the mandatory amalgamation of municipalities as a way of overcoming functional shortcomings in service provision. Most new *Länder* did not wish to risk the political back-lash that would occur if they appeared to threaten the autonomy of municipalities that had only gained their self-government status in 1990. Instead, they created a number of joint administrative authorities, similar to the *Gemeinde* in the *Länder* of the former Federal Republic (see: Petzold, 1993).

Ireland

For local government purposes the Irish state is divided into twenty nine county and five county borough (city) areas of equivalent status, each with a separate elected council. The five county borough corporations represent large urban populations (in Dublin, Cork, Waterford and Limerick) existing within their respective county boundaries. Below this tier of local government is a lower tier of representative authorities in the smaller urban areas of counties and county boroughs: there are five borough corporations, forty nine urban district councils and twenty six town commissioners (Government of Ireland, 1996a:97). There were originally a set of rural district councils too, but these were abolished and their powers transferred to the county councils in the 1920s (Sinnott, 1995:254).

Although the counties and county boroughs have equivalent legal status as the main units of local government in rural and urban areas respectively, some functions are carried out by county councils throughout the entire county, including the urban areas represented by county boroughs.[9] Similarly, at sub-county level some functions that are legally vested in urban authorities are exercised on their behalf by the county council on foot of local agreements (Government of Ireland, 1996a). Though the county is the most important unit of local government, its range of functions is limited, relating primarily to physical infrastructure and public recreation facilities (Sinnott, 1995:255). These include the provision and organization of public housing, local road networks, water supply, waste management and sewerage, the maintenance of public amenities and a limited role in environmental protection. County councils also have some secondary functions in the areas of education, health and welfare, though in these areas they are subordinate to the specialized state-sponsored bodies responsible for each of these areas.[10]

State-Sponsored Bodies (SSBs) are 'autonomous public bodies, other than universities, neither temporary in character nor purely advisory in function' (IPA, 1997:128). There are five types of state-sponsored bodies: commercial, developmental, health, cultural and regulatory/advisory. Not surprisingly, developmental SSBs are the most significant for regional development, providing a range of support services to industrialists, farmers and others. These include: *An Bord Trachtala* - The Irish Trade Board; *Bord Fáilte* - the Tourism Board; *Cóillte* - the Forestry Board; *FÁS* (*Foras Aiseanna Sáothair*) - the Training and Employment Authority; *Forbáirt*, providing a range of science and technology services and programmes for enterprise to facilitate the development of Irish business; *Forfás* - the policy advisory and co-ordination board for industrial development and science technology; the Industrial Development Authority (IDA) - designed to create employment by providing incentives to foreign enterprises to set up in Ireland; and *Teagasc* - the Agriculture and Food Development Authority. The creation of numerous state-sponsored bodies and the transfer of functions to them that might otherwise be the responsibility of local government typifies Irish government attitudes to policy delivery whereby practical problems are often solved at the expense of democratic accountability. The development of the 'managerial system' in Irish local government further illustrates this point.

The basic principle of the managerial system is a 'legal dichotomy of reserved powers of councils and executive functions of managers', each provided for by central government legislation (Bromage, 1954:93). The main functions reserved for elected members include: the adoption of the annual estimate of expenses; the fixing of annual rates and amounts to be borrowed to meet these expenses; the making of development plans and by-laws, house-building programmes; and assisting other local bodies in providing service and amenities. These various functions can be exercised only on the passing of a resolution. Executive functions, which are the responsibility of the county/city manager, include: arrangements made by the manager in relation to staff; acceptance of tenders; making contracts; fixing rents; making lettings; and deciding on applications for planning permissions. Following the Local Government (Planning and Development) Act of 1963, the increasing emphasis on local development through planning, zoning, acquisition of land and site assemblage, and urban renewal initiatives, resulted in managers playing an ever larger role - often taking a leading part in the development of their areas (Chubb, 1992:278; Bannon, 1991:44).

City and county managers are appointed by the local authority on the recommendation of the Local Appointments Commission, (a three-person body set up in 1926 to select and recommend to local authorities persons for appointment to principal offices). Though internal promotions to the post of manager are not permitted, nearly all managers have had previous service with local authorities and it is exceptional when a person outside the local authority service succeeds in being recommended by the commission (Dooney and O'Toole, 1992:138-40). As permanent, professional and salaried officials, the manager and her staff are often in a stronger position to influence policy formulation and implementation when compared to the unpaid, part-time and perhaps transient, elected councillors to whom they give their service.

By the early 1990s, there was a growing consensus that local government was ripe for reform (Adshead and Quinn, 1998). Typically, this view did not stem from any radical desire for change, but rather from a realistic appreciation that after years of *ad hoc* responses, the plethora of agencies operating at sub-national level had become an 'administrative jungle' (Chubb, 1992:263). Coupled with the acceptance of the need to improve sub-national structures was an enormous increase in development activities at this level - exemplified by the variety of local activists from different organizational backgrounds - much of it driven by EU initiatives. Although these initiatives have varying aims and objectives, it is possible to identify common approaches. There has been an emphasis on the creation of partnerships that have fostered innovation, bringing together actors from statutory, voluntary, public and private sectors in a manner that has gained international recognition (OECD, 1996).

New approaches to local development have resulted in local authorities acquiring new functions: instead of operating as administrative agents of central government, with responsibility for a limited number of services, they now act as central co-ordinators for the ever widening arena of actors in sub-national development. The 1994 Programme for Government stated that 'the local authority must become the focus for working through local partnerships involving local community-based groupings, voluntary bodies, the private sector, and public agencies' (Government of Ireland, 1994:70). In this regard, the Operational Programme for Local Urban and Rural Development 1994-1999 (OPLURD) supported this new view of local authorities and provided significant evidence of local authorities taking a new approach to partnership initiatives at local level. Without supporting institutional reorganization, however, it is not clear how permanent this change might be.

Britain

In 1992, when the Conservative government was re-elected for a fourth term, they set about the further reorganization of local government. Their main objective was to decide 'whether in any area a single tier of local government could provide better accountability and greater efficiency' (Wilson and Game, 1998:59). As a result, they created 46 new unitary authorities in areas previously covered by non-metropolitan counties. The number of non-metropolitan county councils was reduced to 34 (now comprising only 238 district councils); the six metropolitan counties were abolished (leaving in place the 36 metropolitan district councils); and the Greater London Council and ILEA was also abolished (leaving in place the 32 London Borough Councils and the City of London). In Scotland the three island authorities were retained, whilst 32 unitary authorities were created in place of the previous regional and district authorities.

The irony of Conservative reforms aimed at simplifying local government structures is that the range of bodies now responsible for the provision of local government services is potentially unfathomable.[11] Moreover, continued attempts to deregulate, privatize and contract-out local government service provision have increased central government powers. The legislative programme of the 1980s, aimed at 'setting the citizen free', resulted in the acquisition by central agencies and ministers of over 400 new reserve powers (Williams, 1993:106). The logic was that before 'empowerment' could begin, those blocking it had to be disempowered. It has since been argued that this wide dispersion of powers and responsibilities is now combined with an absence of local authorities that hold a broad enough geographical responsibility to take a strategic view of economic development in their area. Greater Manchester, for example, was previously a metropolitan county presenting a fairly coherent economic unit. There are now ten different authorities, each responsible for a wide range of functions in an area of roughly three million people, the borders of which have no obvious economic logic and do not reflect other patterns of work or population flow (Davies, 1993:92; see also: Barlow, 1995).

It is this proliferation of bodies that has challenged traditional characterizations of British local government. To note that there has been a dramatic shift in the balance of power towards the centre, is to state the obvious: equally significant, though much more difficult to quantify, is the huge diffusion of authority that has occurred as a result of powers and functions being granted to appointed boards or to functionally specific bodies, trusts or initiatives. However, precisely because of their non-government status, statistics regarding these bodies are scant. Morris (1990) notes that government statistics give information only about nationally appointed boards and bodies, omitting the growth of such boards and bodies at the local level. He refers to the growth of a new 'lay elite', which has taken away many of the functions and responsibilities from elected councillors, as the creation of 'the new Magistracy'.

Stewart and Davis (1994:29-36) argue that the 'new Magistracy' has grown in response to the raft of changes at local level. Local authority representatives were removed from District Health Authorities and from Family Health Service Authorities (which replaced Family Practitioner Committees). Appointed boards were set up to run Health Service Trusts. The creation of Training and Enterprise Councils ended direct local authority involvement in regional training programmes and decisions. Self-appointing boards of governors took responsibility from local authorities for further education colleges and sixth-form colleges (subject to the requirements of nationally appointed funding councils). Schools were encouraged to opt out of local authority control and become grant-maintained and financed by new nationally appointed funding councils.

Table 2: The new local governance

FORMAL LOCAL GOVERNMENT		**INFORMAL LOCAL GOVERNMENT**		
Locally controlled service delivery	*Locally purchased services*	*Nationally controlled service delivery*	*Nationally regulated*	*Regulatory agencies*
Non-opted out schools	Private contractors delivering public services (eg. rubbish collection & cleaning)	Opted-out schools houses	Inner city initiatives	Privatized utilities
Planning Social services		Training and Enterprise Councils	Local enterprise agencies	Private sector developers
Social services		Housing Action Trusts	Urban Development Corporations	
			Public/private partnerships	
			Urban Regeneration Agency	
			Enterprise zones	

Source: King (1993:206)

Housing Action Trusts and Urban Development Corporations were appointed to take over responsibilities for housing stock regeneration and urban regeneration more generally. Finally, local authority control over policing matters was diluted by proposals for newly appointed police authorities only partially composed of local authority appointed members. King (1993:194-218) argues that as a consequence of all of these changes a 'new local governance system' has been created, combining both the traditional formal local government sector plus a new informal local government sector (see Table 2). The latter has grown at the expense of the former. This so-called 'informal local government' includes a series of authorities and boards 'established independently of local government, holding significant powers over the same jurisdictions and discharging policy-making functions that might logically have been assigned to local authorities' (King, 1993:205).

Below this tier of government, in the non-metropolitan areas of Britain lies a network of 'sub-principal' authorities. In England there are approximately 10,200 parishes, of which around 8,000 (mostly in rural areas) elect parish or town councils (Wilson and Game, 1998:69). In Wales there are around 900 'communities' at sub-county level, of which around 750 have established councils. Elections to both parish/town councils and community councils take place every four years. In Scotland, a similar number of community councils were set up as a result of the Local Government Act of 1973, though their role is more limited in that they are regarded primarily as local advocates to the relevant county councils and functional authorities. Elsewhere, community and town or parish councils hold discretionary powers relating to the provision of local services such as allotments, recreation areas and public amenities. They may also act as consultative bodies for local planning applications and development.

Town, parish and community council income is derived from local charges, collected on their behalf by the relevant county council. These charges vary from county to county depending on the council tax bands of property in the areas of collection. In 1997, the Conservative government extended the powers of sub-principal authorities with the Local Government and Rating Act. It provided for more local consultation between county and parish councils over planning and development, a share of reduced business rates to local councils, transport powers enabling local councils to initiate car-sharing and voluntary bus schemes, and crime prevention powers allowing local councils to set up surveillance cameras and run community policing schemes. Crucially, the Act did not provide any extra funding from central government to cover additional expenditure incurred as a result of exercising their new-found authority. As a result, the chief function of most local councils is to act as local advocates and lobbyists to other statutory authorities and functional bodies discharging services in their area.

Financial organization

Developments in the financial organization of sub-national government (most particularly in relation to regional policy) have contributed to changes in the position of sub-national government in all of the states considered. In Germany, the financial dependence of the new *Länder* upon the Federal government not only affected all of the *Länder* (either directly or indirectly), but also the German federal system as a whole, contributing to a trend of increasing centralization of development responsibility. In Ireland, local authorities need of finance has led them to become involved in a variety of new partnership arrangements and contributed to a re-definition of their role as key co-ordinating bodies at sub-national level. In Britain by contrast, responsibility for regional development has neither moved up to central government, nor down to local government, but been diffused amongst the wide range of new bodies operating at sub-national level and contributed to a fragmentation of policy authority at sub-national level.

Germany

According to Ossenbühl (1990), the core piece of the German federal system is the financial system, which includes both vertical and horizontal types of revenue-sharing and is derived from Articles 106 and 107 of the German constitution. Horizontal revenue sharing refers to the equitable redistribution of income between the richer and the poorer *Länder* and constitutes a central plank of Federal government regional policy. Vertical revenue sharing refers to the distribution of tax revenues, between the Federal government, the *Länder* and local authorities and forms the basis of *Länder* financial arrangements. The *Grundgesetz* stipulates that the disparate financial power of the states should be balanced.

Regarding vertical distribution of tax revenues, the federal system makes provision for both the Federal and *Länder* governments to raise taxes to which they each have *exclusive* access. In addition to federal grants-in-aid, the *Länder* are also entitled to shares in a number of joint taxes, the exact level varying depending on the type of tax under consideration. These rights are qualified by Article 106(3), which stipulates that the *Länder* and Federal government should have an equitable claim to revenues in order to *promote uniform living standards across the country*. Thus, for example, the allocation of the joint turnover tax, between the Federal government and the *Länder* is dependent upon the relative disparities between expenditure and revenue at these two budgetary levels (Smith, 1994:69). In short, whenever there are disparities at the federal level, the allocations from the turnover tax are revised.

The distribution of revenues from turnover tax comprises the chief instrument of horizontal revenue-sharing. 25% of the revenue from turnover tax is distributed among the financially weak states. Differences between states are equalized by the setting a country-wide average (of tax benefit) per inhabitant, each state is then entitled to at least 95% of the average (on a pro rata basis). The redistribution is effected so that any excess over this average, received by the more well-off *Länder*, is either totally, or partially taken away from them for redistribution among less well off *Länder*. In addition, financially weak *Länder* receive federal supplementary grants, which are derived from the federal revenue share of the turnover tax. The Federal government allocates approximately 2% of its share of turnover tax for this purpose (Eckey, 1991:707).

Not surprisingly, following unification, disputes over tax shares and allocations became increasingly tense. If the new *Länder* were to be fully integrated into pre-existing regulations for revenue sharing, extremely high transfer payments would result because both their economic performance and their tax revenue was only half that of the *Länder* in the former Federal Republic. In 1991, Eckey (1991:709) calculated that the net transfer cost could be as high as DM24 billion. As it turned out, this was a conservative estimate. Rather than risk losing the support of the *Länder* of the former Federal Republic and in order to avoid uncomfortable political consequences, a number of transitional agreements were reached.

One of the transitional arrangements involved sharing the spoils of *Länder* VAT receipts. Initially, a compromise agreement ensured that the five new *Länder* would each receive payments sufficient to increase their financial standing to a 55 % share of VAT revenue (using the number of inhabitants as a proxy guide to revenue shares). This transfer was to begin in 1991 and by 1994 it was envisaged that, with improvements in their economies, the new *Länder* could increase their share of VAT revenues incrementally to 70 %. In February 1991, however, the rapid rise of public sector debts and the prospect of bankruptcy in many authorities in the new *Länder*, led to a change of heart: the new *Länder* would receive a full share of VAT revenue immediately. Whilst the necessity for more investment was widely understood, many *Länder* from the former Federal Republic feared that they could not support such a burden on their own finances. They argued that revenue shares should be allocated according to the ability to raise revenue, rather than the proxy of counting inhabitants. After a series of heated discussions between Federal and *Länder* governments in March 1991, the Federal Finance Minister, Theo Waigel announced that despite the recognized need for investment in the new *Länder*, any spending over DM35 billion of public funds would be unwise (*Süddeutsche Zeitung*, March 1991). The arguments were abated, though far from conclusion.

Under the terms of federal fiscal equalization across the German states, the new *Länder* represent the chief spatial priority of German regional policy and their restructuring is supported by massive public financial transfers. The Federal government's gross contribution amounted to approximately DM400 billion over the period 1991-1994 and transfers in 1995 were estimated to exceed

DM150 billion in 1995 (Drerup, 1997:339). Much of this money is channelled through pre-existing policy arrangements and instruments. The Federal Transport Plan (*Bundesministerium für Verkehr*) plans to invest DM540 billion on the construction and extension of transport infrastructure up to the year 2012, of which DM180 billion is earmarked for the new *Länder* (*Bundesministerium für Verkehr*, 1993). The Federal *Telekom 2000* Plan invested approximately DM60 billion in the new *Länder* over the period 1990-1997 (*Deutscher Bundespost Telekom*, 1994). Production-related infrastructure projects are supported by the Joint Tasks, or GRW fund (*Gemeinschafts Aufgabe für Verbesserung der Regionalen Wirtsschaft Struktur*): by the end of 1994, DM16.3 billion of regional aid had been granted to the new *Länder* for investments totalling DM22.5 billion; and private investment worth more than DM130 billion was granted financial aid (Drerup, 1997:339).

The distribution of tax revenue between Federal and *Länder* governments continues to be a matter for dispute. With the increasing financial heterogeneity of the *Länder*, especially since unification, the difficulties of reaching compromises over tax sharing have increased. Originally, the *Grundgesetz* gave the *Länder* legal control over revenue from income and corporation taxes. In 1955 the Federal government was given a share of this revenue (Shonfield, 1965:268). Given, however, that there are no means of determining the exact level of consumption in each of the *Länder*, the number of *Land* inhabitants is used as a proxy upon which to base the relative shares of VAT revenue. The problem with this method is that it assumes uniform patterns of consumption across all *Länder* - an assumption that has become increasingly problematic with the absorption of the *Länder* of the former Democratic Republic. As a consequence of this system, the weaker revenue-raising power of the new *Länder*, has been ameliorated at the expense of the better-off *Länder* of the former Federal Republic.

Ireland

There are two aspects to the funding of Irish local authorities: capital and revenue expenditure. Capital expenditure is normally financed by borrowing from the Local Loans Fund, operated by the Department of Finance. Commissioners of Public Works, acting on the behalf of the Department of Finance, sanction loans if the project applied for is deemed satisfactory and within the remit of the local authority. As a consequence of increasing financial rectitude, local capital expenditure (taken as a proportion of the Public Capital Programme), decreased from around a quarter in 1977 to less than a fifth in 1992 (McManus, 1993:37). This trend has continued with the Irish government's financial commitments to Economic and Monetary Union.

Revenue, or current expenditure, is met from three main sources: rates, government grants and miscellaneous receipts from property and other charges. As a consequence of a *Fianna Fáil* election promise in 1977, domestic rates were abolished and replaced by a state grant in compensation for lost revenue. The government initially agreed to provide a 100% recoupment of the lost revenue to local authorities but in 1983, this was amended to a fixed annual total and local authorities were empowered to levy local service charges. Despite elaborate waiver provisions made for the less well-off, service charges proved extremely unpopular and were strenuously resisted. Few local authority areas were able to introduce them and those that did had great difficulty enforcing them. Although a popular national vote-catcher, the decision to abolish rates on domestic property meant that the financial dependence of local authorities upon central government was greatly increased: local revenues were, on average, diminished by half (Chubb, 1992:274).

The determination of central government to decide the maximum increases in the rates that remained not only hit local revenues, but also severely curbed local government autonomy. The abolition of domestic rates was the final major transfer of decision-making power to central government (Hederman O'Brien, 1989:341). The chair of the government appointed Commission on Taxation (1980-1985) reported that 'it might have been expected that such a transfer would have been marked by a recognition of its implications, some policy or plan for the new situation. The apparatus of local machinery was left in place and no significant change was made to its structure' (Hederman O'Brien, 1989:342). The fact that the abolition of domestic rates was carried out initially without legislation only underlined the power of central government vis-à-vis local authorities. This power has been further increased by the centralized nature of the grants system now in operation (McManus, 1993:39).

As a result of abolishing domestic rates, state grants form a larger part of local revenue, at around 44% (Dooney and O'Toole, 1992:147). Several government departments are responsible for different types of grant to local government, including Agricultural Grants given to replace 'lost rates' from agricultural producers, housing subsidy grants to meet loan repayments on local housing schemes, road grants, and some subsidies towards sanitary services such as water supplies or sewerage schemes. A further category of general grant, known as the rate support grant, may be used at the authority's discretion. These grants are allocated to individual authorities, by the Minister of Environment (responsible for local government), on the basis of proposals from them, the level of need in each area, and the state of on-going works in the locality.

The last category of revenue, miscellaneous receipts, arises as a consequence of charges for the provision of goods and services, the biggest earner being housing in the form of either rents or payments of house loans. Attempts in 1983 to reintroduce some local fiscal flexibility, allowing local service charges (for water, sewerage, refuse collection etc.), were for the most part a failure: in many instances local authorities refused to accept such a 'political hot potato', whilst other authorities with members in favour of such a move, found that they could not pass such a resolution at local level.

By 1994, it was evident that local government was financially hamstrung and if - as the government had promised - it wished to develop its role as a key player amidst the ever widening arena of sub-national actors, some financial reform was necessary. In 1995, the Rainbow coalition introduced an income tax allowance in respect of local authority charges. Since, however, the 1977 rates removal applied only to domestic properties, businesses increasingly felt that they were bearing a disproportionate burden of local government finance.[12] In 1997, the Local Government (financial provisions) Act enabled local authorities to claim the revenues from road taxes and from certain duties and fees charged under other enactments. This was widely perceived as a stop-gap measure until more comprehensive arrangements could be made as consequence of the central government sponsored review of local government finance. There have been no other reforms as yet.

Britain

When the Conservatives came to power in 1979, they were convinced that state intervention in the economy, far from being a potential cure for Britain's economic decline, was the major cause of the problem. The government's desire to curb public sector expenditure was reflected in attempts to reduce central grant support (Aggregate Exchequer Grant) to local authorities, largely through a change in the structure of the grant system. The old system of grant support, incorporating an assessment of both needs and resources, was replaced by Grant Related Expenditures (GREs). The methods used to measure GREs were also changed. Whereas 'needs' had traditionally been calculated using local formulas, incorporating value judgements (such as the dependencies of single parent families or special needs areas); the GREs were calculated using direct measures of client numbers that attempted to avoid, as far as possible, the use of past expenditure data and so reduced the possibilities for feedback (Gibson, 1992:58). Furthermore, in order to highlight 'over-spending' authorities, measures of expenditure needs were published in the annual grant settlement.

In 1981, the government introduced a composite 'block grant' based on an assessment of GRE, which included a reduction (known as the taper) in the rate of grant support on any expenditure above the government's pre-determined threshold. This was usually some ten % above the GRE measurement of the authority's needs. More significantly, that same year the government established a system of expenditure targets: local authorities failing to meet with these were then subject to grant penalties for over-spending. Following the Conservative re-election in June 1983, a government White Paper (HMSO, 1983b:1.22) noted the widespread increases in local authority charges and suggested that 'the root cause of this large increase in rates has been local government's failure to meet the Government's spending plans. Had it done so, rate increases would on average have been below the general rate of inflation'. The government took action with a series of measures.

The 1984 Rates Act made possible the operation of both selective and general rate limitation schemes, giving the central government unprecedented new powers to control local government. In 1986, the system of target expenditure and penalties was removed in favour of straightforward rate-capping for selected over-spending local authorities. The responsibility for high rates was placed on a minority of 'over-spending' authorities and a number of measures were introduced to reduce their autonomy: a series of changes largely extricated the control of education, housing and health from local authorities; the Greater London Council (a notorious Labour strong-hold) together with the Inner London Education Authority (ILEA) and the other metropolitan county councils were abolished (Williams, 1993:99-103). The government assumed that its problems with local government were over.

In partial response to the special study report of the Audit Commission (the body created by the government during its first term to oversee the audit of local authorities and given the power to institute 'special studies'), and also to the increasing disquiet over local rates increases, the government felt obliged to consider alternative means of financing local government. The publication of the Green Paper, *Paying for local government* in January 1986, set out radical proposals for the reform of the system of local government (HMSO, 1986). The rates system was widely regarded as an unfair tax, weighing disproportionately on owner-occupiers - particularly single occupants - with relatively large houses, regardless of income. Local business rates were also criticised for giving local authorities the power to tax local wealth creation in order to create revenue for social-spending purposes: the government argued that these were a significant determinant of business location decisions that could mitigate against economic development in certain higher-spending local authority areas. The government's central argument against the weaknesses of the rates system was its lack of local accountability. The fact that rates charges did not reflect the use of local services was referred to as the absence of the 'beneficial principle' in local taxation (see:

Gibson, 1992:63-67; Davies, 1993:88-91).

In 1989, significant reforms for the financing of local government were introduced. Chief amongst them were: an end to *full* rates rebates for those on the lowest income levels; the simplification of the central government grant system (now called the Revenue Support Grant), replacing the GREs with simple Standard Spending Assessments (SSAs); the substitution of non-domestic rates with a nationally uniform tax, the proceeds of which are distributed to local authorities on the basis of an equal amount per adult; and finally, the replacement of domestic rates by a flat-rate tax, called the 'community charge' in each local authority area (see: Flowerdew, Francis and Lucas, 1994).

The political upheaval that followed the British government's substitution of 'community charges' - more commonly known as the poll tax - for domestic rates is legendary. The fall-out included the ousting of Mrs Thatcher from the Conservative party leadership, as well as the eventual replacement of the poll tax by a more politically acceptable Council tax (a banded property tax based on capital values with a twenty five % reduction for single occupiers and various other categories of persons). With regard to the other reforms however, little changed. There was no change in the system of uniform non-domestic rates, or in the methods of estimating local authorities' needs assessments, the Standard Spending Assessments. As a consequence, financial reforms reinforced other administrative reforms, decreasing local government autonomy by increasing their dependence upon central government finance. Davies (1993:90) argues that because the essential links between taxing and spending have been broken, the interests of different tiers of government tend to diverge so that 'local authorities see themselves primarily as 'spending' agencies and identify their main task as being to attract grants from central government for the benefits of their area'.

Both the relatively small size and the number of these numerous second-tier governments militates against their ability to attract funding. The reforms have led to a dramatic reassignment of the local tax burden, whether measured between households, individuals or areas. On an area basis, average local tax bills seem to be lower in areas that previously sustained high domestic rates, and higher in areas that previously sustained low domestic rates (Gibson, 1992:66). The borders to local authorities do not group richer and poorer areas to form balanced taxing units. One consequence of local government reform is that it both 'creates fiscal difficulties and also tends to push responsibility for taking a strategic view of economic development up to the central government' (Davies, 1993:92). London, for example, now has thirty-three different local authorities, some almost entirely composed of socially deprived areas with very weak local tax bases (Davies, 1993:91). There is now, however, no mechanism for fiscal equalization between the least well-off local authority areas and the better off, compared, for example, to the previous system of tapering grant support (Keating and Midwinter, 1994). The financial bases of local authorities are thus being undermined not only by central government but also by damaging competition with other local authorities for access to the same scarce resources.

Concluding remarks: policy environment and network potential

The aim of this chapter has been to illustrate how different institutional environments impact upon the structure of regional policy networks in each of the states. This helps us to anticipate the kinds of network structures that are most likely to form in different state systems. In Germany, for example, the strong tradition of regional self-government, the functional organization of the German federal system and the importance of the *Rechtsstaat* concept in public administration, suggest that German regional policy networks will be relatively formal in terms of their organization and structure. We can expect the organization and administration of regional policy competencies to be highly prescribed and the resulting policy networks to be relatively stable and enduring.

In Britain and Ireland, both unitary states where the institutions and organization of sub-national government are not constitutionally protected, central government plays a more significant role in determining the form and structure of sub-national government. In Ireland, central government approaches to sub-national government have been characterized by pragmatism. This is reflected in the institution of the managerial system for local government and a range of expedient responses to localized problems, evidenced in the massive growth of state-sponsored bodies and different organizations and agencies created by central government. Despite the proliferation of regional agencies, plus a little tinkering with the organization of local government, there has been no substantive reform of sub-national government. Instead an 'administrative jungle' has grown and thrived as a result of central government's relatively short-term approach to the organization of sub-national government. Within this institutional environment, it not clear what kinds of regional policy networks will emerge - only those that will not. Regional policy networks will not, for instance, be legally constituted, formally prescribed or rigidly structured. The exact form of networks will depend to a very great extent on the behaviour and attitudes of regional policy actors who constitute their membership.

In contrast to Ireland, British central governments have shown a much greater enthusiasm for reform of sub-national government - albeit it equally short-term and non-strategic. The reorganization of British local governance throughout the 1980s has been variously characterized; as 'an end in itself' (R. Leach, 1994:345), or a 'classic example of policy drift' (S. Leach, 1993,

1994a,1994b) emerging 'as much through accident as by design - a by-product of the Thatcherite conflict with local government in the 1980s' (Williams, 1993:96). Not only has control of British regional policy institutions become more centralized, but it has also been increasingly subject to the influence of the private sector. As a consequence, we can expect both central and private sector actors to have a strong influence on the structure of regional policy networks. However, the fragmentation of regional policy responsibilities and institutions between a wide range of different actors, suggests that the structure of British regional policy networks will be much more dependent on the approach taken by central government, than is the case in Ireland. This is because central government has taken an increasing share of management control over sub-national government and also because many of these institutions have been established for a much shorter period of time. As a result they are not so deeply imbedded into the institutional architecture of sub-national government and have only a limited operational experience.

The material in this chapter allows us to relate longer-term trends in the organization of sub-national government in each of the states to patterns of change in policy networks. Thus, we might expect the institutional environment of regional development policy in Germany to be reflected in stability in regional policy networks. British sub-national government, by contrast, has experienced such a massive and radical reorganization of policy structures and institutions that we can expect a significant degree of instability in the policy networks found there. In terms of the impact that sub-national government structures have on network formation, we can expect the experience of Irish regional policy networks to lie mid-way between Germany and Britain. On one hand, the relative inertia of central government to tackle the issue of local government reform could be said to contribute to a degree of stability in sub-national government. On the other hand, the lack of constitutional or legal protection for sub-national government in Ireland means that it is still vulnerable to any significant change in central government approaches to the regions. The impact that different central government approaches to regional development can have upon the formation of regional policy networks is discussed in detail in the following chapter.

Notes

1. The *Grundgesetz* was designed 'to bring a new order to political life for a transitional period'. The term *Verfassung*, or constitution, was reserved for the document that would govern a reunified Germany.
2. In 1898, the Local Government (Ireland) Act, transferred the functions of the grand juries (non-

elected gentry held responsible for law and order in their own localities) to democratically elected county councils under the same doctrine of *ultra vires* that pertained in Britain.

3. In 1888, the Local Government Act established 62 elected county councils and 61 all-purpose county borough councils in England and Wales. It was followed by a parallel act in Scotland in 1889. In 1894, a second Local Government Act established within the county areas a network of 535 urban district councils, 472 rural district councils and 270 non-county borough councils. It was followed by an equivalent act for Scotland in 1900. The 1899 London Government Act established within the London County Council area a network of 28 metropolitan borough councils and the city of London Corporation (Wilson and Game, 1998:42-48).

4. The city acts included Dublin City Management Act, 1930; Limerick City Management Act, 1934; and Waterford City Management Act, 1939.

5. The 1963 Local Government (Planning and Development) Act was intended to give local authorities greater freedom to expand their developmental role without need of constant referral to central government. In practice, however, it served primarily to strengthen the role of the county managers at the expense of elected council officials.

6. After a difference of opinion between the leader of the Labour party, Dick Spring, and the leader of the *Fiánna Fáil* party, Albert Reynolds, in November 1994, the coalition government comprising these two parties collapsed. In the same month, John Bruton, leader of the opposition *Fine Gael* party entered into coalition with the previous Labour party office holders plus a smaller left of centre party - Democratic Left, led by Pronsiás de Rossa. The three-way split in government soon became known the 'Rainbow coalition'. See: Finlay, 1998: 205-266.

7. The 32 boroughs were allocated housing, social services, non-metropolitan roads and libraries, leaving the GLC with strategic functions - fire, ambulances, main roads and refuse disposal. However, a concerted attempt to preserve the education system built up under the former LCC resulted in the creation of a special committee of the GLC, known as the Inner London Education Authority (ILEA), which retained responsibility for education in the 12 inner London Boroughs.

8. Schleswig-Holstein, the Saarland and the three city states of Berlin, Hamburg and Bremen do not have *Regierungsbezirke*. In Schleswig-Holstein and the Saarland, the Ministries of the Interior assume the functions of the *Bezirke*, delegating administrative tasks to local government. In each of the city states, although there are no *Mittelstanzen*, the *Senat* is responsible for delegating a number of functions to the city districts for administration.

9. These include motor taxation, library services, fire, building control, emergency planning, generally national and regional roads, and most aspects of pollution control.

10. The Vocational Education Committee (VEC) for education and the eight regional Health Boards that deal with health and welfare.

11. William Waldegrave, in a debate in the House of Commons on 24th February 1994, claimed a reduction of such bodies from 2,167 to 1,389 (Stewart and Davis, 1994:29). Another survey by the *Guardian* (19/11/93) suggested that there would be some 7,700 such bodies by 1996.

12. In the period 1984-1994, rates on businesses increased by 102%, whilst the consumer price index increased by only 33%. Business representatives argued that they were being unfairly burdened with the cost of local service charges because they had little electoral influence when compared to the mass of domestic voters who did not wish to pay local charges. See: Collins and Walsh, 1995.

Chapter 3

Managing Policy Networks: Central Government Approaches to Regional Development in Germany, Ireland and Britain

Introduction

Having examined the institutional and organizational landscapes that shape and structure policy networks in the three states, we turn now to central government approaches to regional development in order to evaluate how these too might have impacted upon the formation of policy networks. The first section outlines traditional policy approaches in each of the states and shows how different conceptualizations of regional development led to quite different policy outcomes. Despite this, throughout the 1980s the evolution of regional policy in all three states was influenced significantly by the co-option of new actors into the policy area. The second section looks at the incorporation of these new actors into regional policy and reviews the role played by central government in the mediation and/or management of policy change. The resulting policy programmes, initiatives and instruments are described in the third section, whilst the fourth section examines the impact of alternative financial arrangements in each of the states. The chapter concludes with an indicative assessment of how different policy approaches influence network formations.

Traditional approaches to regional development

This section illustrates the significance that central government approaches to regional policy have upon regional policy outcomes. For example, despite the highly decentralized system of administration and political accountability in the Federal Republic of Germany, regional policy remains fundamentally a responsibility of the Federal government. This is because the high degree of integration between the Federal Republic's system of financial, fiscal and economic equalization between the German states, makes it difficult to separate out regional policy from other federal equalization policies. Similarly, in Ireland for some time it was difficult to separate out regional policy from national industrial policy because of government assumptions about the nature of development and economic growth. In contrast to both Germany and Ireland, however, British regional policies have not usually been integrated with other policy areas. This situation reflects both the traditional reluctance to acknowledge regions in a unitary state, as well as the traditional antipathy towards strategic policy planning.

Apart from the obvious importance of alternative policy contexts, this section also highlights the significance of particular policy trends in each of the states. For example, both Irish and British approaches to regional policy have altered dramatically in recent years. In Ireland this change is reflective of a wider shift in emphasis regarding the management of public policy. The gradual development of this shift means that it commands consensus support. Paradoxically, in Britain dramatic policy change co-exists with a long-standing tendency to eschew any form of comprehensive, policy planning in favour of *ad hoc* initiatives and programmes. As a consequence, the high degree of consensus surrounding policy change in Ireland has not been matched in Britain. Ironically, despite experiencing the greatest political upheaval (as a consequence of unification), German approaches to regional policy have changed the least. Arguments that unification has led to increasing centralization in the Federal Republic fail to take account of the fact that this trend was in evidence for some time before unification, or of the fact that in regional policy at least, the new *Länder* have succeeded in using the European Union to buttress their autonomy from the Federal government (Yuill, Allen *et al*, 1995; Yuill, Bachtler and Wishlade, 1996).

Germany

German regional policy is derived from Article 72 of the *Grundgesetz,* referring to the standardization of living conditions across the state, and is inextricably bound up with the notion of fiscal equalization between the *Länder* in the federal system (Ossenbühl, 1990). The need to counter regional imbalances was first recognized in 1951, with the establishment of a regional development programme primarily aimed at assisting economic development in deprived rural areas. This was supplemented, in 1953, by aid to the former Federal Republic's 'frontier corridor' (*Zonenrandgebiet*), stretching from the Baltic zone in the north to the south-eastern corner of Bavaria. With the inclusion of Berlin and those rural *Landkreise* with very poor levels of agricultural production, these areas were collectively designated as development areas (*Fördergebiete*) in the late 1950s.

In general, regional policy sought to decrease income and employment disparities between these areas and other parts of Germany through a series of *ad hoc* measures designed to attract investment and development. The limited success of these various initiatives and investment incentives, however, led to the development of a more coherent policy strategy throughout the 1960s.

As well as increasing budgetary allocations, the 1965 Regional Development Act (*Raumordnungsgesetz*), provided the three essential goals of regional policy: growth goals, stability goals and equilibrium goals (EURES, 1995:162). 'Growth goals' refer to the promotion of regional growth as a means of increasing overall economic growth in the state. 'Stability goals' comprise three objectives: full employment, price level stability, plus the reduction of economic monocultures and special programmes designed to prevent large-scale employment and income losses in regions with structural problems. 'Equilibrium goals' aim to standardize living conditions across the state, by decreasing disparities in income and the provision of public and private services. Additionally, the *Länder* of Bavaria, Lower Saxony and North Rhine-Westphalia were empowered to designate their own development areas (*Landesausbaugebiete*).

In 1969, an amendment to the *Grundgesetz* (para.91a) empowered the Federal government to share with the *Länder* responsibility for the 'promotion of improved regional economic structures' (it was using this provision that some of the direct investment in the new *Länder* was later made). This so-called joint responsibility soon became one of the essential instruments of regional policy together with provisions for 'Regional Action Areas'. Both the designation of development areas and the determination of eligibility criteria became 'joint tasks' (*Gemeinschaftsaufgabe Verbesserung der regionalen Wirtschaftsstruktur - GWR* for short) shared between the Federal and *Länder* governments. During this period, the concept of 'growth centres' was adopted, with over 300 areas classified as 'Federal Development Centres'. Three grades of assistance were established, to be deployed in order of need.

The increasing involvement of the Federal government in both the development and determination of regional development centres brought more opportunities for centralized control of regional policy. Meanwhile, the creation of joint responsibility and joint tasks heralded the tacit acceptance from the *Länder* that *alone* their efforts were not sufficient to counter-act regional imbalances. This view was further substantiated in 1975, by provision for the Federal Regional Planning Programme, or *Bundesraumordnungsprogramm*, designed to co-ordinate regional policies across and between the *Länder*, in order to promote uniform development throughout the states. From this point onwards, it became impossible to isolate German regional policy from the fiscal system, or overall economic policy (Smith, 1994:78).

Throughout the 1960s and 1970s, Federal government attempts to manage the federal economy, through the accretion of greater powers for financial equalization and redistribution between the *Länder*, have been cited as evidence of increasing centralization in the Federal Republic (Hesse, 1987, Jeffery, 1994). Nevertheless, the historical, political and legal bases through which the *Länder* derive their autonomy ensures that they retain substantial powers in the formulation and implementation of regional development policy. Arguments about increasing centralization in Germany should therefore be understood within the context of the elaborate provisions for, and divisions of competencies between, different levels of government in the German federal system. Clearly, however, the economic and budgetary strains involved in the incorporation of the new *Länder* in the process of German unification brought an added saliency to this debate.

Ireland

In the years after Irish independence, development was associated clearly and exclusively with central government economic policy: regional development referred only the equitable spread of the benefit. It was assumed that successful national policies, designed to attract investment and increase industrial activity, would benefit the whole of Ireland through a 'trickle-down' effect whereby less well-off regions would be lifted by a rising tide of development throughout the state. Responsibility for development resided either with the central government or with agencies appointed directly by central government.

Despite a variety of regional initiatives, local government was largely excluded from the drive for regional development. The designation of local authorities as developmental agencies in the Local Government Planning Act of 1963, was one of the few innovations in the Irish local government system since its establishment in 1898 (Coyle, 1990:23). Under this Act, all local authorities were required to prepare development plans for their areas. In practice, however, many authorities were simply too small, lacking the financial and technical resources necessary to carry out this role. The envisaged re-organization of local government and strengthening of its financial basis, which would have made such a role feasible, was not carried out. Centralized sectoral planning remained the norm, with little effort to achieve sectoral integration, institutional co-ordination or local participation (Walsh, 1993:3). Essentially, development policy was a top-down process, controlled by central government and motivated largely by economic considerations. The national agencies implementing government policy in the regions, despite being regionally dispersed, could not be regarded as genuinely *regional*.

Throughout the late 1960s and early 1970s, several proposals were put forward to improve regional development, including the Buchanan Report (1969) urging concentration on a small number of growth centres, and the Devlin Report (1969), which suggested establishing a Department of Regional Affairs. Over time, it became clear that the government favoured the growth centre approach. In 1968, a Regional Development Organization (RDO) was established for the Limerick region to plan and co-ordinate development programmes across the mid-west. The following year, eight RDOs were set up across the country. By 1972, the creation of the RDOs (each publishing regional development plans) and the state-sponsored Industrial Development Authority (whose strategy included regional industrial plans), reflected the increasing significance that the government attached to regional development.

Despite such explicit concern for balance and economic dispersal, regional development remained constrained by governments' preoccupations with tackling macro-economic problems related to fiscal imbalances and rising unemployment (Walsh, 1992). With the movement towards freer trade and attempts to promote industrial development, industrial policy moved to the centre of Irish economic policy (O'Donnell and Walsh, 1995:200). After 1972, regional development became identified almost exclusively with the regional component of industrial policy. Central government's preoccupation with macro-economic development and national development objectives left scant room for regional development initiatives. From about 1975, the commitment to regional planning declined not only as a consequence of economic recession, but also because EC membership led to change of policy emphasis. Instead of focusing on internal regional disparities, the new priority was achieving greater convergence between Ireland as a whole and the more developed parts of the EC (Walsh, 1993:3).

Ironically, it would not be long before both of these conditions led to a policy turn-around later in the 1980s. During this period, changing attitudes to government policy-making facilitated a change in the structure and style of regional policy. Moreover, in conforming to EC regional policy reforms, the Irish government was obliged to give greater voice to regional policy interests. Since it was widely felt that sub-national government needed revision, reforms at European level became a vehicle for initiatives already underway at sub-national level to achieve greater recognition within the policy process. From the mid-1980s, the synergy of forces created by changes in practice at national, European and sub-national levels of government, led to a complete overhaul of Irish regional policy (Adshead and Quinn, 1998). The changed approach to public policy has been characterized in Ireland as the advent of 'partnership' government, in reference to the inclusion of agreed 'Social Partners' in the policy process. It is illustrated in regional policy by the incorporation of a variety of new local actors and agencies into the policy process.

Britain

Until the Blair government of 1997 expressed an interest in regional devolution, British regions were of no real importance as political entities in their own right, much less as recipients of any coordinated regional policy. It is even argued that the British may have a 'natural antipathy towards strategic planning and thinking' and that often what might otherwise appear to be 'random and pragmatic behaviour' is perceived in Britain as a sign of 'getting things done' (Roberts, 1993). 'Getting things done' in British areas of regional decline resulted in a variety of *ad hoc* policy programmes and initiatives, instead of long-term strategic planning for disadvantaged regions. Only in the early 1970s was there a serious discussion of problems confronting the major cities and a belated recognition these would be better 'tackled at source'.

The first major policy development affecting urban areas was the phasing out of the 'Urban Programme' (the collective term used to describe a number of projects and activities carried out under the Local Government Grants (Social Need) Act of 1969) and its replacement by the Inner Urban Areas Act in 1978. Under this act central government argued that local authorities had obtained 'special powers to promote regeneration, including the ability to designate industrial or commercial improvement areas and make grants or loans within them for environmental improvements or to promote the provision of new employment initiatives'(HMSO, 1995:7). Taken together these measures were known as the City Grant and Derelict Land Grant regimes.

The Urban Programme survived in a limited number of areas and a much more simplified form throughout the 1980s. In 1987, it was replaced by arrangements whereby fifty seven local authorities in England were specified as 'designated recipients' and were thus eligible to *submit bids* for government support (HMSO, 1995:6). The submission of bids in competition with other local authority areas highlighted the change in central government's attitude towards local government in general and regional policy in particular. Parkinson (1989:3) suggests that until 1979 and accession of the Conservative party to power, urban re-development and inner cities policy rested upon two assumptions: first, that social and welfare services were as important to this process as were economic or wealth-creating policies; and second, that the public sector had a central role to play in the regeneration of inner city areas. Local authorities were therefore key policy actors with significant responsibility for the majority of services that were seen to be centrally involved in urban regeneration (Gray, 1994:146).

After the election of the Conservative government, however, there was a general shift of priorities at the local level away from social welfare objectives and towards economic development goals. This change has been described as 'the shift from welfare state to enterprise state' (Cochrane, 1990) leading to a 'marketization of local governance' (Atkinson and Moon, 1994) where private sector interests have a bigger role to play than ever before, largely at the expense of local authorities declining competencies. Accounts of urban regeneration initiatives in Britain now emphasize the increased importance of inter-organizational coalitions between the public and private sector, with business interests becoming more influential (Harding, 1991; Shaw, 1993). The co-option of new interests into regional development is discussed in the section below.

Co-option of new actors into policy field

For a variety of reasons, traditional approaches to regional policy were challenged in each of the states as a consequence of central government desires to incorporate new sets of actors into the policy process. The most striking and obvious example of this is the incorporation of the former Democratic Republic into the Federal Republic of Germany in the process of German unification. At issue here, was the ability or otherwise of the former Democratic Republic to adapt to policy institutions and processes used by the Federal Republic. The question of making changes to Federal Republic institutions and policy processes was never seriously considered.

In Britain, by contrast, the entire organization of regional policy was subject to change. Under the leadership of Mrs Thatcher, the Conservative government pursued a more aggressively 'free-market' approach to economic management than most other developed countries (Davies, 1993:80). Traditional policy responsibilities were removed from local government control to new administrative boards appointed by central government and in many cases this affected the organization of regional development initiatives considerably. Political power became more centralized as the powers of locally elected authorities were curtailed and a range of other private interests were co-opted into policy over whom only central government had direct control.

Only in Ireland was the experience of change relatively even-handed. The Irish government did substantially alter its approach to regional development but here, policy change was negotiated between the full range of actors and agencies involved in regional development. Details of this and alternative processes of policy change in Germany and Britain are discussed below.

Germany

The co-option of the former Democratic Republic into the Federal Republic of Germany was a largely asymmetrical exercise in 'institutional transfer' (Lehmbruch, 1994). For regional policy and for all other policy areas, the West German model was extended over - and to a large extent superimposed upon - the area of the former Democratic Republic. The changeover was driven forward by exogenous and endogenous actions (Wollman, 1997). Exogenous factors refer to the massive transfer and influx of administrative personnel from west to east in what was termed 'administrative aid' or *Verwaltungshilfe*. Endogenous factors refer to the influence of the local political and administrative personnel whose task it was to implement this transfer.

The process of personnel transfer comprised of two major initiatives. First, as well as encouraging *Land* partnerships between states from the former Federal Republic and the former Democratic Republic, a series of partnerships (*Städtepartnerschaften*) were set up between east and west German counties and municipalities. A survey conducted by the Association of Local Authorities (*Deutscher Städtetag*) showed that by the end of 1991, all east German municipalities with more than 20,000 inhabitants, together with 95% of those with between 10,000 and 20,000 inhabitants, had been twinned with another municipality in the west (Scheytt, 1993:80). About half of these partnerships involved material assistance and consultancy. Whether through exchange visits, phone-call conversations or more formal forms of information exchange, these *Städtepartnerschaften* provided an opportunity for the induction of new administrative personnel in the former Democratic Republic into the administrative systems and institutions of the Federal Republic.

The second initiative comprised of a range of special funding programmes set up jointly by the Federal government and the western *Länder*, designed to encourage west German officials and administrative personnel to relocate to the east. These were both temporarily and permanently arranged in order to provide a transfer of expertise and institutional knowledge into the new *Länder*. By 1993, it was estimated that approximately 4,000 west German municipal experts and employees had moved to work in the east, representing a significant influx of west German administrative know-how (Wollman, 1997:326).

Regarding the endogenous factors affecting institutional transfer from west to east, Osterland's (1993) portrayal of local government personnel in the new *Länder* outlines a series of common traits that were widely substantiated in the twenty seven interviews carried out in east Germany as part of the primary research for this work (see also: Berking and Neckel, 1991).

The new state personnel of the former Democratic Republic are generally 'outsiders' to the political and administrative system within which they operate. They are new, not only to their positions but also to the job of politics in general. Many have technical and scientific training and worked in the old regime in fields unrelated to politics or administration. Often, though they were tolerated because of their technical skills, their careers did not flourish as a result of their disassociation from politics in general and the Communist party in particular. After unification, many of these workers found their names being put forward for positions in the new regime. Mostly male, in the 45-55 age group, the majority have attended a polytechnic or university, following their apprenticeship (Osterland, 1993:10). As a consequence, though they are well-educated and able, they often lack the type of skills common to most west German bureaucrats. Most are unfamiliar with the federal legal system and the process of law, which since it forms the basis of all policy in the German *Rechtsstaat*, is frequently cited as a difficulty.

Typically, personnel from the former Democratic Republic are highly committed to their work, though enthusiasm is relatively rare (Osterland, 1993:11). Many find themselves under a double workload as they struggle not only to carry out the difficult task of reconstruction in the east, but also to come to terms with new ways of working, new procedures and often a completely new job. Sometimes this leads to a feeling of frustration with themselves, or with the system, or with the west German officials and bureaucrats who seem always to 'know better'. Above all else, however, administrative and political personnel from the former Democratic Republic share a massive desire for autonomy and freedom. The experience of democratic centralism in the former Democratic Republic has left a widespread and generally held cynicism for centralized power that is often misdirected at any perceived 'interference' from *Land* level officials or politicians (Osterland, 1993:12).

Sometimes, these attitudes are illustrated by a lack of regard for proceduralism, more often they reflect a lack of patience with it. More generally, they are evidence of a strong sense of commitment and desire to discharge their duty. Consequently, the notion of a *complete institutional transfer* between west and east is a misnomer: development in the east cannot be fully understood without acknowledging the significant role played by the people of the east.

Ireland

Throughout the early 1980s, the large-scale external shocks to the Irish economy - such as the oil crisis, world-wide recession and the emergence of stagflation - illustrated serious flaws in Irish development policy. Across Europe, as many governments sought to pursue broadly similar strategies, they often ended up 'competing against each other for key projects so that the net beneficiaries in this zero-sum game were the large mobile corporations' (Walsh, 1993:6). As a result policy emphasis changed, reflecting a keener interest in new technologies and product innovation: Irish governments began to place a renewed emphasis on the 'development of the indigenous sector and the development and promotion of small and medium sized enterprises' (Quinn, 1996). At the same time, attempts to create export-led growth led to Ireland's total participation in, and inextricable ties to, the international economy (O'Donnell and Walsh, 1995).

In seeking both to reform the economy and respond to the demands of the international market, Irish governments attempted to introduce greater flexibility in production processes and the organization of labour by introducing a system of national concordat with the major representatives of business and labour. The 'National Understandings' of 1979 and 1980 marked a subtle shift in the nature of Irish decision-making.[1] 'They began the integration of management and trade unions into the formulation of public policy' (Lee, 1979:20). This trend was inhibited by the turnover of governments and the recession of the early 1980s, but later re-established in a yet more developed form towards the end of the decade.[2] The *Programme for National Recovery* (1987-90), the *Programme for Economic and Social Progress* (1991-93), the *Programme for Competitiveness and Work* (1994-1996), and the lastest *Programme 2000* illustrate successive governments' commitment to reaching a *consensus* regarding the appropriate levels of growth and *agreed* measures to achieve them. The making and implementing of these agreements shows how closely employers' associations and unions have become involved, not only in public policy-making, but also in its administration (Chubb, 1992:128). It has come to be known in Ireland as 'partnership government'.

The advent of 'partnership government' was but one of a series of developments that heralded a new approach to the management of regional policy in Ireland. There was a growing consensus that local government structure in Ireland was inadequate, over-burdened, and unable to respond to local needs. After years of ad hoc reforms, the plethora of agencies operating at sub-national level had become an 'administrative jungle' (Chubb, 1992:263). There was also a growing appreciation of the relative failure of centralized approaches to solve the country's social and economic problems and also an increasing desire to countervail central control with local initiatives. Finally, the implementation of European Community pilot programmes and new initiatives in Ireland provided a range of opportunities to formulate new approaches to regional development that were later incorporated into Irish regional policy. The way in which this occurred was, however, by no means straightforward.

In 1988, the negotiations resulting in the reform of the EC Structural Funds presented a 'mixed blessing' for the development of Irish regional policy. Irish negotiators believed that if the more prosperous Eastern region, especially Dublin, were evaluated in isolation from the rest of the country; it might well be excluded from the benefits of the Regional Fund. Furthermore, the Community's developing competition policy would more than likely prevent the state from giving out industrial development grants or investment inducements. Whilst the negotiations cemented Ireland's successful bid for a lion-share portion of structural funding, this came at the price of treating Ireland as a single region. Nevertheless, as a consequence of the reforms, the Irish government was obliged also to set up a number of '*sub-regions*', (sub-regions because under EC funding criteria, the whole island of Ireland is treated as a *region*), in order that they might contribute to the preparation of a four-year National Development Plan (NDP) being submitted to Brussels.

In fact, the development plan submitted in 1989 was based on a national programme rather than a regional one and the input of regional groups was regarded by central government largely as a 'cosmetic exercise' in order to satisfy EC funding criteria (Coyle, 1990:11). Despite this, however, the promotion of specific measures aimed at *rural development* succeeded in establishing a framework for alternative future policies (discussed in more detail in the succeeding section). This, together with the desire to make the best use of Structural Funding - through attempts to coordinate development activities and to avoid duplication of efforts or costs at local level - did contribute to pressures for change that had already built up elsewhere in the system. Even though the NDP did not address itself specifically to the issue of Irish regional development, it was obliged to acknowledge the operation of a variety of programmes, initiatives and pilot schemes as part of regional consultation exercise, so that by the time the second National Development Plan was introduced, a discernable shift of emphasis was apparent.

The second National Development Plan, submitted to the European Commission in October 1993 for the period 1994-1999, included a specific Operational Programme devoted to Local Urban and Rural Development (OPLURD). The government presented OPLURD as a 'key element' in the strategy of the plan, 'building upon the experience gained from the implementation of initiatives stemming from EC actions' (Government of Ireland, 1995:12). The inclusion of a structured local development programme in the National Development Plan was not only a major innovation in national planning, but also an important political response to demands from local and regional interests that the spirit of partnership as envisaged in the 1988 reform of the EU Structural Funds was not being fully addressed in Ireland (Walsh,

1995:13).

Since much of the substance of the Operational Programme is derived from the experience of previous and in some cases on-going development initiatives, it is fair to argue that OPLURD's main purpose is to legitimate such practice and formalise their incorporation into the presentation of an over-arching National Plan. In essence, OPLURD did not *introduce* regional policy to Ireland: it simply *recognised* and *promoted* those development strategies that were already in existence and attempted to support their implementation within a coherent national framework.

Britain

The most evident feature of British urban policy in the 1980s was the dominance of development interests (Stewart, 1996:146). The government sought the involvement and support of the private sector not only to curtail government spending (both local and central), but also to invoke market-based solutions, such as competition and entrepreneurship, to the problems of urban regeneration. This approach both transformed and fragmented the mechanisms for policy delivery (Stewart, 1996:147). The resulting proliferation of organizations associated with regeneration shifted the balance of interests in regional policy-making: local authorities were relegated in status, whilst private interests, especially property developers, became more significant. This trend began with the Heseltine initiatives of 1981, which sought to strengthen the contribution of local and national businesses in the process of urban regeneration, and was firmly established with the 'Action for Cities' initiative, launched in 1988 (HMSO, 1988).

'Action for Cities' introduced a number of new urban initiatives and attempted to co-ordinate development strategies that were the remit of different government departments. All the projects, including the establishment of Urban Development Corporations (UDCs), Task Forces, and City Action Teams (CATs), incorporated the private sector (HMSO, 1991). For the most part, initiatives concentrated upon infrastructure, environmental works and site preparation for the private sector, as well as projects to promote local training and housing improvements. The primary aim however, was clearly to attract *private* investment in attempts to create jobs.

Thirteen Urban Development Corporations were created to reverse large-scale urban decline. Equipped with statutory powers that usually included planning responsibilities, UDCs were allowed to buy and sell land in their area in order to encourage industry and commerce and to develop local housing and amenities. Some UDCs were accused of alienating local authorities, as well as being autocratic and remote (DCC, 1985; GLC, 1984). Many suffered badly as a consequence of the down-turn in the property market at the end of the 1980s but others continued to operate effectively because they were able to react more quickly to the needs of the private sector than local authorities (Lawless and Brown, 1986). Not all UDCs alienated their local authorities. The Merseyside Docklands Development Corporation, for example, managed belatedly to achieve a co-operative relationship with the local authority and some local authorities, such as Trafford, Birmingham and Cardiff, actively sought UDC status (Dawson and Parkinson, 1991; Deakin and Edwards, 1993).

Inner city Task Forces, were intended to bring together and focus the efforts of government departments, local government, the private sector and the local community to regenerate inner cities (HMSO, 1995:40). Task Forces were not permanent, but designed to create some synergy of actors at local level, which could then be 'handed on' to existing local organizations after the life-span of the Task Force. Other programmes were also created to 'draw in' the private sector. The City Challenge Initiative was launched in May 1991 to enable local authorities, in partnership with the private, public, and voluntary sectors in local communities to draw up 'imaginative, comprehensive and realistic programmes designed to regenerate key areas over a five-year period' (HMSO, 1995:31; see also Atkinson and Moon, 1994). The Safer Cities programme, introduced in March 1988, awarded contracts to organizations managing crime prevention initiatives in inner city areas. In 1988, Housing Action Trusts (governed by executive boards made up from local representatives, nominated local councillors and central government appointees) were created and charged with regenerating severely run-down council housing estates and. English partnerships, introduced in April 1994, involved the setting up of a number of government agencies to promote the development of vacant, derelict and contaminated land. Designed to draw together public, private and voluntary actors in joint development initiatives, in 1994 it assumed the functions previously carried out by local government under the City Grant and Derelict Land Grant schemes respectively, as well as the work of English Estates.

The implementation of urban regeneration policy has been characterized by administrative complexity: it is a multi-area policy, carried out by a range of different bodies, which has resulted in an increased role for central government in the supervision and co-ordination of policy tasks. Moreover, as a result of the reforms, any common cause or solidarity that local authorities might have felt against central government cut-backs was dissipated by their competition against each other for funding (Atkinson and Moon, 1994:95). Other initiatives, such as the City Action Teams (CATs), further cemented the policy authority of central government. Acting as co-ordination agencies operating joint ventures between the Departments of Employment, Environment, Trade and Industry, CATS were later subsumed within the Integrated Regional Offices in April 1994. Created in November 1993, the Integrated Regional Offices combined the former regional offices of the Departments of Environment, Employment, Trade and Industry, and Transport and are sometimes referred to as Government Offices for the Regions. Whilst the new offices represented an acknowledgement of increasing policy fragmentation, they also served to further buttress the authority of central government in regional regeneration policy.

Policy programmes, initiatives and instruments

In relation to the nature and substance of policy, all three states differ widely in their conception of 'regional development' and what constitutes the most appropriate role for central government. In the German federal system, for example, the main aim of policy is to equitably distribute opportunities for economic growth and development throughout the country. Regional development is thus conceived in terms of the equitable advancement of *economic* development across Germany. In this policy framework, the Federal government plays a crucial role through its central control of the federal financial system, which has implications for the resourcing of policy both across the federal states and between the federal levels of government.

In Ireland, by contrast, the government's incorporation of a variety of alternative development projects into one all-encompassing national programme, reflects a newly emerging definition of regional development whereby *social* and *economic* aspects of development are regarded as equally important and interlinked. Within this policy framework, the importance of the Irish government is not so much linked to its ability to determine policy outcomes, as it is to its pivotal position and capacity to co-ordinate the range of policy initiatives going on in the state.

Compared to both Germany and Ireland, Britain has a much narrower view of what constitutes regional development. There is no policy mechanism designed to distribute development opportunities equitably around Britain, nor is there any distinctive emphasis on developing human capital. Since the 1980s, the chief aim of regional development policy has been to attract more private (and less public) sector investment in lagging regions, as a means of 'kick-starting' economic regeneration. Within this policy framework, the importance of central government has increased, first because it sets the terms and conditions of private sector investment in regeneration and second, because it controls the allocation of funding to the public sector.

In relation to the organization and administration of policy, the states can be arranged along a continuum according to the degree of influence that central government can wield over policy aims and objectives. In Germany, for example, the objectives are formally provided in the German constitution, as is the division of policy responsibilities between the different levels of government in the federal system. As a consequence, the operation of regional policy is closely bound up with federal economic and fiscal policies and, to a lesser extent, other policy areas that either impact upon or are themselves influenced by regional development programmes and initiatives (such as trade, commercial, agricultural, industrial and environmental policies). Although the Federal government has a decisive influence over all of these areas, it cannot ignore the provisions of the Federal constitution, or the opinions of constituent federal states, or other institutional policy actors within the federal system.

In Ireland, the aims and objectives of regional policy are set out in the National Development Plan (NDP) agreed between the Irish government (through negotiation with the Social Partners) and the European Commission. The Operational Programme for Local Urban and Rural Development (OPLURD) is in effect a compendium of contracts negotiated between the range of regional development actors involved in projects emanating from European, national and sub-national levels and represents the government's effort to guide the direction of development by co-ordinating the efforts and outcomes of different policy initiatives.

In Britain, the aims and objectives of regional policy are determined exclusively by central government. Since the early 1980s, the operation of regional policy has been closely bound up with a range of quasi-autonomous agencies designed to lever in private sector support. The regulation and control of these bodies is a matter for central government and as a consequence the practice of regional development has been further centralized.

Finally, regarding the degree of integration achieved between different policy areas and also between different policy actors, in each of the states it is clear that central governments are in the best position to affect the level of policy co-ordination or integration. They have, however, each gone about this task in different ways. The German Federal government, for example, regulates the impact of different policy areas on each other through a system of comprehensive planning. Regional policy in Germany is strongly codified by law, highly proceduralized and often formulaic. This system of policy administration requires a significant level of bureaucratic management but the resulting policy is a highly integrated (between different parts of the federal system and between different policy areas), and there is a clear division of competencies between policy actors regarding the methods by which to achieve specified policy aims.

In Ireland also, a high level of policy co-ordination has been achieved between a wide range of policy actors including the European Union, state-sponsored agencies and institutions, the national Social Partners, as well as local communities and groups. There is, however, no permanent, formalized system of co-ordination between these groups: the entire policy structure of the OPLURD is designed to last only as long as the Community Support Framework that funds it. There is, therefore, no guarantee that this level of integration will continue, though the fact that it has been achieved so successfully to date may also reflect the organizational advantages that Ireland enjoys as a consequence of its relatively small size and population compared to other European states. Still, without central government support, it is not clear how long this level of policy integration could endure.

Compared to both Germany and Ireland, Britain has achieved only a negligible degree of policy co-ordination or strategic planning. The change from Conservative to Labour government did not result in significant policy reform. The Labour government has made numerous statements that seem to support the view that existing approaches are less than satisfactory. It asserts that co-ordination, strategic planning and effective partnerships are all desirable approaches to regional development. Yet still there are no concrete proposals for a change in approach. Perhaps the absence of an alternative strategy accounts for the reticence in rejecting the current approach.

Germany

The goals of regional harmonization, provided for by Article 72 of the Grundgesetz, are sought by four policy measures: locating government industries and services in problem regions; deterrence measures (such as levying extra taxes) in over-crowded areas to control development in non-problem regions; enticement policy, directed at the mobilization of fixed capital investments; infrastructural improvements in the structurally weak regions (Hahne, 1985). Of these measures, infrastructural development and mobilization of capital investments have generally been the preferred means of achieving an improvement in the overall economic situation. As a consequence, regional policy in Germany is primarily a matter of regional *economic* policy and regional *structural* policy. Three major policy instruments are used to co-ordinate policy, these are the joint responsibility principle; the economic programmes of the Federal government; and the operation of fiscal equalization. The first two of these instruments are considered below. Consideration of fiscal equalization is left until the following section, dealing with the financing of regional policy.

The principle of joint responsibility for 'improving of regional economic structure', derived from Article 91 of the *Grundgesetz*, is the cornerstone of

German regional policy. This has been opreationalized, however, at the cost of complete *Länder* autonomy: the Federal government must agree to the execution of measures, as well as the determination of areas. The cooperation is coordinated by a Planning Committee, chaired by the Federal Economics Minister. Decisions are made by a three quarters majority: the *Länder* each have one vote, and the Federal government has the same number as all the states together. More recently, this structure has been augmented by two new committees: the 'Inter-ministerial Committee for Regional Economic Policy', which seeks to inform other Federal ministries on Joint Task matters; and the 'Working group for Regional Economic Policy', which acts as a briefing meeting for sub-*Land* authorities and economic and social interests. It is the task of the Planning Committee to determine the intervention areas and the development approaches within these areas. In general, a 'national framework plan' lasts for four years, but may include a number of additional *annual* framework plans. The *Länder* governments are responsible for policy, so long as they concord with the overall framework plan. One consequence of this system has been an increasing standardization of regional interventions by the *Länder*, together with a decrease in *ad hoc* interventions in so-called 'emergency areas' (Kruse, 1990).

'Joint responsibility' tasks, or *Gemeinschaftsaufgaben*, are co-financed - half by the Federal government and half by the respective *Länder* involved. The choice of areas chosen for development is based on labour market potential, combining districts or cities that are not well-serviced in terms of infrastructure and accessibility for commuters. This determination is important, since it is used for many other regional initiatives and promotion measures taken up by the Federal government. The level of support is determined by a formula comprising factors such as the average gross annual salary, average unemployment rate, infrastructure and labour market trends. The five new *Länder* have all been defined as areas in need of development under these criteria.

In addition to regional development promotions carried out under joint responsibility, there are five major federal measures designed to promote regional development (Neupert, 1986). The first of these is a system of capital grants based on tax incentives for investment and is designed to stimulate job creation through commercial enterprise. Companies may apply for this themselves at the tax office or through the federal Ministry for Economics. The second measure comprises the dispersement of federal financial aid in accordance with Article 104a of the *Grundgesetz*: this measure is only available to public bodies, but is not regionally targeted. The third measure constitutes preferential loan arrangements for the promotion of investment in economic growth in regional and municipal areas respectively. These ERP promotion programmes originated immediately after the Second World War and were established by the United

States for reconstruction in Germany. The economic agreement is still in effect and ERP funds are administered by the Federal Economics Ministry. The fourth measure relates to investment credit from the Credit Institute for Reconstruction - another measure originally conceived for rebuilding the German economy after the war that has gained increasing significance since unification. It comprises of preferential loans for small and medium sized companies in the manufacturing sector. Finally, the fifth measure relates to favourable status accorded to the areas that formerly bordered the Democratic Republic as a result of their peculiar circumstances and peripheral location in the former Federal Republic.

Ireland

Since the Operational Programme for Local Urban and Rural Development (OPLURD) represents the Irish government's attempt to envelope the wide range of sub-national development activities within a single national framework, it is best understood by a brief review of those initiatives that have been consolidated by its creation.

During the period 1988-90, the Pilot Area Programme for Integrated Rural Development was the first attempt to apply the principles of integrated rural development in a systematic way. Administered by the Department of Agriculture and Food, the general objective of the programme was to improve employment opportunities, earning potential, quality of life and sense of community identity among people in rural areas (O'Malley, 1992). The emphasis was on encouraging viable private and community sector enterprises based on the full utilization of the abilities and talents of local people.

Twelve sub-county areas were chosen, each of which had between 6,000 and 15,000 inhabitants. A rural development coordinator was appointed to each area to act as 'animator', stimulating and co-ordinating local effort and facilitating linkages between local groups and various statutory agencies. Animators were not intended to be leaders or initiators and their first task was to assemble a 'core group' of local leaders. Each core group had the responsibility for deciding on local development priorities and ensuring their implementation. As there was no special fund for the programme, apart from a small amount for technical assistance, the core groups and the animators took on a brokerage role in their approach to the mainstream funding sources (Walsh, 1995:5). Another important feature of the programme was an emphasis on shared learning through workshops and other forms of networking. This approach was followed by the LEADER initiatives (Liaisons entre actions de developpement de l'economie rurale) for the period 1991-94, which gave locally-based integrated development strategies a new lease of life.

The objective of the LEADER initiative was to find innovative solutions to development that incorporated different sectoral measures and that might also be used as a future model for all rural areas. Accordingly, in March 1991, the European Commission (through its Irish intermediary body - the Department of Agriculture, Food and Forestry) invited local groups to prepare and submit 'integrated' business plans for their areas. Thirty-four groups submitted and following negotiations with the Commission, sixteen were selected, covering areas representing 61% of the land area of Ireland and almost 30% of the population (Kearney, Boyle and Walsh, 1995:ii). The success of the LEADER model encouraged a similar approach in urban areas.

In 1990, the National Economic and Social Council highlighted the problem of long-term unemployment and advocated a specialized government programme, directed specifically towards localized area-based responses, so that local people might be empowered to direct development towards specific local needs and priorities (NESC, 1990:74). Under the government concordat entitled *Programme for Economic and Social Progress* (PESP), an area-based response (ABR) to long-term unemployment was established on a pilot basis as 'an integrated approach designed to implement a community response in particular local areas to long-term unemployment and the danger of long-term unemployment' (Government of Ireland, 1991b). Twelve ABR areas were selected (eight urban and four rural), each with a board of directors comprising six directors from the local community, six from the social partners, and six from the state agencies in the area.

In September 1992, following negotiations with the Irish government, the European Commission established the Global Grant for the period 1992-95, comprising a 64% contribution from the ERDF and 36% from the ESF. It was valued at IR£8 million and was to be administered by Area Development Management Ltd (ADM), an intermediary organization established for this purpose in October 1992 (Haase, McKeown and Rourke, 1996:6). The Global Grant continued to support the twelve area-based partnerships set up under the government's *Programme for Economic and Social Progress (PESP)*, as well as a number of other small-scale, local development groups.[3] The condition of support for all projects was the submission of 'an integrated area action plan drawn up in consultation with such other local groups and bodies, public agencies and local representatives of the social partners, as the eligible body sees fit. This plan will set out the basic strategy whereby it seeks to achieve its objectives of economic and social revitalization in its area' (CEC, 1993b: Art.4).

In 1994, the establishment of OPLURD marked the government's resolve 'to bring about social and economic development at local level, to involve and to enable local communities to be involved in that development in a formal way, and to achieve physical improvements to the environment' (Government of Ireland, 1995:11). The Programme comprises three sub-programmes of developmental initiatives. The first, relating to local enterprise creation and development, is intended to support services for small and micro-enterprise initiatives (employing less than 10). The primary vehicles for this policy action are the thirty five County Enterprise Boards (CEBs) covering county and urban local authority areas. They were established first in 1993 and are organized according to a partnership model that includes representatives of public agencies concerned with enterprise development, the private sector, farming, trade union and community interests and elected members of the local authority. The Executive Manager of the Local Authority is also a member.

The second sub-programme, relating to integrated socio-economic development of designated disadvantaged areas, extends the operation of PESP and Global Grant area-based partnerships to 33 designated areas of disadvantage (adding an extra 11 urban and 10 rural areas). All allocations made under this programme are conditional on the presentation of an integrated socio-economic plan that has been mediated through local representative structures and prepared jointly by local community groups and agencies involved in development. The objectives and conditions of this programme are the same as those pertaining to the first Global Grant, covering the period 1992-95.

The third sub-programme, relating to urban and village renewal, aims to develop a comprehensive programme of urban and village renewal through the rehabilitation of built environment and restoration and conservation of urban architecture and heritage buildings. Overall, this sub-programme funds twenty-nine projects throughout the state. As well as supporting urban development, this sub-programme is intended 'to complement measures being implemented on foot of the [European] Commission's discussion document *The future of rural society*' (Government of Ireland, 1995:41). A particular aim is to co-ordinate development strategies arising from a variety of European Commission sponsored initiatives aimed at developing rural societies. More generally, it is intended to consolidate all local development projects in a given area, in order to achieve maximum impact.

In 1995, the 'rainbow' government highlighted its commitment to local development through the establishment of a 'Local Development Liaison Team' - a small group of civil servants seconded to the *Taoiseách's* Office with special responsibility for improving the coordination and cooperation between local development actors and agencies across Ireland.[4] The Local Development Liaison Team was designed to support the operation of County Strategy Groups (CSGs) in every county, reflecting the government's desire to ensure that local development actors and agencies worked as effectively as possible together.

Following a change of government in 1996, CSGs were dropped in favour of Strategic Policy Committees (SPCs). Carrying out a broadly similar role to the CSGs, SPCs were established for all major service areas in each local authority. Their membership is comparable to that of the CSGs, with the addition of a local council member to support the broader inclusion of public representatives. SPCs have been augmented with the creation of City/County Development Boards, charged with the task of preparing integrated strategies for local economic, social and cultural development and taking cognisance of all locally delivered associated public services. Strategies are due for completion by January 2002.

Britain

In May 1997, a Labour government was returned to power and the election promises of devolution for Scotland and Wales, as well as the introduction of Regional Assemblies across England, suggested that a radical change in regional policy might be afoot. Whilst the referendum for devolution in Scotland was unquestionably successful, the Welsh referendum was only a 'qualified success'.[5] As a result, the plan for regional assemblies in England was compromised and they were allocated a position much lower down on the government's list of priorities. All of the policy initiatives begun by the Conservative government continued to run and - save the large-scale plans for devolution - no new programmes were introduced by the Labour government.

The government did, however, add a rider onto the fourth round of bidding for the Single Regeneration Budget Challenge Fund. In July 1997, they issued supplementary guidance for SRB bids, outlining the government's new priorities for determining the 'winning bids'. 'Ministers indicated that they want resources to be concentrated on the areas and populations of greatest need, partly in pursuit of their overall policy objective of achieving a more equal society, and partly in order to make the best use of limited resources' (DTER, 1998:3). In order to attempt a more strategic approach to development, Ministers asked the Government Offices for the Regions to draw up regional frameworks for this round of bidding. However, since the government gave only a short period of notice for this request, 'the frameworks were not intended to represent long-term regional strategies' and 'given the short timescale for preparation, these were necessarily drawn up by the GORs without consultation with other SRB stakeholders' (DTER, 1998:6).

Fundamentally then, a change of government brought little substantive change in the operation of regional policy. A DTER review of regeneration programmes acknowledged that they had grown up in a piecemeal way and did not operate to a single strategy at national, regional or local level (DTER, 1998).

It also noted that progress has been slowest in the most deprived areas and that regeneration programmes have had a positive impact where large and continuous sums of money have been spent. Still, however, numerous references to different types of regional problems and an acknowledgement that regeneration is most difficult in areas where these problems come together, suggests that there is only a limited appreciation of the interconnectedness of development issues.

This view is reinforced by the government's assertion that regeneration policy cuts across a number of government departments and that most spending within targeted areas will come from a variety of different departmental programmes. Yet there is no mechanism by which to co-ordinate the policy outputs from these programmes. Furthermore, the government argues that any regeneration programme should take account of other existing initiatives, such as EU funding, Lottery funding, Welfare to Work and measures to tackle social exclusion, yet again there is no mechanism by which to co-ordinate the work of these initiatives. Finally, the DETR assumes that whatever model for future regeneration policies and programmes is adopted, it should be capable of being implemented either through Regional Assemblies or existing mechanisms. This suggests that even if a change in policy is proposed, it will not offer any significant alternative to the current 'top-down' model of development. In other words, a policy that can be delivered as easily through existing policy mechanisms as through new assemblies, does not indicate any radical change in its approach to decision-making or community involvement.

Financing regional development

Different allocative mechanisms reflect quite significant differences in the policy processes of each of the states. In Germany, for example, policy parameters set in federal and state constitutions make for a highly bureaucratized and formulaic approach to funding. In Ireland, the partnership approach to government has led to a system of funding that places a premium on local community involvement and that has been described as a move towards more participative democracy. The result is a more informal and negotiative approach to policy finance that is less bureaucratic than the German system of allocation but also less transparent. In Britain, increasing emphasis on private sector involvement in regional regeneration, plus the proliferation of new development bodies and agencies, has militated against an integrated or strategic policy approach, making it more difficult for community involvement in policy - either directly or through local representatives. These themes are explored in more detail below.

Germany

A crucial point of change, bearing both on Federal-*Länder* relations and on the ability of the Federal government to grant aid to regions, occurred in 1967 (Smith, 1994:60-76). The Stability and Growth Act of 1967 (*Gesetz zur Förderung der Stabilität und des Wachstums der Wirtschaft*) and later, the fiscal and constitutional reforms of 1969, each had important implications for the co-ordination of policy between different levels of government. The reforms of 1969 included: the *Länder* Revenue sharing Act (*Länderfinanzausgleichsgesetz*); the Budget Basic Rules Act (*Haushaltsgrundsätzegesetz*); and the creation of a new legal basis for inter-governmental relations regarding joint planning, decision-making and financing (*Gemeinschaftsaufgaben*). Under these reforms, principles of budgetary authority were to apply equally to the Federal and *Länder* governments (the act obliged the *Länder* to pass their own legislation and accordingly a series of budgetary regulations were passed between 1970-1972) (Smith, 1994:64). The Budget Basic Rules Act (*Haushaltsgrundsätzgesetz*) further bolstered the Stability and Growth Act, by ensuring that Federal and *Länder* budgets would take account of overall economic objectives. Subsequent Federal legislation (*Bundeshaushaltsordnung*) explicitly provided for the establishment of budgetary principles 'applicable to both the Federation and the *Länder*' (Bundesministerium der Finanzen, 1990:109.3). This Act could be regarded as a compromise between the need to protect *Länder* sovereignty - by preventing Federal encroachment upon their legislative authority - and the need to obtain some overall basis for cooperation between the two levels of government when framing budgetary policy.

The basic thrust of all the financial reforms was provided by the Stability and Growth Act of 1967, namely the acknowledgement of a central role for Federal government in the determination of regional development. The 1967 Act created a reserve fund (*Konjunkturausgleichrücklage*) at the Central Bank (*Bundesbank*), which was to be used to either slow-down or stimulate the economy as required. If there was inflationary pressure in the economy, the fund could effectively decrease the circulation of capital and in times of recession, the fund could be used to support *Länder* governments in need of help. Contributions were set at a maximum of 3% of the total *Länder* tax revenue from the preceding year. The Federal government was empowered to raise taxes by up to 10% in order to top up the reserve fund, only if it was deemed necessary to restore *Länder* equilibrium.

The Federal government's ability to make reserve fund support conditional on the *Land* government's pursuance of policy in line with overall macro-economic policy afforded the Federal government an unprecedented degree of influence over *Länder* economic policy. The Federal government could, for example, issue decrees obliging *Länder* to limit borrowing and/or repay funds to the *Bundesbank*. Despite the fact that such decrees required the *Bundesrat's* approval, the Federal government nevertheless gained significant influence over *Länder* fiscal policies, particularly in times of severe economic recession when it was empowered, if it deemed it necessary, to place restrictions on *Länder* budgetary policy (Smith, 1994:61).

It was soon apparent that if policy resulting from the reforms was to be effective, it was necessary for the Federal and *Länder* governments to co-ordinate their policies more effectively. In consequence, the Fiscal Planning Council (FPC) was established. Chaired by a representative of the Federal Minister of Finance, the FPC draws up economic plans and projections with a view to co-ordinating the budgetary policy between the *Länder* and Federal government. The FPC's wide membership, including representatives from different level government institutions, political parties and the *Bundesbank*, means that policy change can only occur through persuasion and accommodation. Still, its membership ensures that once a compromise has been reached, it has a great deal of influence over budgetary policy.

One weakness of the 1967 legislation has been the difficulties associated with defining when 'macro-economic imbalance' has occurred. In 1989, the Federal Constitutional Court sought to clarify matters by issuing a number of guidelines concerning Federal borrowing requirements. The increasing budget deficits since the Court's decision, especially as a consequence of unification, have resulted in these guidelines acquiring a new significance. Smith (1994:61) notes that in effect they give further constitutional sanction to the deficit financing required to assist the new *Länder*. The demands of financing unification, in terms of a growing German budget deficit and increased tax revenues going to the Federal government, has intensified the discord felt between some *Länder* governments and the Federal government. Existing divisions between the richer *Länder* in the west (mainly Baden-Württemberg, Hesse, Bavaria and North Rhine-Wesphalia) and the poorer *Länder* in the east (as well as the Saarland, Bremen, Lower Saxony and Schleswig-Holstein), were further complicated by the addition of the five new *Länder*. All of the poorer *Länder* have sought Federal government aid in times of financial difficulty: the Saarland, for example, has taken the lead in forming an alliance with Bremen and the new *Länder* to put pressure on the Federal government for increased aid (Sturm, 1992:123).

Since unification, the balance of power between rich and poor *Länder* in the *Bundesrat* has shifted so that the less well off and poorer *Länder* now constitute a majority in the Federal Republic. Although this cannot *per se* damage the constitutional basis of the Republic, it can impede consensus formation among the *Länder* and as a result weaken their position as a whole vis-a-vis the Federal government. Schmidt (1992:3) argues that the Federal government is now in a particularly strong position to adopt a 'divide and rule' strategy against the *Länder*. This could take the shape of a coalition between the Federal government and poorer *Länder*, against the richer *Länder*; or an alliance between the Federal government and *Länder* of the same political complexion. However, it might equally be argued that precisely because of the scope for different sorts of alliances, German federalism is now stronger.

The importance of EU subsidies for German regional policy was negligible until unification, when all of the new *Länder* were classified as Objective One areas for EU regional aid. With the incorporation of the former Democratic Republic, Germany became the sixth largest beneficiary of EU Structural Funds (after Spain, Italy, Portugal, Greece and Ireland). According to the Structural Funding criteria, the new *Länder* were entitled to 2 billion Ecu's worth of assistance. However, in order to avoid difficulties with other EU states in receipt of Structural Funding, the Federal Republic agreed to limit EU subsidies to the new *Länder* to 1 billion Ecu. Following unification, a special Regulation was made by the Council that provided for an allocation of Ecu3 billion to the new *Länder* for the period 1991-93. In 1991, the European Union gave a special ERDF grant of 1.5 billion Ecu to the new *Länder* and eastern Berlin for a three year period. A further 1.5 billion Ecu was committed through the European Social Fund and the EAGGF. The ERDF contribution was spent on productive investment and production-related infrastructure (Drerup, 1997:340).

Total Structural Fund transfers to Germany amounted to Ecu6,431 million for the period 1989-93 and increased significantly to Ecu21,729 million for the period 1994-99. The total scale of interventions, including national, local and private sector matching funding, amounted to Ecu24,481 million for the period 1989-93 and Ecu83,727 million for the period 1994-99 (CEC, 1997:22). Since all of the new *Länder* have been designated as Objective One areas for EU regional aid, the level of EU Structural support varies enormously across Germany. In the new *Länder*, support for the period 1994-99 amounted to an average of Ecu145 per capita per annum, compared to annual averages of Ecu37 and Ecu26 per capita per annum for recipients of EU aid, under Objectives 2 and 5b respectively, in the former Federal Republic (CEC, 1997:22).

The new *Länder* have been able to benefit significantly from EU assistance not only because they satisfy the EU criteria of need, but also because the German system of federal fiscal equalization satisfies all of the conditions of EU support. The formulaic calculations for regional assistance in each of the

German *Länder* mean that the Federal government is easily able to demonstrate the additionality of EU funding. Furthermore, the requirement of comprehensive *Land* development plans satisfies EU requirements for programmatic and strategic development planning. As a consequence, EU funds have been deployed almost exclusively in support of Federal government regional policy objectives.[6]

Ireland

All the measures in the Operational Programme for Local Urban and Rural Development (OPLURD) are co-financed by the Irish government and European Union Structural Funding. Some projects attract additional funding either privately from local sponsors, or publicly from community groups and fund-raising. Other projects draw on additional EU funding from the operation of specific Community Initiatives in selected areas.

Sub-programme One, designed to promote local enterprise is based on four policy measures: measure one, preparation/review of county enterprise plans and promoting enterprise culture; measure two, business information, advice, counselling and mentoring support; measure three, financial assistance; and measure four, the provision of management development. Measure four is funded through the ESF and the other three measures through ERDF. This sub-programme also envisages a considerable level of private funding, especially for measures two and four.

Sub-programme Two, designed to promote integrated socio-economic development in disadvantaged areas, combines ERDF support for enterprise creation and development (measure one) with ESF support for education and training (measure two). The sub-programme is managed and controlled by ADM. Funded by the European Commission's Global Grant, ADM sponsors 38 Partnerships and 33 Community groups and selected organizations. On average, the amount of money allocated to each partnership (at around IR£2.1 million) is four times greater than the amount allocated to each Community Group (around IR£0.5 million) (Goodbody, 1997:104).

Sub-programme three, designed to promote urban and village renewal, operates through five measures: measure one, five separate inner city initiatives in major cities; measures two and three, the upgrading of the physical environment in towns and villages throughout the state; measure four, conservation of the built environment in cities and towns; and measure five, the development of the Temple Bar area in Dublin as a cultural, residential and small business centre. This programme draws down approximately IR£110 million over the period 1994-99 and is intended to be used in conjunction with other national policies that support more general development objectives. Participants in this scheme reported that its chief advantage was the fact that physical improvements and urban/village renewal initiatives could be *planned* in advance.

Instead of working to annual budgets, as was previously the case, local authorities can now plan a programme of regeneration five years in advance. As a result urban/village renewal projects can be factored in to other development initiatives taking place in the area, making it easier to lever in matching funding for development initiatives and also facilitating a more strategic approach to planning that combines different local development projects into a wider development framework. The experience of carrying out this type of development has meant that Irish community groups have been adept at attracting other forms of EU support from the a variety of Community Initiatives and more recently the Cohesion Fund.

The total Structural Fund transfers to Ireland amounted to Ecu4.5 billion for the 1989-93 period and Ecu5.6 billion for the 1994-99 period (CEC, 1997:73). On an annual basis this is equivalent to Ecu253 per capita per annum and Ecu262 per capita per annum respectively. When the national and private sector matching funding are included, the scale of intervention amounts to Ecu10.3 billion and Ecu10.4 billion for the two periods respectively. In addition, Ireland received Ecu 144.4 million from the Cohesion Fund in 1993, with an indicative allocation of Ecu1.3 billion for the period 1994-99 (CEC, 1997:73).

Britain

In 1992, the Urban Programme was discontinued. In November 1993, it was replaced by the Single Regeneration Budget (SRB), which is now managed by the by the Integrated Regional Offices (IROs), under the leadership of a single Regional Director. As well as managing SRB allocations between a range of government agencies, IROs also co-ordinate the competition for SRB funding between a number of other smaller programmes such as the Safer Cities and Estate Action projects. Bids under the Single Regeneration Budget are assessed and approved by ten Cabinet Ministers together with the Department of the Environment's Inner Cities Minister: together they make up the Ministerial Committee for Regeneration (the EDR), which agrees the resources available to regional offices throughout the country (Stewart, 1996:148).

In the financial year 1994-95, the total SRB amounted to £1,300 million (HMSO, 1995:29). The government decided to honour commitments under pre-existing programmes but from 1995-96 onwards, as these commitments expired, the money was to be allocated under a new bidding procedure - the Single Regeneration Budget Challenge Fund. The deadline for the first round of bids was September 1994. A total of 469 bids were received and in December 1994, the government announced that 200 had been successful (HMSO, 1995:29). When the new Labour government took office in 1997, it announced that it would stick to the spending totals prescribed by the previous government (*Financial Times*, 3/7/97:32). The government guidelines for the fourth SRB Challenge Fund, announced in July 1997, stated that 'as a working assumption, and subject to the finalization of public expenditure plans, potential bidders should prepare bids on the basis that around £80 million will be available nationally in the first two years' (HMSO, 1997). The guidelines also advised potential bidders that 'the position on resources in some regions is very severely constrained as a result of pressure from commitments from earlier Challenge Fund rounds, and that in those cases no substantial spend may be possible in 1998/99' (HMSO, 1997).

The introduction of competitive bidding for government funding has been described as a way of being seen to allocate 'fairly' diminishing resources for urban regeneration with decisions based on the market principle, rather than on the assessment of need. The system has been criticised on three main counts. First, central government assistance based upon competition between public/private partnerships does not leave any room for assessment of needs. There is no apparent relationship between the success of a bid and a bidder's place in the Department of Environment's own ranking of multiple deprivation (Atkinson and Moon, 1994:95). Despite a change of emphasis with the new government's issuing of 'supplementary guidelines', the underlying principle of *competition* for regeneration funding has not changed. Second, the objectives of the initiative - 'to tackle problems that are perceived by residents and potential investors as being crucial to regeneration' - are potentially contradictory. It is worth asking to what extent the preferences of local residents and would-be investors on policy priorities will coincide. Third, despite the Department's recommendation that SRB Challenge Fund initiatives should 'fit in' to the wider economy, no regional or local strategies exist to achieve this aim. As a consequence, the success of the bid may well depend on the strengths and/or abilities of the local/regional economy and business partnerships: this leaves areas in greatest need of assistance doubly disadvantaged. Moreover, the failure of development and property markets in recent years has put much of the urban regeneration process at risk, raising important value for money questions about the extent to which public leverage resources have been dissipated as a consequence of the development recession (Stewart, 1996:146).

Developments in the financing of urban regeneration must be viewed in tandem with other reforms affecting sub-national government in Britain. The organizational reforms resulted in policy responsibilities being contracted out to so many different agencies that there is no coherent *local* forum with strategic responsibility for local economic development. Whilst a number of different localised agencies may coordinate some of their local development initiatives, it could reasonably be argued that a certain synergy of effect is missing. Added to this, financial cutbacks have exacerbated competition for scarce public resources between an increasing number of bidders, again at the cost of a more integrated or strategic approach to policy. As the competencies and role of local government have diminished, responsibility for regional development has been left largely to central government. However, the central government's desire to invoke market-based solutions to the problem of development, through decreased government intervention and increased support for private sector development means that it has been unwilling to take a central co-ordinating role in regional development policy.

This approach is at odds with European Union sponsored forms of assistance for regional development, whose criteria stress the need for planned policy responses through strategic partnerships involving local communities affected by development programmes. Furthermore, the British government's continued desire to view European funding as a substitute for national funding has militated against Britain's receipt of Structural Funding support because it contradicts the EU principle of additionality (Thomas, 1992; McAleavey, 1992, 1993; LAA, 1994). Taken together, these two issues have led to an under utilization of British entitlements to Structural Funding from the European Union. The great irony of EU Structural Funding assistance to Britain is that despite a range of criteria that stipulate the need for concerted, integrated development action, the EU principle of additionality (ie. its requirement of matching funding for EU assistance) exacerbates even further the competition between regional development actors in search of scarce resources.

Total Structural Fund transfers to the UK (including Northern Ireland) amounted to Ecu5239 million for the period 1989-93 and to Ecu12,981 million for the period 1994-99 (CEC, 1997:124). The regional policy process in Britain makes it more difficult to evaluate policy finances than in other states. 'Lack of public expenditure data at regional level and the problems of securing information on the regional spread of expenditure under a number of interventions preclude precise calculations' (CEC,

1997:126). However, the European Commission estimates that EU spending in Objective One regions amounted to Ecu100 per capita per annum for the period 1989-93 and will amount to Ecu119 per capita per annum for the period 1994-99 (CEC, 1997).

Concluding remarks: policy management and network potential

The aim of this chapter has been a cross-national evaluation of central government approaches to regional development with a view to assessing the impact that different approaches might have upon the formation and development of regional policy networks. It examined the changing regional policy contexts in each of the states and the ways in which these have been reflected in the structure and finance of regional policy initiatives. On the basis of this, we can begin to adduce the most likely forms of network association in each of the states.

The German conception of regional development as the provision of equitable opportunities for economic growth, following policy objectives prescribed in the constitution, leads us to expect network memberships to include a significant proportion of economic, business, legal and bureaucratic interests in regional policy networks. Both the central co-ordinating role of the Federal government and the distinctive division of policy responsibilities between the different tiers in the federal system might lead us to expect regional policy networks to be hierarchically organized and bureaucratically managed in accordance with the legal principles of the federal system. Despite unification, there has been no significant change in regional policy processes and practice, and as a result we can expect relatively stable policy networks.

In Ireland, both policy processes and practice have undergone significant change. Regional development is no longer associated solely with attempts to achieve export-led growth through inward investment, but now focuses equally on the development of indigenous productive potential. This has led to a re-conceptualization of regional development with an emphasis on the creation of partnerships that have fostered innovation, bringing together actors from statutory, voluntary, public and private sectors in a manner that 'blurs familiar distinctions between public and private, national and local, and representative and participative democracy' (OECD, 1996:9). This changed approach to development indicates that we can expect networks membership to be made up from a wide range of interests, in accordance with the partnership principles supported by the Irish government and European Commission. We can expect policy organization in these networks to be inclusive of, and negotiated between, a wide range of development interests.

This is not the case in Britain, where emphasis on the need for competition between development interests in order to deliver 'best practice' and 'value for money' in regional development initiatives has led to increasing fragmentation of policy delivery. In this environment, we can expect regional policy networks to be much less co-ordinated than their German and Irish counter-parts and to be more subject to the influence of professional and private-sector interests. Together, the lack of central government co-ordination of regional policy and the requirement to compete for regional policy resources suggests that British regional policy networks will be relatively unstable and impermanent. In the following chapters, we take a look at alternative regional policy networks in each of the states and see whether or not they bear out our expectations.

Notes

1. Both National Wages Agreements were negotiated directly between the government, the Irish Congress of Trades Unions, and employer organizations (Chubb, 1992:125-30; Lee, 1989:537-40).
2. Between 1981 and 1982 there were three elected governments in Ireland: from 30:06:81, a Fine Gael/Labour coalition claiming 48.2% Dail support; from 09:03:82, a Fianna Fail government claiming 48.8% Dail support; and from 14:12:82, a Fine Gael/Labour coalition with a slim majority of 51.8% of Dail support (Coakley and Gallagher, 1993:272).
3. 28 other local community groups, as well as the Dublin Travellers Education and Development Group (DTEDG), a self-help group for Dublin-based Irish travelling communities, also received assistance.
4. In 1996, in its reorganization of governmental responsibilities, the new *Fianna Fáil*/Progressive Democrat government relocated the Local Development Liaison Team to the Department of Tourism, Recreation and Local Development.
5. Although Scottish voters supported the referendum on devolution by a majority of three to one, only one in four of the Welsh electorate were shown to support Welsh devolution when a majority of less than 7,000 voters nudged the referendum outcome marginally in its favour. The disappointing Welsh referendum result was widely represented as a serious blow to Labour's plans to decentralise power from Westminster (*Financial Times*, 20/9/97).
6. Until the Agenda 2000 reforms, fourteen Community Initiatives allowed certain targeted groups (such as women returning to work, border regions, rural areas etc.) to apply to the European Commission directly for funding in support of their projects (CEC, 1994f). However, both the small amount of funding available (compared to Structural Funding assistance) and the small number of groups eligible for such assistance, meant that the impact of these programmes was marginal in the new *Länder*.

Chapter 4

Case Study: Thüringen, Germany

Introduction

In contrast to the British and Irish experience of EU Structural Funds assistance, the designation of the eastern German *Länder* as an area for Objective One funding did not alter the nature of German regional policy substantively at all. The first tranche of EU support given to the new *Länder* for the period 1991-1993, concentrated its investment entirely upon supporting the two Federal regional policy priorities under the Joint Tasks (*GRW*) initiative, that is, productive investment and local economic infrastructure. Negotiations over the second tranche were more controversial when the European Commission supported the new *Länder* in their bid to 'de-couple' EU regional aid from the Federal 'Joint Task' programme. The Federal Ministry of Economics insisted that Structural Funds expenditure should be subject to its own *GRW* aid criteria rather than the slightly broader criteria laid out by EU Objective One guidelines. The new *Länder* governments, however, were keen to broaden their discretion over regional development to the maximum.

As a result, in mid-1994, the Federal government (under mounting pressure from the new *Länder* to release their aid) finally allowed the *Länder* governments to deploy part of the EU money allocated to them outside of the *GWR* framework - a gesture that had already been made to the old *Länder* in the late 1980s. Despite the arguments that Structural Funds assistance for the period 1994-1999 helped to broaden the scope of regional assistance, still none of the EU support measures conflict with any Federal government policy instruments or measures. In this respect, Federal government references to 'equalization of living conditions' as articulated in the *Grundgesetz* are not out of place with European Union references to the development of 'economic and social cohesion' as articulated in the Single European Act and the Draft Treaty on European Union. Although Berlin, Brandenburg, Saxony and Mecklenburg-Western Pomerania have all 'de-coupled' parts of their Structural Funds aid, EU financial resources are still for the most part incorporated directly into the existing *GWR* regional policy framework (outlined in Chapter 3).

The remainder of this chapter examines the formation and implementation of regional development strategies in Thüringen, one of the 'new' German states. In order to facilitate comparison with other case studies, policy-making structures and processes are described, insofar as possible, using network concepts and terminology. The first section, which looks at the establishment and organization of the policy domain is described in terms of 'network formation'. The next section dealing with 'network membership' outlines the key policy actors in terms of who they are and what they do. The third section looks at the 'network resources' in terms of the financing of policy measures and other relevant resources available for network members. The fourth section looks at 'network dynamics' by examining the relations between key policy actors and agencies. The fifth section provides an overview of the policy process and gives a preliminary view of the impact that the network's structure and form has upon the policy process. The connections between different network forms, policy processes and the level of integration between policy actors is considered in detail in chapter seven, which gives a comparative overview of the case study material.

Network formation

Despite the relatively brief existence of current political and administrative arrangements, the Thüringen policy network benefits from both widespread support and a ready supply of capable personnel. The historical origins of the *Land*, the subsequent political and administrative development throughout its area, and its final incorporation into the Federal legal system following German unification have resulted in a network that is clearly structured territorially and functionally.

In spite of its relatively small size, the strong desire to 'recover' the old federal states that existed prior to Germany's division after the second world war, means that Thüringen's traditional *Land* borders are well-established with a history pre-dating the GDR regime itself. Moreover, the end of the second world war and the imposition of a Soviet occupied zone on east Germany, did not entirely remove its federal structure. Thüringen remained as an administrative area, with its own regional planning and housing development offices, until its dissolution and replacement by three administrative districts in 1952. In each of the three districts - Erfurt, Gera and Suhl, newly established offices for area, town and village planning were set up. Qualified personnel, already available in Weimar were divided out between the newly created districts. Originally coordinated by the Ministry for Construction, in 1965, offices for State

Construction and for Territorial Planning were created. Infrastructural planning was also carried out by a third set of offices, under the direction of the State Ministry for Transport. The particular skills and expertise of these administrative personnel, most especially those from the Territorial Planning Offices, enabled the newly recreated *Land* administration of Thüringen to recruit locally from a wide range of technical and specialist experts.

The rapid and secure establishment of a binding legal framework for the incorporation of the new *Bundesländer* into the Federal Republic, meant that in principle the entire body of German Federal law was instantly applicable to the new *Länder* from the 3rd October 1990 (Goetz, 1995:6). After unification, Thüringen enjoyed the constitutional autonomy, powers, rights and responsibilities, bestowed by German federal law immediately. With these came a prescribed legal and procedural framework within which to operate development (and all other *Land*) policy. Thüringen was the first of the new *Länder* to devise its own planning law, *das Thüringer Landesplanungsgesetz (ThPlG)*, in July 1991. The *ThPlG* provides the basic legal framework for all development in the *Land* and its four chief planning regions. It sets out the objectives of regional development and the rules governing its organization in terms of planning and development procedures at *Land* level and the four 'sub-*Land*' area planning regions.

Article two of the Thüringen planning law, *das Thüringer Landes-plannungsgesetz (ThPlG)*, sets out fifteen basic principles of spatial planning, detailing the overall objectives for development in Thüringen, and also objectives for development in certain fields. It provides for two basic planning levels, relating to general *Land*-wide planning and more specific area planning in four planning sub-regions. It is the task of the *Land* administration, under the authority of the government, to produce the Land Development Programme, or *Landesentwicklungsprogramms* (LEP), setting out the general targets and fields for development across the *Land*. These are then more concretely iterated in the four regional spatial plans, *regionalen Raumordnungspläne* (RROP) produced by the regional planning boards, or *regionalen Planungsgemeinschaften* (RPG), made up from the representatives of *Landkreise*, *kreisfreien Städte* and *Gemeinde*, according to their size.[1] The RROP set out practical guidelines or development criteria for their regions, specifying what form development in the region should take, in terms of the general development objectives for the area, and the specific targets to be achieved. The *ThPlG* also provides for regional advisory councils, *regionale Planungsbeiräte*, comprising all major interests to guide the work of the RPG.

The legal/procedural definition of policy parameters within the German federal system leads, inevitably, to a highly structured policy network: it also raises the potential for the creation of a *closed* policy network. In other words, it is possible that by referring specifically to certain fora and agencies in law, the *ThPlG* confers status upon selected policy actors in the network, which might militate against the inclusion of others. This is avoided, in theory, by the broad definition of development in the *ThPlG*. Development is outlined as a process that must take into consideration the infrastructural, ecological, economic, social and cultural requirements in the *Land* (*ThLPlG*, 1991, Art. 1). Legal provision for Advisory Councils to all planning boards (*regionale Planungsbeiräte*), with members from organizations representing the interests of local parishes, chambers of commerce, farming and forestry groups, trades unions, employers associations, churches, higher education and recognised environmental interests, further facilitates the representation of a variety of policy interests in the network. (*ThLPlG*, 1991, Art. 7). In principle then, almost any interest in the policy domain has the right to a recognised status in the policy network. In practice however, this openness is constrained by the realities of political and economic reconstruction in the new *Länder*, which means that public officials and certain economic-oriented interests are afforded more influence over the policy process (Interview 27). This differentiation between network members is discussed below.

Network membership

Article 72 of the Constitution charges the German government with the responsibility of decreasing regional disparities and balancing regional development across the state. In addition, a series of legislative acts throughout the 1960s and 1970s (detailed in Chapter 3), designed to enhance the Federal government's role in the coordination and direction of regional development, resulted in the intertwining of regional policy, national fiscal policy, and overall economic policy to such a degree that it is no longer possible to completely differentiate one from another (Smith, 1994:78). These developments, together with the more recent so-called 'big-bang' approach to unification (OECD 1996b:127), have had major consequences for the memberships of regional policy networks in the way that they have shaped the organization and representation of development interests.

First, they have secured a view of regional development whereby 'development' is conceived of as a more narrowly defined *economic* project rather than a more broadly defined socio-economic or political process. Second, they have secured the position of government sponsored development interests in regional policy networks, both directly by cementing the position of public representatives and officials and indirectly by assuring those interests closest to government thinking a position of influence. This was particularly true in relation to unification process where the strategy for transition was controlled by government-appointed agents in the form of the *Treuhandanstalt* (Breuel, 1994; Timmins, 1998). Together these developments reinforce the importance of government sponsored network members and clearly facilitate the separation of regional policy network memberships into two distinct sets.

In Thüringen, policy formulation is clearly the responsibility of public officials and elected representatives - indicatively in the terms of the *Landesentwicklungsprogramms* (LEP), and concretely in the determination of *regionalen Raumordnungspläne* (RROP) by the *regionalen Planungsgemeinschaften* (RPG). Policy implementation, however, is the responsibility of a wide variety of agencies and organizations whose functional remit impacts upon development in the region and whose involvement is officially recognised by the *ThPlG* in its provision of Advisory Boards to the RPG and consultation with local interests over all development issues. In this sense, the policy network is clearly divided between 'insiders' and 'outsiders' - the former being able to shape the form and substance of policy, and the latter having a role in its implementation, though no substantive influence over its form. Alternative categories of network member are discussed below.

The Land government

The *Land* government has three main functions (Interviews 20, 21). First, using its political and electoral mandate, it determines the 'development agenda' for the *Land*, establishing the development priorities for *Land* policy reflected in the LEP. Second, it negotiates budgetary allocations according to the territorial and functional requirements prescribed by law. This is done through a *Landtag* committee system where membership is divided out between all political parties according to their electoral support. Through both of these roles, it fulfils its third task, providing political accountability for development throughout the *Land*. Since the last *Landtag* election on October 16th 1994, Thüringen has been governed by a coalition comprising the CDU and SPD parties.[2] Despite their differing political orientations, once in government both parties quickly reached an accommodation with each other (Interviews 20, 21).

The *ThPlG* (1991, Art.3). specifies that political responsibility for *Land* planning and development lies with the 'responsible *Land* ministry'. Initially, this was the Ministry for the Environment, but it was replaced by the Ministry for Economy and Infrastructure. Save for this move, the *Land* government has left the management of development policy entirely to the responsible ministry (Interview 21). The government's 'hands off' approach to the day to day management of policy illustrates how the formal structuring of the policy network serves to depoliticize policy decision-making. Policy formulation is determined in accordance with legal norms set by the *ThPlG* and according to the consultation procedures set up by the LEP and RROP. The Ministry's coordination and organization of these interests is discussed below.

The Land administration

The Ministry for Economy and Infrastructure is responsible for drafting the Land Development Plan or *Landesentwicklungsprogramms* (LEP). The LEP provides the legal framework that ensures uniformity of planning standards between regions (in relation to environmental standards and infrastructure for exampe). It also outlines appropriate forms of development and prioritizes planning objectives (*ThVLep*, 1993: Teil A, 2.1-3). The structuring of development is further facilitated by the provision of functional classifications for villages and towns. These are: localities with special area development functions, which are intended to function as a 'hub' for surrounding development; localities that should develop their potential as trading/business areas; those that are primarily residential; and those with tourist potential (*ThVLep*, 1993: Teil A, 2.4-3.5). The intention is that development initiatives should concentrate on area specialization and regional diversity in order to realise maximum development potential (*ThVLep*, 1993: Teil B). The four sub-*Land* regions decide on plan contents and specifications for their own regions, subject to Ministry approval (Interview 9).

The main objectives for the region of South Thüringen, for example, include the strengthening of traditional manufacturing industries already in the area and the development of a service sector. These are to take place, with due consideration for the nature sites and places of particular historical interest in the area that are important for the development of the region as a centre for tourism and culture (*ThVLep*, 1993: Teil A, 3.4). Mid-Thüringen aims to develop its strategic location as the 'growth engine' for development around the rest of the *Land* since it contains the *Land* capital Erfurt, and the largest concentration of skilled labour in the region (*ThVLep*, 1993: Teil A, 3.2).

Even where detailed plans exist, the need for investment has led to a degree of flexibility in their implementation. Where an investor is keen to develop a particular location, not designated for development in either the regional or *Land* level plans, the outcome has often been a judicious interpretation of local planning regulations that enable the project to go ahead (Interview 25). Furthermore, in the competition to attract investment and develop the regional economy in Thüringen, it became clear that investors and entrepreneurs often need quick decisions. This led the *Land* administration to 'customise' the planning process, which was widely regarded as being too time-consuming and bureaucratized in its procedures.

The introduction of the *Regional Entwicklungs Koncept* (REK, or 'regional development concept') into the Thüringen planning process is unusual in that it has no formal legal basis. Officials in the Ministry of Economy and Infrastructure argue that in this respect, the organization of policy making in Thüringen is 'a step ahead' of the old *Länder* because it promotes real (not just planned) local development. It was developed by the Ministry of Economy and Infrastructure in 1994, as a way of getting small-scale projects and initiatives off the ground as quickly as possible, without subjecting them to lengthy planning procedures. Accordingly, the Ministry gave public notice of its desire for project proposals from a variety of representatives in local communities. The proposals are vetted by local political representatives (to check that they accorded with regional development objectives) and, subject to local approval, allowed to go ahead. The Ministry usually provides 20-25% of project funding, and the rest comes from development actors in the region (Interview 25). A REK can come from an area much smaller than the Regional Plannungs Gemeinschaft. It can be a *Kreis* or a *Kommune*, or a particular association or area covering a couple of county boundaries. According to the Ministry, this is 'subsidiarity in action' (Interview 11). Still, however, REK are the exception to development planning rules and facilitate the implementation of small-scale local projects. Larger-scale development issues remain subject to normal planning procedures described above.

Kreise, Städte and Gemeinde

At sub-*Land* level, *Landkreise*, *Städte* and *Gemeinde* are entitled to send between one and five representatives to sit on the regional planning boards, or *regionalen Planungsgemeinschaften* (RPG), responsible for drafting the *regionalen Raumordnungspläne* (RROP) and in this respect they are quite influential. On the one hand, the clear outlining of competencies and responsibilities apportioned to sub-*Land* institutions in the federal system in general and in relation to development policy in particular, confirms the authority of *Landkreise*, *Städte* and *Gemeinde* in the network. On the other hand, the strong desire for as much local autonomy as possible results in network members who are willing to use the status and policy authority that they have to maximum effect (Interview 3). Following unification, Thüringen's 1,717 independent *Gemeinde* were reduced to 1,021. All but 20 of these, together with Thüringen's 129 *Städte* are members of the *Gemeinde- und Städtebundes Thüringen*, a legally recognised voluntary association, designed to share information and expertise between members in order that they may each develop their administrative capacity (Gemeinde- und Städtebundes Thüringen, 1996:5). The organization is represented throughout the *Land* by county associations (*Kreisverbände*), whose members meet regularly through a range of standing committees and plenary sittings designed to support the exchange of ideas, know-how and experience across its membership.

Additionally, the *Thüringischer Landkreistag* (the representative assembly of the counties) acts as the official representative organ for all *Kreise*, and sees itself as a powerful local lobbyist vis-a-vis the other *Land* institutions (Interview 24). Undoubtedly, one of the reasons for its strong influence, is the fact that its members share a common view about what is important for Thüringen's development. In this regard *Landkreistag* representatives admit that in principle the *Land* administration has not opposed them but that the strength of feeling and development impetus comes predominantly from sub-*Land* level (Interview 24). This view was confirmed by *Gemeinde* representatives who argued that it was the strength of feeling on the ground that helped contribute to the consensus between political parties in the *Landtag* (Interview 3). This strong consensus at sub-land level about the priorities for development policy, reflected again at *Land* level in the development priorities of the LEP, has contributed to the elevated importance of business interests in the network and facilitates the 'insider' status of certain local business interests who share the same view. The significance of business interests in the network is discussed below.

Local business

The Federal Republic's wide-spread re-development projects in the new *Länder*, combined with rapid privatization and large-scale capital investment, led inevitably to a quick configuration of business interests, centred around trade, business and finance. Moreover, the collapse of numerous combines from the former GDR, which occurred as soon as they were exposed to competition with the west, and resulting mass unemployment (see Grabher, 1997) led quickly to a widely-held consensus that regards *economic* development as the major priority. Together, these circumstances, the fact that Federal law mandates private companies to join the *Industrie- und Handelskammern* (IHK), or Chambers of Commerce, and the *ThPlG*'s provision for IHK representation on the advisory councils for each of the four regional planning boards, contributes to the status of the *Industrie- und Handelskammern* (IHK) as the chief representative of business interests in Thüringen.[3] There are three main branches of the IHK in Erfurt, Suhl and Gera and they regard themselves - both individually in their own regional planning areas and collectively at *Land* level - as a powerful interest group and effective lobbyist (Interviews 1, 2, 13).

The IHK seeks to exert its influence through both formal and informal channels. Formally, the IHK is represented on each of the advisory councils to the four regional planning boards. Although a range of other interests are also represented on these advisory councils, the IHK benefits most from the network's consensus about the terms and objectives of development policy for the region. With only a limited number of large-scale firms in Thüringen, and the chances for attracting foreign investment dependent on a range of factors outside the control of local government, development hopes are pinned firmly to the growth of a strong *Mittelstand* as the engine of regional development.[4] The IHK represents the constituency of interests most likely to achieve this and as a consequence, their opinions on the advisory council are often persuasive (Interview 2).

Informally, the IHK is also enjoys good relations with the *Land* administration, through a number of personal contacts in ministries with responsibilities for the economy, construction, business, finance and to a lesser extent, some social and environmental issues. Thüringen IHK officials keep in touch with individual *Landtag* members and officials, as well as making organizational representations to the party factions. Most IHK officials were certain that the combination of *informal* as well as formal links to the *Land* administration helped to ensure that their view of development was pursued by the *Land* administration. Nevertheless, all IHK representatives admitted that the policy process was such that they could never claim complete influence over it.

Perhaps the greatest responsibility for the success of the IHK in promoting its views, and for the extent of its influence over development strategies in Thüringen, lies in the fact that the IHK view of development coincides with the prevailing economic orthodoxy and government approach to development in the new *Länder*. In this sense, IHK involvement in Thüringen development is imbued with 'insider' status in the policy network. Other groups, such as the trades unions and organizations that are critical of the transition process, have remained outside the main development policy process. The German Trade Union Federation, or *Deutscher Gewerkschaftsbund* (DGB), for example, prefers to push for a change in policy by exerting pressure from outside government, rather than allowing itself to be co-opted into a policy position that it does not support (*Deutscher Gewerkschaftsbund*, 1994:14). In April 1993, when the Minister for Economy presided over 'solidarity talks' between a range of development interests in the region, the DGB sent only a token observer and refused to participate fully in the talks, acting in protest against the *Land* government's 'hands-off' approach to development. Actions such as these are tantamount to refusing a place with the 'insiders' in the policy process. Yet in this respect, at least the DGB had a choice over the extent of its involvement with other key policy actors. The same cannot be said for other community groups in the network that are discussed below.

Community groups

The growth of 'community-based' development initiatives, comparable to CBEDs in Merseyside, or community partnerships in Limerick (detailed in chapters five and six), has been limited in Thüringen. The legal provisions that establish the terms of development policy are designed to incorporate representation of local communities through existing *Land* institutions (such as the *Gemeinde, Städte* and *Kreise*), and through their representation in planning bodies such as the *regionalen Planungsgemeinschaften* (RPG) and their advisory councils. As a result, local development, even at *Kommunen* level, is already fully provided for by the *Land* administrative arrangements. There are, however, a small number of community groups that have grown in rural areas. Seven have arisen around EU LEADER initiatives and one under the EU CARREFOUR project.

Community groups set up with direct assistance from EU initiatives are in an unusual position vis-a-vis other established development actors because they are established without reference to them. The director of one local development group explained how the group's autonomy from the 'recognised policy set' resulted in their 'outsider' status (Interview 22). He argued that the institutions established by the Federal government in the new *Länder* can stifle local initiative and referred to the west German notion of subsidiarity whereby the representation of 'those at the bottom' is always provided for by laws and administrative arrangements determined by 'those at the top' (Interview 23).

Even with official recognition from the *Land* administration, setting up a project with local initiative in the Thüringen is still difficult. The strong bias in favour of *economic* development tends to overshadow local initiatives aimed at social and cultural development. Despite the introduction of the *Regional Entwicklungskoncept* into the planning process (discussed above), which gives local groups the opportunity to submit their own proposals for local projects, still decisions over which REKs are implemented remain with the *regionalen Planungsgemeinschaften* (RPG) who tend to be 'only interested in economic development and tourism but rarely social or cultural projects'(Interview 23). The strength of the consensus that exists around the importance of *economic-oriented* development provides further evidence of the way the network's structure distinguishes between its members: 'insiders' are responsible for formulating policy priorities and objectives, whilst 'outsiders' may be involved in different aspects of policy implementation but unable to shape its formulation.

Agencies involved in policy implementation

There are a range of agencies associated exclusively with policy implementation whose terms of reference are provided for by the objectives and targets of set out in the LEP and RROP. In Thüringen, as in other new *Länder*, development of small and medium sized enterprises is seen as a priority. For the most part, growth in this sector relies on smaller sized firms that are usually hi-tech, innovative or established in response to a specialised demand (Interview 5). They are often a combination of all three. Nevertheless, the difficulties associated with acquiring 'risk capital' has led to too great a concentration on the service sector in Thüringen (Interview 10).

In order to compensate for this tendency, the implementation of Thüringen's development strategy is designed to maximize support for growth by limiting the damage caused to developing new firms by unnecessary and damaging competition in their start up phase. It does this by providing for functional specialization in each of Thüringen's regions. Under the provisions of the LEP, four technology and enterprise centres, one in each of Thüringen's planning regions, were set up by the *Thüringer LandesWirtschaftsförderungs-gesellschaft mbH* (TLW), or Economic Promotion Company. Each centre provides business space at low rent and common office facilities for newly established, small scale firms.[5] The centres run in-house training and enterprise programmes for their tenants and provide other advisory and back-up services to new businesses. Each of the centres, however, concentrates on its own particular niche specialism: in Jena, university and business links in the region have led to a concentration in hi-fibre optics and related technologies; in Erfurt, the location and business links have led to a concentration on light industry and related expertise; in Ilmenau, the technology centre aims to develop current links with the technological university and focus on electronics and other related specialist areas (Interviews 5, 6, 8). The work of each centre is thoroughly integrated into the regional development plan, in order to provide the maximum intra industry and service linkages for the region.

Regional development plans are further supported by state sponsored agencies, such as the *Landesentwicklungsgesellschaft* (LEG) or State Development Company and the *Thüringer Aufbaubank* (TAB) or Thüringen Bank for Reconstruction. The LEG, which was set up under the *Gemeinschaftsaufgaben*, is based in Erfurt with three sub-offices in the other planning regions of north, south and east Thüringen (Interview 7). LEG offices provide the first port of call for offer advice and help with business start-ups, providing information about grant and assistance opportunities and sometimes helping out with the proposals and applications (Interview 7). In doing so, the LEG cooperates quite closely with another *Land* institution, the *Thüringer Aufbaubank* (TAB).

The TAB exists to promote existing business development through grant subsidies and low cost loans. It works mostly with small sized firms to help overcome the specific difficulties that firms encounter in the early phase of their development and expansion. The director of one TAB branch suggested that; 'Although the development of the *Mittelstand* has been very good, it still needs help in order to grow into big business and bigger medium-sized business' (Interview 12). The TAB helps small firms raise investment capital through secured, low cost loans and often offers seed funding to support business expansion.

Personnel from the LEG and the TAB maintain close links, with each other and with other development institutions and organizations in the region. The TAB in south Thüringen, for example, has combined with the IHK in Erfurt and Suhl, to offer advice and training to local businesses (Interview 12). Both the LEG and TAB act as consultants to another IHK sponsored body, the *Thüringer Aussenwirtschafts-Fördergesellschaft mbH*, or Thüringen Export Promotion Company, which uses the IHK membership network to provide a range of foreign contacts and export advice to Thüringen companies looking towards marketing their products outside the region and outside Germany (Interview 2). By cooperation between agencies and specialization within them, the implementation of development policy in Thüringen ensures that network members are not in direct competition with each other, and thus not wasting network resources by duplicating tasks. The resource dimension of the network organization is discussed in more detail below.

Network resources

The centrality of the financial system of fiscal equalization in the German federal system has already been referred to in the previous two chapters. One consequence of these extensive provisions for the redistribution of income between *Länder* is that revenues available to *Land* governments are a matter of entitlement. This entitlement is determined according to long-established federal laws and procedures. The terms of reference for granting regional financial assistance are determined by criteria laid out in the GRW. After unification, the GRW became a major source of funding for reconstruction in the new *Länder*, providing approximately DM 113 million annually, half paid by the *Bund* government, and half by the *Land* for development in Thüringen (Interview 14). The other major source of finance is the European Union, through its Objective One programmes and grant assistance. Since however, the GRW criteria establish very clearly what funds the *Bund* contributes to regional development vis-a-vis those contributed by the *Land*, there is no difficulty establishing the *additionality* of EU funding. As a result, EU funding is mixed in with the *Land* funds to create an overall development budget.[6]

In Thüringen this budget supports the LEP, which provides for certain areas of development *without* specifying concrete projects for development. The money available for each development objective, or *fachliche ziele*, is determined independently to these plans by federal policy and procedures. Budgetary allocations are made by the *Land* government, following negotiation between the various *Landtag* committees *Landtag* committees, whose membership is divided out by the party factions in the *landtag*. Funds are allocated on either a functional or territorial basis, in accordance with minimum requirements that are set by law and federal policy procedures. As with all other *Land* governments, the Finance Ministry in Thüringen has a department devoted to budgetary planning. Regarding development finance in Thüringen, all policy action is governed by the *ThlPg* and the *LEP*. As a consequence, the room left for manoeuvre is quite small. The *Land* government may shuffle expenditure allocations from one area to another, but this must be done in consultation with the *Landtag* committees and in accordance with the LEP criteria. The degree of consensus over development priorities, between the two government parties and all of the key groups responsible for policy formulation in each of the planning regions, means that there is very little to argue about in terms of finance.

This level of consensus is maintained for a number of reasons. The enormity of the task of reconstruction of east German *Länder* has resulted in the shared view amongst many policy actors from both east and west that development will be a long slow process. Everyone accepts that the struggle for development is difficult and that there are no quick fixes - financial or otherwise. Added to this, the widespread acceptance of federal procedures for fiscal equalization in Germany tends to decrease the scope for conflict between policy actors: if disputes over finance do arise, they are more likely to occur at federal level in relation to *Bund* politics over the allocation of resources across the Republic between different *Länder* (Interview 14). Finally, the structuring of the network is such that those groups with an alternative view of development - outsider groups, such as trades unions and community groups discussed earlier - who might well argue for a different distribution of resources have been relegated to a position of only notional influence over policy formulation.

Network dynamics

The fact that the policy network is structured by law and procedures that clearly set out the rights and responsibilities of membership, enables all of its members to play a part in policy, whether in terms of the formulation or implementation of the development plan, or in the representation or negotiation of development interests outlined within it. It also facilitates the separation of policy responsibility into two distinct groups. The first represents the core or 'insider group' of the policy network and is made up almost exclusively of public officials and local elected representatives who are associated primarily with *policy formulation*. The second area relates to those groups associated with *policy implementation* and incorporates a variety of actors with different functional responsibilities that impact upon the *Land*'s development.

The structuring of the network also facilitates consensus building within it. In relation to policy formulation, the fact that 'insider' groups share the same views about the problems and priorites for development increases their capacity to build consensus. Regarding policy implementation, the fact that all network members are able to refer to their role in development in accordance with an agreed plan that prescribes regional differentiation and area specialisms, enables a range of different development actors and agencies to complement rather than compete against each other in their attainment of agreed targets for development. This leads to network stability, which helps promote the consistency in outcomes and shared values between members, again supporting good relations between network members.

In addition to the network's structure, the attitudes of network members towards the organization and operation of policy is also crucial to understanding the dynamics of network relations. In Germany, the predominant policy paradigm promoted by the federal system is one of compromise and consultation. This feature is referred to in federal policy making as the *Gegenstromprinzip*, literally translated as the 'opposing power principle' (Interview 24). It is the *Gegenstromprinzip* that underscores the dynamics of interest negotiation and policy formulation in this network. First it legitimates the range of interests that are deemed important in development policy. In Thüringen, these are already referred to by the *ThPlG* and also in the preamble to the LEP, which states that 'successful development is achieved as a result of a conglomeration of political, economic, social, cultural and religious interests' (*ThVLep*, 1993:710). Second, the *Gegenstromprinzip* refers to the recognised authority of *Landkreise* and *Kommunen* to negotiate between and on behalf of these interests in the determination of development policy (*ThVLep*, 1993:710).

The combination of west German proceduralism with strong elements of east German personalism and localism, has lent a new meaning to the *Gegenstrom prinzip* in Thüringen. The strong localism that developed in the former GDR, was widely referred to by many east Germans (Interviews 2, 3, 7, 12, 22, 23). In the former GDR central planning left only a small number of areas where local officials could exercise their own discretion: these were jealously guarded and, in the absence of alternative rewards, often cultivated as bases for local patronage. Whilst some argue that this attitude has helped to inhibit the 'bottom-up' style of local development in east Germany, others are optimistic that it holds the key to future development, because it is indicative of a strong culture of self-help.

The culture of self-help is perhaps one way of explaining east German attitudes to administration. One senior executive at a regional IHK branch, explained the 'east German position': 'For long enough, we had enough pressure from above. We know what that feels like, and we won't have it again. Forty years of central planning has led, to what you might call, a 'healthy disrespect' for red-tape' (Interview 2). Moreover, even lawyers closely associated with the planning process believe that since unification, the extent of legal proceduralism in the new *Länder*, compared to the west, has decreased (Interview 17). They point to the fact that the need to combat widescale economic difficulties in the east, necessitated a quicker and more flexible planning process.

This less-bureaucratic attitude towards federal policy-making and proceduralism in the east is further supported by the high degree of personalism in east Germany. One east German, the director of a regional Technology Centre designed to support the establishment and development of small hi-tech firms, suggested that his approach to management was typically east German: 'You could say I'm a typical *Ossie* Manager. We always talk to each other and say very simply what's what. We don't stand on our pride' (Interview 8). *Ossies*, is the slang expression formed in the west that refers pejoratively to east Germans (stemming from the German word *Ost* for east). This manager's use of the term is ironic, since it acknowledges his difference but suggests that the 'Ossie way' is an alternative, not an inferior, approach.

The less formal and more flexible attitudes of the 'ossies' have been augmented by those of the west Germans who volunteered to transfer to east Germany to assist in its transition after unification. Some saw the move as an opportunity to avoid many of the routinised procedures used in the west. A west German official from the Ministry for Economy and Infrastructure noted that in contrast with his fifteen years experience in the former Federal Republic, policy-making in Thüringen involved closer and more direct relations with the actors and agencies involved: 'We each speak with one another very frequently. It's already known that our Department is routinely out there [in the towns and villages]. We leave our base, and go out to visit them. There's nobody so high and mighty here as there is perhaps in other *Länder*' (Interview 9).

Evidently both the network's structure and the attitudes of the actors within it impact significantly on network dynamics. Additionally, the unique conditions created by the unification process also played an important part determining network interrelations. Many interviewees referred to the strong sense of purpose and enthusiasm engendered by unification, which was shared by east and west Germans alike and probably helped to develop a common bond between network personnel. Taken together these attitudes refute the notion, inferred in much of the unification literature, that a west German policy model was simply supplanted on to the east of Germany. This network is not an example of simple policy transfer, it is policy learning in action.

Concluding remarks: characterizing the network and the policy process

Table 3 provides a summary of the main themes raised in this chapter. Taken together they suggest that the Thüringen regional policy network resembles very closely the ideal type *policy community* outlined by Marsh and Rhodes (1996) and discussed in chapter one.

In relation to the formation of the network, this chapter illustrated that despite its relatively short-lived existence since unification, Thüringen has a strong regional identity that supports the *Land*'s political and administrative arrangements. Since the policy architecture for regional development coincides exactly with the institutions of sub-national government and administration, the regional policy network is heavily structured by institutions that help to reinforce its legitimacy and stability.

Regarding the network's membership, the evidence suggested that it is strongly differentiated according to status and functional responsibilities of regional policy actors. First and foremost, the federal system of government divides out policy making responsibilities between the different tiers of the federal system: at state level, the *Land* government and *Land* administration; at county level, the *Kreise*, *Städte* and *Gemeinde*; and finally at ward level, the *Kommunen* representatives plus a variety of network actors operating locally in wards and districts throughout the Land. Added to this, the network membership is further distinguished according to 'insider' or 'outsider' network status. This highly structured participation in the network is illustrative of the 'hierarchial organization of interests' that, according to Marsh and Rhodes, typifies policy communities. It is significant also in that it enables policy competencies to be divided effectively between the membership so that there are no difficulties associated with conflicting areas of policy competencies or uncoordinated

Table 3: Characterizing the Thüringen policy network

Dimension	**Network features**
Formation	Well-established, recognised and accepted boundaries for policy operation. Structured by law and federal policy-making institutions. Commonly accepted and agreed.
Membership	Hierarchial organisation of membership dominated by public servants and political representatives. Structured between insider and outsider groups, with some groups consciously excluded.
Resources	Basic relationships are exchange relationships based on formulaic distribution of funding through federal system. All participants have resources, thereby minimising occassions for budgetary disputes.
Dynamics	Highly Institutionalised and routinised interaction provided through representative system of government and policy planning process. Membership, values and outcomes persistent over time. All participants share basic values and accept legitimacy of policy outcomes.
Power	There is a balance of power among members. Although one group may dominate, the policy community supports positive-sum outcomes, which ensure their continued support from members of the group.

development action across the network. It also enables representatives of different elements of the network membership to 'deliver' their own group in the negotiation of policy: the *Kreis*, *Städte* and *Kommunalen* representatives negotiate on behalf of their constituencies; the IHK negotiate on behalf of business interests, and so on.

In relation to the resources available to the network, this chapter illustrated how network finances are distributed according to territorial and functional divisions of labour. The comprehensive planning procedure means that all network members agree on the main development deficiencies (as outlined in the LEP) and share a consensus on the measures devised to tackle them (reflected in each of the RROP). This, combined with the formulaic entitlement to finance across many areas of policy activity arising as a consequence of the federal system of fiscal equalization, facilitates consensus building between network members by removing the need for damaging competition between network members over finances. In this respect, the network's key feature is not the amount of funding it receives - though the vast sums spent in east Germany since unification and the significant European Union assistance are important - but rather the *means by which they are disbursed.* The notion that in a policy community 'the basic interaction is one involving bargaining between members with resources' is substantiated by the arrangements for the distribution of resources in this network.

Network dynamics are conditioned primarily by the structure of the network's membership which is highly organized, stable over time, and helps to support consensus building. The Thüringen policy network is based on a bureaucratic model of politics. Its formation is institutionally based and legally guaranteed, resulting in quite formal inter-organisational relations between policy actors. The policy-making processes of the federal system support stable and structured regional policy networks, which elevate the status of a few key groups, provide for the representation of a wide range of development interests, and effectively exclude some altogether (such as some self-selecting voluntary or community groups that are not formally recognised in the decision-making process and some trades unions, which despite being 'recognised' are not willing to compromise their position by joining the policy community). The distinction between 'insider' and 'outsider' groups in the network membership also supports Marsh and Rhodes' view that 'policy communities have limited participants, often dominated by professional or economic interests, with some groups consciously excluded'.

'Insider' groups are responsible for policy formulation and are comprised primarily of government officials, elected representatives and select business interests whose views coincide with those of the government. Within this core, there is 'frequent and high quality interaction' between these 'insider' groups that reflects the 'consistency of membership basic values and broad policy preferences' associated with Marsh and Rhodes' ideal type policy community. 'Outsider' groups comprise the mass membership of the *policy community* responsible for policy implementation. Although the 'insider' group is relatively small, because policy formulation is a process based on consultation with a range of 'outsider' groups responsible for policy implementation, the scope of network membership is very wide indeed. This supports Rhodes' assertion that 'policy communities are either dominated by the government, or they serve the interests of all the members of the community, given that over time they develop common interests' (Rhodes and Marsh, 1992:184).

In addition to the structural features of this network, the behaviour of actors is also conducive to good network dynamics. The unique conditions caused by the speed of transition in the new *Länder* meant that many officials seconded to the new *Bundesländer* from the west, adapted their behaviour accordingly. Some saw it as an opportunity to moderate or innovate the application of old procedures to new circumstances in the east, whilst others saw it as an opportunity to avoid the restrictive routines of the west (Goetz, 1995:9). Many referred to the 'enthusiasm' and almost 'missionary zeal' with which the reconstruction process in the east was begun. Many officials, from all areas of administration worked long hours and missed holidays. In doing so, they were joined by equally committed east Germans, many of whom already held a range of skills and experience gained in the former GDR and were thus able take up their position in the network from the beginning. Despite comparable training and qualifications to their colleagues from the former Federal Republic, however, the vastly different lifestyles and experiences of those who lived in the GDR meant that they inevitably brought a fresh and alternative perspective to bear upon the operation of policy in the new *Länder*.

As a result, the network presents an interesting mix of stability and flexibility. The incorporation of policy into a legal framework, whereby policy practice and procedures are rooted in administrative law, setting out both the rights and duties of membership presents a secure framework for the development of the policy network. The widespread acceptance and uniform implementation of Federal law, further augments network stability. A degree of flexibility is provided, however, by the inclusion in this network of policy actors who are, for a variety of reasons, willing to adapt or innovate practice and procedures in the context of the alternative policy environment in the new *Länder*. In the concluding chapter, which gives a comparative examination of change in policy networks in relation to the process of European integration, we shall see how the institutional stability created in this network, together with the adaptive approach of new network personnel, serves to condition the process of policy change.

The evidence from this chapter suggests that the highly structured nature of regional policy networks that stems from the institutional arrangements of the federal system, plus the prominent role played by the federal government in the organization of German regional policy, leaves little scope for the EU to exert a significant impact upon the organization of policy. Still, however, the clear-cut institutional and political arrangements concerning the operation of policy do not present any obstacle to EU involvement in German regional policy. This suggests that whilst the capacity of the EU to influence German regional policy processes is limited, the potential for integration between EU and German policy processes remains unaffected.

Notes

1. *Landkreise* and *Städte* with up to 40,000 residents are allowed 2 representatives; between 40,000 and 80,000 - 3 representatives; 80,000 to 120,000 - 4 representatives; and over 120,000 - 5 representatives. *Gemeinde* associations covering areas with over 20,000 residents are also allowed 1 representative (*ThPlG*, Art.6).
2. CDU - the Christian Democratic Union, broadly conservative and SPD - the Social Democratic Party, left of centre.
3. There are two other types of enterprise organisations in Germany, neither of which plays a significant role in the Thüringen. The *Wirtschaftsverbände* (business associations), which help to co-ordinate exportation, marketing, and research and development activities of firms. They also lobby the government regarding tax policy, environmental issues and other matters directly related to running a business (see: Coleman, 1990). The *Bundesvereinigung der deutschen Arbeitgeberverbände* (BDA, the Federal Organisation of German Employers' Associations), is the umbrella organisation for approximately 50 separate sectoral employers' associations, comprising usually between 10-20 regional affiliates. Employers' associations provide a common platform for the interests of their members, and negotiate on their behalf with trades unions. They also lobby the government on policy areas of interest to them (see: Silvia, 1997).
4. *Mittelstand* has no literal English translation. It represents a group of mainly privately-owned, often family run, medium-sized independent businesses, predominantly in the engineering sector. These companies are said to form the backbone of Germany's economy, through a twin focus on advanced technology and niche marketing (see: *Financial Times*, 19/5/1997:12; *Financial Times*, 10/10/1997:3).
5. The *Thüringer Landes-Wirtschaftsförderungsgesellschaft mbH* was dissolved in 1996 and replaced by four sub-*Land* regional development agencies, the *Landesentwicklungsgesell-schaften* (Interview 2).
6. Within the Structural Funds, certain assistance programmes are reserved for particular areas of development, for example: the EAGGF supports agricultural readjustment; the ESF supports training and work-related initiatives; and the ERDF supports investment in trade, business and infrastructure. As a result they are added to the budget allocations covering those areas in the Thüringen *Land* development budget. Still, however all funds assigned for development are treated as a single resource.

Chapter 5

Case Study: Limerick, Ireland

Introduction

Whereas in Germany, the designation of the eastern *Länder* as an area for Objective One funding did not alter the nature of German regional policy, the same could not be said for the Republic of Ireland. Until 2000 and the reform of EU Structural Funds administration, the entire island of Ireland was regarded as a single region under Objective One funding criteria. In attempting to meet the 1988 revised Structural Funding guidelines, the Irish government was obliged to revise its approach to regional development and give greater voice to local and regional development actors. At the same time, it was widely felt that the operation of development policy at sub-national level was ripe for review and as a result, EU Structural Fund reforms became a vehicle by which new and alternative development initiatives were able to achieve greater recognition. This, combined with the evolution of new government approaches towards national policy making and development programming (discussed in Chapter 3), cemented a change of attitude in Ireland towards regional policy formulation and implementation (Adshead and Quinn, 1998). The development of Irish regions has become a more inclusive process, involving partnerships between statutory and voluntary bodies, state agencies and private interests, local activists and local representatives. As a consequence, the design and direction of development now places a greater emphasis on negotiation, partnership and subsidiarity. It marks a shift from what was an exclusive, top-down and economically-oriented notion of regional development, to one that is more inclusive, organized from the bottom-up, and stresses the importance of human, rather than solely economic needs.

The remainder of this chapter examines the formulation and implementation of regional development strategies in Limerick, using the same organizing concepts for comparison as the other two case studies: it examines the formation of a development policy network; its membership; resources; and dynamics. The chapter concludes with a review of the relationship between the policy network's structure and form, and the nature of the policy process.

Network formation

In contrast to the situation in Thüringen, where both the *Rechtsstaat* concept and detailed provisions of the federal system provide clear reference points for the operation of regional development policy, the formation of the Limerick policy network was a much more informal affair. Although the Operational Programme for Local Urban and Rural Development 1994-1999 (OPLURD) set out the aims, objectives and instruments of development policy, it has already been shown in Chapter 3, that really this was a means of legitimizing the range of *pre-existing* development actors and agencies. Because of this, the organizational framework for current development strategies represents an acknowledgement of pre-existing local development borders and boundaries as they have tended to be drawn up in policy practice. The fact, for example, that all Irish interviewees rejected the notion of *regional* development, preferring instead to talk of the advancing interest in *local* development, is reflected in the title of the Operational Programme (for *Local* Urban and Rural Development).

The conversion throughout the last decade, by both policy-makers and practitioners alike, to the 'bottom-up' approach to development means that despite a renewed interest in the reform of local government and even limited moves towards proposals for regional devolution, the small-scale county boundary has remained the most important administrative unit. This has occurred less by design and more by default. In the first place, the 'administrative jungle' (Chubb, 1992:262) created by the differing regional boundaries of the many various state agencies and state-sponsored bodies, renders them meaningless in terms of their ability to define sub-national administrative or organizational units, further justifying use of the one administrative unit that has a long history and wide-spread acceptance. Secondly, the strong culture of localism and personalism in Irish politics, makes the county boundary the largest meaningful political unit for effective local politicking (Gallagher and Komito, 1992; Farrell, 1983). Thirdly in 1995, the establishment by central government of County Strategy Groups (CSGs) and later, City/County Development Boards (CDBs) - designed to secure intra-programme linkages and integration of development policy at local level - copper-fastened the importance of the county unit as the primary unit of evaluation in studies of local development.

Both CSGs and their successors, the CDBs, were required to produce a Co-ordination Strategy Document, outlining procedures for sharing information, identifying the scope for sharing overhead costs, and developing a common approach to the delivery of services (Interview13a). In common with most other counties, Limerick's drafting of its County Strategy Document coincided with the strategic planning phase of each of the other OPLURD programmes. This meant that the Limerick inner city ABR partnership and the two LEADER group partnerships, as well as the county's Local Authorities and Enterprise Boards, drew up their strategic plans at roughly the same time as the County Strategy Group (Interview 14b). This enabled the County Strategy Group to make the greatest use of its co-ordinating capacity to bring about exchange of information and liaison between development groups in Limerick during a key phase of their strategic planning (Interview 14b).

The importance attached in Ireland to strategic planning and programming of development initiatives compensates for the lack of formal/legal policy procedures in the formation of development policy networks. Strategic programming at national and sub-national level gives legitimacy to a range of policy actors, helping to set the parameters of policy and the level of different actors involvement in it. The difference between this kind of policy network formation and the legal procedural process of the German federal system is that in the Irish case development policy networks are formed almost entirely by local consensus. Irish government support for 'bottom-up' development strategies encourages the participation of a wide range of local actors including public bodies, private interests and community groups. The emphasis on integrated planning, however, whereby the same actors are often involved in different projects with different partners, has prevented the formal structuring of this network. There are, for example, no definitive functional or territorial divisions between different network actors, nor any hierarchical relationships between them. Establishing policy coordination in this way, means that network boundaries are not formally drawn by any outside agency. The structure and scope of the network is determined by negotiation and consensus between a range of development actors operating across the county.

Network membership

The Irish approach to development policy, which places great emphasis on partnership in, and local ownership of, the development process has significantly influenced the configuration of regional policy actors (Interview 17). Everyone interviewed in this study, for example, affirmed the strong belief that no relevant interests or interested parties have been left out of the development process. Still, although the number of interests represented in the policy process is high, they are organized in such a way that the policy network can be understood by reference to a few key groupings. It is a mark of the level of integration already achieved in this network that all network members relate to each other and define themselves in terms of these partnership associations. As a consequence, this consideration of the network membership is presented in terms of these groupings, reflecting the way that the members themselves perceive the network's organization.

The Limerick network is made up of the following groups: the County Strategy Group,[1] guided by a member of the central government's Local Development Liaison Team and including all of those bodies funded through the Operational Programme for Local and Urban Development (OPLURD); the Local Authorities (Limerick Corporation, which represents the city borough and Limerick County Council, which represents the outlaying and predominantly rural remainder); the Enterprise Boards, of which there are two, one for the city and one for the county; the three partnership companies that are based wholly in the county of Limerick (one in the city and two in the county); and the various state agencies and state-sponsored bodies, including Shannon Development, which are considered together. It should be noted that in many cases membership of one of these groups does not preclude membership of another. Because of this it is easier to conceive of the organization of this policy network in terms of concentric and overlapping circles, denoting areas of joint activities and functional responsibilities, rather than the traditional organizational pyramid that typifies German regional policy networks.

The County Strategy Group

The Operational Programme for Local and Urban Development (OPLURD) provided for County Strategy Groups (CSGs) in order 'to secure cohesion, from a county perspective, of the various local development initiatives being undertaken by the state and voluntary sectors' (Government of Ireland, 1995:108). Membership of CSGs comprised: the chairs of Enterprise Boards; Partnership companies; LEADER II companies; Community groups; county tourism committees; and the Managers of the local authorities. The setting up of CSGs was facilitated by a team of five staff, based originally in the Department of the *Taoiseách*, and known as the Local Development Liaison Team.[2] In 1998, CSGs were replaced by Strategic Policy Committees for all major service areas. SPC membership remains roughly the same as the previous CSGs, but has been augmented by the addition of elected members from the relevant local authority.

CSGs, and later SPCs, were devised as non-executive bodies with no independent resources. Although they were intended to co-ordinate the provision of development programmes and initiatives, their influence has been constrained by the fact that responsibility for policy implementation remains with the programme operators themselves. Commenting on the work of the Limerick CSG, members of the government's Community Development Liaison Team pointed out that some CSGs were more effective than others but that Limerick's was more successful than most (Interview 13a, 14b, 15c).Before its dissolution, the Chair of the Limerick CSG stated that: 'In fact, it works so well and there are such good relations between the organizations, that we decided that if a new structure comes into being and there are separate structures for the city and county, we are still going to continue co-operating. We've taken the decision that we'll continue to co-operate on an informal basis' (Interview 21). Although CSG members reported few significant gaps or overlaps in service provision, they acknowledged that in some areas, such as business development training, closer co-ordination might be needed (Interview 21). Whether or not this can be better achieved by the creation of different SPCs for different service areas is not yet clear. In 1997, however, a change of government led to the creation of City/County Development Boards (CDBs). Charged with the job of producing integrated strategies for economic, social and cultural development, taking cognisance of all locally delivered associated public services, it appears that the Limerick CSG has survived in all aspects - but for a change of name. Development plans are due for completion in January 2002.

Local authorities

Limerick has two local authorities: Limerick Corporation and Limerick County Council, dealing with the city and surrounding rural areas respectively. Both authorities are involved in all three sub-programmes of the Operational Programme for Local Urban and Rural Development (Interviews 4, 5) The local authority Managers are represented on a range of development related fora: on the Board of the County Strategy Group; on the board(s) of the local Partnership companies; and, together with three elected members of the local authority, on the local Enterprise Board (Interviews 4, 5). As a result, local authorities are associated at some level with all of the local development agencies within the Operational Programme.

Limerick Corporation is responsible for: promoting the commercial development of the city centre; assisting with general economic development in co-operation with other bodies; and promoting community facilities and services (Interview 4). The Corporation contributes to development by providing lands and sites for development and related infrastructural services. Through its planning control policies, it promotes the improvement of amenities and aims to encourage community participation in environmental improvements. Limerick County Council carries out a broadly similar role, though its organization is geared more decisively to rural development. The County Council aims to: encourage the development of the rural economy and the growth of settlements in county areas; and to enhance the amenities of the county either by carrying out work itself, or by facilitating and encouraging amenity works by individuals and other bodies (Interview 5). The County Council co-operates with agencies working to promote and develop tourism in the county by giving advice and guidance to local committees who are undertaking environmental improvements and by encouraging the development of tourism related development across the county, including the provision of tourist infrastructure in suitable locations.

Although local authorities are one of three implementing agencies in the OPLURD, they represent quite different organizational entities to the Enterprise Boards or the Partnership companies. Enterprise Boards, Partnership companies and LEADER groups are relatively new organizational creations, which despite being directly representative of their constituent groups, cannot claim democratic accountability in the same way that the local authorities can. Furthermore, according to the various pieces of planning and development legislation pertaining to local government, these groups are carrying out functions that local authorities could rightly claim to be their own. The reason that this anomaly has developed and been allowed to continue, is that most local authorities have been unable to lead local development initiatives due to lack of funding (Interview 5). Across Ireland, different local authorities demonstrate different degrees of support for the new development agencies. Some carry out their responsibilities in the Operational Programme with efficiency - but not enthusiasm. In Limerick this has not been the case. Both the city and county authorities of Limerick have been successfully co-opted into a variety of partnership initiatives that are discussed in more detail below.

Enterprise boards

The creation of City/County Enterprise Boards (CEBs) in 1993 and their subsequent incorporation into the OPLURD in 1994, signified an acknowledgement on the behalf of government that, heretofore, most of its support for enterprise was concentrated on large-scale industries, either indigenous or multinational, and primarily associated with manufacturing (Interview 16). CEBs were designed to provide state supports to micro enterprises in Ireland, focusing on small businesses of up to ten employees and developing the potential for locally based services in areas like tourism and crafts as sources of local employment creation and as a basis for developing viable local economies (Interview 9). All Enterprise Boards were charged with developing their own Enterprise Plan and allocated funding retrospectively through the Department of

Enterprise and Employment.

Limerick has two Enterprise Boards, one for the city and one for the county. The objectives of each are outlined in their respective Enterprise Plans. The City Enterprise Board aims to: create local enterprise awareness and develop an enterprise culture; provide financial support for small enterprises; act as a single contact point for entrepreneurs and as a referral system between the Board and state agencies; assist community efforts by re-focusing available resources and to influence the allocation of resources from other sources; and to develop the capabilities of local communities in pursuing local development (Limerick City Enterprise Board, 1996). The County Enterprise Board has similar objectives and aims to 'make a positive difference to the economic development of County Limerick, by working with all the agencies in the county, both statutory and voluntary, to enhance the enterprise culture in the county, and to develop and sustain the maximum number of small enterprise projects throughout the county' (Limerick County Enterprise Board, 1996).

As with all Enterprise Boards, both Limerick's Enterprise Boards comprise a chairperson and fourteen members, representing the main public sector agencies, business, trade unions, and community interests, including four elected local councillors each. Staff at both Enterprise Boards describe their job as providing both reactive and proactive support measures for enterprise: the former referring to the disbursement of grants and awards; and the latter comprising 'soft supports', such as management development programmes, business advice and counselling for entrepreneurs (Interviews 9, 10). Both Boards have established strategic alliances with other key players in the local development field. The City Enterprise Board has linked up with the third level colleges in Limerick to produce an action programme, focusing on enterprise awareness and seeking to support and co-ordinate the allocation of resources for small businesses in the city. The County Board has joined with the Ballyhoura Partnership company and the North Cork Enterprise Board, to develop SEED (the Small Enterprises Entrepreneurship Development programme), which provides recipients with grant aid and management development skills (Interview 12). Both Boards joined the Irish Business and Employers Confederation (IBEC) in an EU funded PLATO programme, designed to develop the management skills of between 80-100 small businesses throughout 1997/8.[3]

Partnerships

Partnership companies work according to the principle of subsidiarity, attempting to devolve authority and responsibility for development to the lowest level possible (Walsh, 1995). They are designed to give explicit recognition to the fact that different sets of actors - statutory bodies, the private sector, community and voluntary groups - all have a role to play in local development (Interview 2). There are three partnership companies in Limerick, which between them cover the whole county: the PAUL partnership in Limerick city, Ballyhoura Development Ltd in the south east of the county and West Limerick Resources Ltd in the south west. The Tipperary LEADER group, based primarily in county Tipperary, also crosses over the east Limerick border, covering approximately 9% of the county area. Although all three of the Limerick partnerships are now formally incorporated into the OPLURD, they originate from a variety of government and EU sponsored development initiatives.

Of the three, the PAUL partnership is the oldest. In the late 1980s, community development initiatives in Moyross (one the present targeted parishes) resulted in a series of seminars involving all the groups who had taken part (Interview 22). For the community groups, voluntary groups and state agencies, it provided the initial impetus for a combined partnership approach. Limerick's selection as a model action project for the European Community's third Combat Poverty programme in 1989 gave formal recognition to their attempts at development action through partnership initiatives. In March 1990, the People Action Against Unemployment in Limerick (PAUL) project was set up with a resource base of £1.6 million for a period of just over four years to June 1994 (Interview 2). PAUL's organization reflected the partnership principles on which it was founded, comprising of: five state agencies - *FÁS* mid-west region, Limerick Corporation, the City of Limerick Vocational Educational Committee (VEC), the Mid-Western Health Board and Shannon Development; two voluntary bodies - Limerick Centre for the Unemployed and Limerick Youth Service; and five community organizations - Moyross Partners, Community Adult Reaches Everyone (CARE), St Mary's Parish Awareness and Development Group (PADG), Southill Community Services Board, and Southill Development Co-operative (Interview 2).

In November 1991, the PAUL project was selected as one of twelve government-sponsored pilot schemes (see Chapter 3) designed to provide area-based responses to long-term unemployment (ABR). The initiative arose as part of the national concordat between the government and Social Partners known as the *Programme for Economic and Social Progress* (PESP). This necessitated a re-structuring of the company to include four additional agencies: the Department of Social Welfare, the Irish Congress of Trade Unions (ICTU), the Irish Business and Employers Confederation (IBEC), and St Munchin's Community Information Enterprise Centre. The Limerick Centre for the Unemployed became part of the ICTU representation. With inclusion in the ABR initiative, came access to Global Grant funds for local development in 1992.[4]

Under the ABR initiative, PAUL was given a co-ordinating role in state programmes targeting the long-term unemployed. The partnership expanded its activities, attracting support from a variety of sources including: the Department of Social Welfare for a money advice programme in 1992; the EU HORIZON programme for the provision of education and training for lone parents in 1993; and *FÁS*, for a Community Employment Development programme in 1993 (Interview 2). In February 1994, following the success of the original ABR pilot programme, the government expanded the ABR scheme to include a further 26 area partnerships throughout the state. The thirty-eight area-based development partnerships, including PAUL, formed Sub-programme II in the OPLURD 1994-1999, also partially funded by a second Global Grant from the European Union.

PAUL's focus upon innovative programmes through partnership, has enabled it to attract further support from the EU in the form of pilot schemes and Community Initiatives. The consequence has been successful development actions, locally and nationally. The HORIZON programme that PAUL ran for single mothers between 1992 and 1994, for example, was one of the first European programmes designed to integrate single mothers into the labour market. Following PAUL evaluations, segments of the programme were subsequently mainstreamed by the Limerick VEC and *FÁS*. Another project, designed to provide basic educational skills to older people, especially women with school-age children, has also been adopted nationally by the VEC.

PAUL has been involved in a number of 'take-up' campaigns and welfare activities and in 1996, the OECD noted its particular success in the areas of welfare rights and advocacy on behalf of the unemployed (OECD, 1996:66). By reporting back on its activities to central government, PAUL has achieved a sizeable influence on new legislation relating to unemployment benefit and welfare schemes (OECD,1996:67). PAUL's Money Advice Project, for example, providing low-income families with information, advice and support on how to manage their debts, and helping to organize the supply of low-cost credit to residents of poor areas directly influenced the details of the 1993 Consumer Credit Bill, and was used by the Department of Social Welfare as part of its national money advice programme (Interview 2).

The evolution of the PAUL partnership in the city is mirrored by the development of the Ballyhoura partnership in the county. In 1986, an initiative to regenerate the town of Kilfinane, led to the creation of the Ballyhoura *Fáilte* Society Ltd.[5] The company was set up as a co-operative venture, with the objective of developing tourism as a source of rural employment. By 1988, the *Fáilte* Society had extended its remit to a broader rural development programme, following its selection for a two-year pilot programme for integrated rural development being run by the Department of Agriculture and Food (see Chapter 3). In 1990, the Ballyhoura partnership established a Community Consultative Committee (Interview 12). By 1991, the Partnership area covered a population of 38,856 and had re-constituted itself as the Ballyhoura Development Company in order to qualify for funding under EU LEADER pilot programme (Interview 12).

By 1993, with the support of the LEADER programme, the Consultative Committee comprised over 30 voluntary groups operating in the area and took on its first major project. With the help of technical expertise from the University College Dublin, 500 local volunteers carried out an area audit, collecting data on the skills of 21,777 adults (Interview 12). The audit information collected was subsequently used by the partnership for community planning and was included in the OPLURD 1994-99. Those who took part in the project suggested that aside from the data provided for the Operational Programme, an equally important aspect of the project was the motivation provided to the local community by the audit because it demonstrated their ability to organize and successfully carry out a large-scale project using the partnership structure (Interview 12). By 1995, the partnership had qualified for further funding from the LEADER II programme and been formally incorporated as one of the 38 state partnerships in the OPLURD 1994-99.

The Ballyhoura partnership is currently guiding a number of small-scale development projects. Most recently, they have established a new specialized brand of local cured meat and are planning to expand the operation into international markets using funding from the EU LEADER II programme to finance their marketing and feasibility reports (Interview 12). A review of the partnership's activities in 1995 indicated that 47 communities had been assisted with the production of community development plans (CAAS, 1997:23). Since its formation in 1992, the Ballyhoura Enterprise Support Team (BEST), have assisted local promoters to create 37 new businesses. IRL£3 million that was resourced through Ballyhoura Development Ltd sustained 100 full-time job equivalents in Ballyhoura in 1995 and 500 job equivalents since 1988. Tourism revenue has been increased ten-fold since 1986 (CAAS, 1997:24).

The third and youngest partnership company in Limerick, West Limerick Resources Ltd. was established in 1995, following the group's qualification for funding from the second phase of the EU LEADER programme and its inclusion as one of the 38 area partnerships recognised by the government in the OPLURD 1994-99. Perhaps as a result of the early involvement of both of these programmes, the West Limerick partnership has a strong emphasis on community development through the support of entrepreneurship and also through combating disadvantage. 'It is the central vision of West Limerick Resources Ltd. that local communities be empowered to determine their own personal, social and economic development through the use of the human and natural resources of the area' (Interview 23).

Staff in the partnership believe that their key tasks are to develop working groups that ensure local representation on projects designed to combat particular local issues, and also to help establish networks of groups within the area (Interview 23). Partnership sub-groups have been established to produce targeted policies within the areas of rural tourism, social integration, culture and heritage, enterprise and employment, education and training, and agriculture and natural resources. The partnership has established referral arrangements with the County Enterprise Board and Shannon Development in relation to targeting and supporting local development. It also operates an EU NOW programme in conjunction with the PAUL partnership, aimed at reducing the barriers experienced by women wishing to enter the labour force. Although the partnership is still relatively young, its members believe that they can develop quickly using the experience and examples of best practice already demonstrated by other longer-established partnerships and agencies.

State-sponsored bodies

There are a range of state-sponsored bodies in Limerick that have some role to play in local development. *Bord Fáilte* (the Tourism Board), which was placed under a specific Operational Programme for Tourism in the *National Development Plan 1994-99*, is a member of the Limerick County Strategy Group and has representatives on the two rural partnership Boards. Aside from its own development activities within the terms of the Operational Programme for Tourism, the *Bord* has been involved with the promotion of a number of small-scale tourism initiatives throughout the county.

Coillte (the Forestry Board) and *Teagasc* (the Agriculture and Food Development Authority) are both associated primarily with the county council areas of Limerick. *Coillte*, which manages public forests and related commercial activities, has recently set up a farmer forestry partnership scheme to disseminate best practice in forest management and also provides training on harvesting, forwarding, and environmental management of forestry. *Teagasc* is the national body for providing advisory research, education and training services to the agricultural and food industry. As such, it has been closely involved in the development of the Food Centre at Raheen industrial estate, which together with the Ballyhoura partnership and Shannon Development, is helping to develop the Ballyhoura area as a centre for small food projects (Interview 12).

FÁS (*Foras Aiseanna Saothair*, the Training and Employment Authority), has a high profile in development initiatives. The lion-share of its budget is directed to the long-term unemployed, through the Community Employment Scheme (CES) (Interview 24). Through the CES, local community groups, voluntary bodies and local authorities sponsor employment schemes and - with financial assistance from *FÁS* - provide project-based employment for local people who are long-term unemployed. This is a programme that could not be run without the close co-operation of other development agencies in the area. *FÁS* cooperates closely with Shannon Development, Limerick Corporation, and the two partnership companies - PAUL and West Limerick Resources Ltd.

The pre-eminent state-sponsored body in terms of development responsibilities in Limerick, however, is Shannon Development. The remit of Shannon Development is a wide one and includes responsibility for: the Shannon Free Zone, an export growth promotion centre comprising the regional airport and a number of other export companies; the Shannon World Aviation Park for aviation sector industries; indigenous industry in the region, providing a range of grant supports and consultancy services; tourism development in the region, including product development, marketing, trade services and visitor information services; management and development of the National Technological Park in Limerick (home to the University of Limerick); rural development; and, in conjunction with other agencies, development of the region's tourist potential. The company is responsible for implementation of both the Operational Programmes for Industry and for Tourism across the region (Interview 7).

Shannon Development has been keen to work with and through partnership arrangements across the region (Interview 7). Securing the co-operation of agencies in related tasks, makes Shannon Development's job easier. Furthermore, its broad development remit throughout the region, makes good relations with a range of local agencies common sense. Co-operating with smaller agencies and partnerships does not undermine Shannon Development's competencies and in fact often serves to secure its influence (Interview 7). It is this approach to business that has led to the company's involvement in a range of partnership arrangements throughout the region.

In the city, the company was a founder member of PAUL partnership and has established three enterprise centres in the partnership's targeted areas. Together with Limerick Corporation, the company has undertaken significant responsibilities for the restoration of King John's castle and helped in the development proposals for the inner city area. In the county, Shannon Development has helped to support industrial and business developments with the Ballyhoura partnership and the Women's Business Development Centre located in the University of Limerick campus area.

Commenting on the growth of partnership initiatives involving Shannon Development and other state-sponsored bodies since the mid-1980s, the Chair of the Limerick County Strategy Group suggested that semi-state bodies were obliged to look towards new ways of working, when it became apparent that traditional development approaches were not successful (Interview 21). Working through partnerships is a practical response to the demands of multi-strategic planning and integrated development objectives. It has now become the accepted wisdom of state-sponsored bodies involved in local development.

Network resources

In Ireland, there is no statutory mechanism to ensure an equitable distribution of resources for development such as that provided by the federal system of fiscal equalization in Germany. Yet there are some similarities: there is a degree of indicative development planning in the OPLURD framework that stipulates what types and forms of local development are most desirable; and there is also a greater disposition towards integrated strategic programming and planning of in all aspects of policy implementation. Still, the funding of individual development projects is more akin to the British funding model in that development actors and agencies are expected to tender for funding on the basis of concrete development proposals, and partnership bids between public and private interests are encouraged. The Irish budgetary model for development may be distinguished from the British, however, by its explicit support for *community development* and its positive action in favour of social and economic cohesion. In this respect, the Irish government's approach towards the deployment of EU funding has been designed to encourage cooperation and coordination between local development interests in the network instead of damaging competition. This has been achieved in a number of ways.

Instead of attempting to substitute EU funding for national public expenditure, the government has levered the maximum amount of financial support available from the EU by providing the matching funding required for Objective One programmes. This has helped to eliminate damaging competition for funds, both within and between county networks (Interview 11). Added to this, the incorporation of the EU Community Support Framework for Ireland into the *National Development Plan 1994-99* enables the government to integrate its own public expenditure with that provided by the EU in the most cost-effective way - the goals, objectives and targets of development policy and the instruments used to bring them about in both plans are the same. The government's emphasis on the value of integrated, strategic planning in general, and in particular the prospect of secured funding for partnership companies for up to five years, promotes joint projects between network members. For the partnerships, an effective strategic plan that incorporates as many other network members as possible can maximize their funding potential by increasing their ability to offer matching funding for development grants (Interview 21). For other network members, such as the Enterprise Boards and state-sponsored bodies, co-option onto a local partnership project can help spread the costs of meeting their own objectives, whilst fulfilling their commitment to the integrated, multi-agencied approach to local development that the government desires (Interviews 4, 5). In this way, the government's integration of EU and national policy actively promotes multi-agency, strategic approaches to development.

Finally, the partnership approach adopted by the government at national level (detailed in Chapter 3), further supports a co-operative approach to development policy at sub-national level. This is because as well as optimizing members' access to the network's financial resources, the use of integrated development and strategic planning initiatives promotes the growth and development of partnership skills. 'There is', claimed a senior representative of the Board of ADM, 'a genuine growing understanding, which comes through partnership, of other peoples' positions and points of view ... a greater ability to accept that there are other divergent views and to work with them and work towards consensus around them. You see it replicated all over the place and at national level as well' (Interview 17).

Although the acquisition of partnership skills appears to a national phenomenon, Limerick has benefitted from a longer experience of this process than most. This mixture of knowledge, skills and experience has meant that as well as attracting mainstream funding for projects, members of the Limerick network have been adept at drawing down additional 'add-on' funding that would otherwise not be available to the network. The primary source of this has been EU sponsored pilot programmes and Community Initiatives. The PAUL partnership in Limerick city has drawn funds from EU HORIZON and NOW programmes, whilst the rural partnership companies joined with other Limerick agencies and their counterparts in north county Cork to make a successful bid for Article 10 funding from the European Commission (Interview 9).

In summary, the Limerick network is rich in resources. It benefits not only from the significant financial assistance given by the European Union, but also from the fact that this has been mediated by governments prepared to support local development. In addition, the network also benefits from a high level of knowledge, skills, information and experience in terms of development projects and processes. Most important however, is the willingness of network members to share and co-operate in the deployment of the resources available to them.

Network dynamics

There are a number of features that pre-dispose this network's members to good relations with each other. First, the Irish tradition of self-help is evidenced in an active, large-scale and widespread voluntary sector and in large numbers of community development initiatives, local credit unions and co-operatives. A senior member of ADM suggested that the level of community activism in Limerick, although high, was more or less common place in Irish society and that 'in Ireland people happen to expect less from the state and to expect to contribute more themselves in the community and voluntary sector' (Interview 17).

This attitude flourished in the years following Irish independence because the state did not have much money. Perhaps because of this, the shortage of funding for development initiatives acted as a spur to community and voluntary development groups to organize themselves (Interview 20). In Limerick, the locals responded by organizing themselves and out of that arose the partnership structure (Interview 5). In acknowledging that local authorities were 'starved of cash from 1977 up to 1993', as a consequence of recession, the rates stoppage, and central government's failure to give them the funds that they were promised, one local councillor suggested that instead of being jealous of the new agencies that were being created, local authorities embraced them (Interview 20). Co-operation with the new organizations provided alternative mechanisms for capturing funding that were not available to the local authorities operating on their own (Interview 5). The newly-established organizations, particularly the Enterprise Boards, also created new opportunities for seconding local authority staff into organizations that had the capacity to carry out local authority development objectives.

Undoubtedly, an important feature of the Limerick network that promotes membership inter-actions, is the size and nature of the Irish political system. One member of the government's Local Development Liaison Team, explained how the relatively small county sizes lead to small policy groups that are easily recognisable: 'You're talking about county units where populations are on average 40-50,000 towards 80,000. So the number of players ... in any one county would not be more than say one hundred' (Interview 14b). One of the consequences of working in a relatively small milieu, is that persons with policy-making experience tend to be quite mobile within the policy network. Enterprise Board staff for example, are often seconded from their local authorities. In Limerick, the Chief Executive Officer of the County Enterprise Board is on secondment from the county council (Interview 9). The fact that his office premises are based within the county council buildings, is indicative of the close relations between the Enterprise Boards and local authorities. Similarly, when the partnership companies were established they sought experienced officers from other local development agencies. As a result, all partnership companies and LEADER groups in Limerick have representatives at Board level from *FÁS*, Shannon Development, their local Enterprise Board and their local Council, as well as other relevant statutory agencies (Interview 21).

Close and co-operative relations between network members in Limerick are not solely the result of cultural and political traditions. They are common sense. Since the resources for any single project may be made up from funds gathered from many different agencies and sources, it is only practical to develop good relations, not only with potential sponsors, but equally with potential co-funders. Local authority representatives from both city and county councils expressed enthusiasm for the new ways of working together. One senior council official suggested that by contributing to development projects that were led by alternative development agencies, the council could circumscribe much of the bureaucracy created when the council alone takes on a project using public funding (Interview 4).

Another council official suggested that under the new co-operative arrangements, the council was in a better position to make policy (Interview 5). Councillors could for example, determine the parameters of council assistance, making policy decisions to target certain population levels, or specific target areas, whilst local communities could input on the details of implementation (Interview 5). By co-operating with a range of alternative development agencies, the local authorities are able to maximize the impact of their limited resources, whilst the local partnerships and community groups are beginning to recognise the authorities as partners in local development - rather than the political or bureaucratic fiefdoms that they were once assumed to be.

Another significant feature contributing to good network dynamics is the non-hierarchical nature of relations between members. Sharing resources on a 'project to project basis' prevents the formation of hierarchical relations. This is illustrated by the fact that although a single agency may be involved in a number of projects, it may lead on only one, whilst other different projects are headed by other different agencies. Added to this, the emphasis on multi-agencied approaches to development that stress the importance of strategic planning further cement collaborative relations. The partnership companies, for example, have taken advantage of close relations with other local agencies and secured a commitment from them by including such agencies in their own strategic plans. One community activist explained that when representatives of such agencies are involved in the drawing up of a partnership's strategic plan, not only do they volunteer their expertise and experience, they also implicitly give their support. It then becomes very difficult for them to withdraw from involvement at later stages of the plan's implementation, when for example a partnership is seeking matching funding or some other form of assistance (Interview 23).

Without doubt, the significant amount of technical and financial assistance that has come from the European Union has helped to cement these attitudes by providing the necessary experience amongst development actors to support partnership approaches. The Chief Executive of the County Enterprise Board explained how many local informal inter-actions between development agencies were formalized by their incorporation into EC programmes (Interview 9). The decision of Irish governments to promote local co-operation and co-ordination between development interests as a matter of policy, can be clearly traced to the early pilot programmes in local development sponsored by the European Community and in this respect, both the city and rural areas of Limerick are fortunate in having a broader experience of working in EU programmes than most.

As a consequence, the Limerick network boasts a high level of co-operation and inter-action between its members. One senior member of the Limerick CSG suggested that high levels of co-operation stem from the way that member groups perceive their role: 'most CSG members, but particularly the partnership companies, view themselves first and foremost as facilitators of development projects, rather than development actors in their own right' (Interview 21). The specific desire of such groups to be responsive to community needs and inclusive of community membership illustrates the extent to which 'bottom-up' approaches to development that stress the importance of empowerment and social animation have taken hold. An independent appraisal of the co-ordination of local development in Limerick concluded that:

> The impression gained during the course of this study was of a complex yet flexible and responsive approach to local and rural development that worked in practice despite its complexity, largely through effective networking at formal and operational levels. The potential for duplication is high, especially in the provision of "soft supports" such as training, but was largely avoided in practice because of the high level of inter-action among the agencies concerned (CAAS, 1997:40).

Concluding remarks: characterizing the network and the policy process

Table 4 provides a summary of the main themes raised in this chapter and illustrates how the Limerick network conforms closely to the model of a *policy community* in the Marsh and Rhodes (1996) network typology (discussed in Chapter 1). Unusually, however, the membership of this network is open and

Table 4: Characterizing the Limerick policy network

Dimension	**Network features**
Formation	Responsibility for regional policy is decentralized to local level. Network boundaries determined by personal interactions negotiated order achieved through strategic planning and partnership initiatives.
Membership	Wide-ranging and inclusive membership which is non-hierarchically and informally organized into a few key groups, representing a mixture of public, private, community and voluntary organizations.
Resources	All participants have equal access to resources, so that basic relationships are exchange relationships.
Dynamics	Highly personalized, non-hierarchical relations between policy actors blurring the distinction between 'government and governed'. Negotiated order which is constantly 'worked at' through pragmatic innovation and accommodation.
Power	There is a balance of power among members which supports positive-sum outcomes. All members perceive themselves to be sufficiently better off in this set up to ensure its continuance.

non-hierarchical and because of this, it is perhaps useful to refer to the ideal type policy community characterized by Richardson and Jordan (1979). Whereas Marsh and Rhodes (1992) emphasized the importance of exclusive memberships that were often hierarchically organized, Richardson and Jordan (1979) emphasized the importance of interpersonal relationships between policy actors. Their model of a policy community is characterized by the disintegration of policy-making authority, with policy-making negotiated amongst sub-systems made up of government and/or government agencies and other interests. Negotiation is achieved through pragmatic improvization and accommodation.

Regarding the network's formation, the Irish emphasis on programmatic government, evidenced in the nine Operational Programmes that together make up the *National Development Plan 1994-1999*, supports the notion that in Ireland policy-making has been divided into a series of governmental sub-systems.[6] Since, however, the Objective One designation covered the whole island of Ireland until 2000, it played no significant role in shaping regional boundaries to areas for development action in Ireland. Similarly, despite specific programmes aimed at rural or urban areas, the OPLURD initiative set up by the Irish government to integrate EU support into Irish development strategies did not prescribe regional development areas either. Thus, the institution of County Strategy Groups under the OPLURD initiative, and later Strategic Policy Groups and City/County Development Boards, represents the establishment of a core set of policy actors, with no clear bounded periphery.

The organization of regional policy actors was dealt with in greater detail in the section dealing with network membership. Lacking formally constituted borders for development action, the network is entirely constructed by personal links and associations between the range of development actors on the ground. This is possible because the number of relevant actors is small enough - with sufficient overlapping functions and responsibilities - that everyone can join the core, and also because of the culture of personalism and localism in Irish politics. The range of state sponsored bodies, government departments and associated agencies, each organized according to their own administrative borders, yet with some involvement in development activities across the Limerick county, is typical of the 'administrative jungle' of Irish sub-national government (detailed in Chapter 2). Arguably, the only reason that such a chaotic and haphazard mosaic of organizations continues to interact effectively is because of the relatively small scale of Irish counties as focal points for development action.

In other respects, the success of the three partnership companies operating in Limerick points to the negotiated consensus between policy actors over policy preferences and desired outcomes suggested by Richardson and Jordan's (1979) model of a policy community. There is widespread evidence of highly personalized and informal relations between development actors throughout this network. Moreover, the adoption of 'bottom-up' approaches to development where emphasis is placed upon building the capacity of the population through enabling principles such as *partnership* and *subsidiarity* has brought together actors from statutory, voluntary, public and private sectors in 'a way that blurs familiar distinctions between public and private, national and local, and representative and participative democracy' (OECD, 1996:9). As in the Richardson and Jordan model of policy communities, the distinction between 'government' and 'governed' is often difficult to maintain (Richardson and Jordan, 1979:61). The Limerick policy community is based on a negotiated order and environment, which is achieved through pragmatic improvization and accommodation. Interviewees referred to the supportive system of information exchange and co-ordination - a feature that is facilitated by the high level of cooperation within the network.

The Limerick network also reflects the typical policy community features outlined by Marsh and Rhodes (1996) relating to the distribution of resources. The Limerick network has adequate finances, which are deployed effectively between a variety of agencies that are encouraged to co-operate with each other, supporting Marsh and Rhodes' (1996) proposition that in a policy community all members of the policy network have resources, so the links between them are exchange relationships. Thus the basic interaction is 'one involving bargaining between network members with resources, so that there is a balance of power, not necessarily one in which all members equally benefit but one in which all members see themselves as in a positive-sum game' (Rhodes, 1997:43). This view of network relations was substantiated in the fourth section dealing with network dynamics.

Whilst the evidence from the Limerick case study tends to corroborate the view of a 'self-regulating' policy community; lacking any permanent, formal structure, the temporary nature of the current OPLURD related policy fora means that the future of this network is uncertain. On the one hand, the OPLURD initiative reflects adaptive structuring of Irish policy institutions in order to incorporate EU involvement in regional policy and this 'flexibility' has enabled the European Union to have a significant impact upon the *current* organization of regional policy. On the other hand, the impermanence of those institutions and structures that facilitate EU involvement in regional policy means that the level of integration between EU and Irish policy processes is heavily dependent on elite attitudes in favour of, and government support for, European integration. The relative significance of institutional versus government and elite support for EU involvement in policy is given comparative consideration in the concluding chapter, which gives a comparative evaluation of change in policy networks in relation to European integration.

Notes

1. This body has since been superseded by City/County Development Groups (see Chapter 2).
2. The Local Development Liaison Team has since been relocated to the Department of Tourism, Recreation and Local Development.
3. PLATO, built on a Belgian model, is a business training network. Small businesses are encouraged to learn from one another and from local large enterprises, who act as facilitators of small working groups.
4. The Global Grant combines monies from the ERDF and the ESF to support an integrated package of measures aimed at socio-economic development. It is administered by an independent state-sponsored company, Area Development Management Ltd. For more details see Chapter 3.
5. *Fáilte* - the Irish word for welcome.
6. The *National Development Plan 1994-1999* (Government of Ireland, 1993:161) comprises of the following Operational Programmes: Industry; Tourism; Transport; Environmental services; Economic infrastructure; Agriculture, Rural Development and Forestry; Fisheries; Human Resources; and Local Development (County Enterprise Boards, Area-based approach to disadvantaged areas, Community Employment Development Programme and Social Employment Scheme, Urban Renewal).

Chapter 6

Case Study: Merseyside, England

Introduction

Merseyside's designation as an EU Objective One region, marked a significant turning point in the evolution of development policy in the area. It was important not only because it signalled the introduction of the European Union as a new and potentially powerful regional actor, but also because it marked the introduction of new approaches to regional regeneration in the UK. Chief amongst these were the emphases placed by the European Union upon strategic programming and planned assistance, together with a desire to build *social* as well as *economic capital* in areas of regional decline. When Merseyside was first declared an Objective One area for EU assistance in 1992, the introduction of such 'European style' approaches to development was not welcomed by the then Conservative government. The desire of the EU to promote regionally-oriented, community-based and strategically planned development was not regarded by the UK government as an opportunity to reconsider 'traditional' approaches to development. Instead, it was widely assumed to be evidence of unwelcome European interference with British policy practice.

In November 1993, Merseyside's first bid for Objective One funding - described by one local government official as 'essentially a shopping list sent from central government to Brussels' (Interview 15) - was rejected by the European Commission. Lloyd and Meegan (1996:83), who were employed by the European Commission to act as independent advisors on the bid, suggest that the document was not so much a plan for concerted action, as a account of how EU funds could be dispersed in Merseyside: 'The Single Programming Document (SPD) was not a "plan" nor did the UK authorities see such an approach as appropriate.' In the subsequent reapplication, the new authors[i] (none of whom were from central government) devised a more structured and integrated programme, which was accepted by the British government and the European Commission in July 1994 (Interview 12).

The revised SPD outlines five 'key drivers for change'. The first four 'drivers' comprise of four sets of measures designed to promote economic development. Together they are designed to set out a strategy by which 'Structural Fund support is packaged and directed towards creating the conditions under which the private sector will invest in Merseyside' (CEC, 1994c:28). The first 'driver' relates to the key corporate sector enterprises, and establishes a series of project initiatives designed to support the preparation, servicing and accessing of strategic sites for large companies and significant inward investors. Infrastructure spending, marketing and improving the region's image are also covered under this set of measures. The second 'driver' relates to home-grown small and medium-sized business sector. SMEs are encouraged to grow through the use of EU money to help fund training, services and advice through the TECs and Business Links. There is provision for a Merseyside Special Investment Fund set up by the clearing banks but with EU money used to subsidise interest rates for business loans. The third 'driver' relates to knowledge-based industries and advanced technologies, which are supported through a series of measures that give special attention to technology transfer between Merseyside's two universities and industry, particularly SMEs. One idea, for example, is a graduate retention programme with local industry to keep more people in the area after qualifying. The fourth industry 'driver' relates to the promotion of cultural, media and leisure industries in which Merseyside has established strengths.

Finally, the SPD's specific inclusion of a 'strategy for investing in the people of Merseyside' as the most important of the five key drivers for change, marked a significant shift of focus (Interview 12). Under this 'driver', the 'Pathways to Integration' initiative set up 38 area-based partnership structures across the region that were intended to provide a channel of access between identified areas of social exclusion and EU development projects (CEC, 1994c:33). This introduction of the concept of 'social exclusion' is notable since it challenges the traditional British view of development as a process that is centred around physical regeneration and the attraction of business and investment into an area (see: Stewart, 1996). In this respect, the Pathways programme illustrates the introduction of 'European approaches' to development that place an emphasis on building the capacity of the population through measures designed to bring about social animation (Interview 1). Whilst the Pathways programme represents an acknowledgement of this view of development, it does not indicate a clear change of policy practice (Interview 15).

The Single Programming Document outlines development activities that are eligible for Structural Funds support, but it does not provide a specific programme of action through which such activities can be discharged (Interview 12). In all cases, the responsibility for obtaining EU assistance is vested entirely with those in need of it: that is to say that neither British government nor its regional outpost, the Government Office for Merseyside, plays any part in attempting to attract Structural Funds assistance into the region. This is particularly important in relation to the need to demonstrate the additionality of EU funding. Without matching funding, many groups entitled to EU assistance are unable to avail of it. The requisite competition for national sponsorship of regeneration initiatives in the form of the SRB allocations system, means that groups already entitled to EU assistance must compete against one another in order to draw down the matching funding they need to obtain it. Moreover, the lack of coordination between EU and UK development initiatives prevents groups from citing national projects or policy instruments as providing 'added value' that can be costed in the presentation of matching funding.

The remainder of this chapter examines the impact of this environment on the formulation and implementation of regional development strategies in Merseyside. Using the same organizing concepts for comparison as the other two case studies, it examines the formation of the development policy network, its membership, resources and dynamics. The chapter concludes with a summary characterization of the Merseyside policy network and the regional policy process that supports it.

Network formation

The formation of the Merseyside network differs from both the Thüringen and Limerick networks in that, with the exception of its designated EU Objective One status, nothing holds the network together. The *Merseyside region* has no real legal or political status to afford it any administrative autonomy from central government. Neither does it benefit from a sense of regional or local identity, which might facilitate more informal or personalist networks. In fact, the *Merseyside region* has only ever been defined by agents outside of Merseyside.

The Department of Trade and Industry (DTI) identified Merseyside as a region in its designation of the area that is eligible for DTI Regional Selective Assistance grants. Merseyside was also targeted by other government initiatives designed to arrest regional decline: the Merseyside Task Force in 1981; Action for Cities and the Safer Cities programme in 1988; the City Challenge initiative in 1991; and English Partnerships in 1993 (all detailed in Chapter 3). Referring to the range of government initiatives in general, and the DTI selective assistance programmes in particular, Lloyd and Meegan (1996:78) argue that 'this is consistent with an overarching view which has no concept of the region other than as a *container for programmes* of various kinds operated under the auspices of national government'.

The Metropolitan Counties, set up in 1974, were the closest Britain came to a regional tier of government (Interview 15). In their establishment, however, they cut across pre-existing and longer-established county borders, so that even their abolition, with the notable exception of the Greater London Council (GLC), was mourned by few, save the politicians and local government bureaucrats most affected by the changes (Leach, 1994). For many then, Merseyside is an artificially constructed region, its tradition reaching back only as far as 1974 and lasting only until 1986, when it was abolished by Conservative reforms to local government.

There are five local authority areas in Merseyside: Sefton, St Helens, Knowsley, Wirral and Liverpool. When the Metropolitan County Council of Merseyside was dissolved in 1986, many of the links between the district authorities (for example, in relation to planning and joint economic development initiatives) were severed (Interview 15). Some administrative links were retained for services that operate across the districts (such as police, fire, health and education), but in the absence of common structures the local authorities each adopted independent approaches towards regional development in their areas (Interview 18). This has led to a widely acknowledged lack of coherence in development policy strategies across the region (Interview 18). It was not until Merseyside received its Objective One status in 1994, that the regional boundary assumed a new significance.

The introduction, in November 1993, of the Single Regeneration Budget (SRB) might be seen as a move towards area-based policy assistance in terms of urban regeneration as it placed urban policy initiatives under a single funding mechanism in an attempt to concentrate resources and integrate policy measures in distinct geographical areas. Still, it occurs at a scale below that of the region and is based on competitive bidding between areas, rather than strategic targeting of resources across the region. By contrast, the EU terms of assistance for Objective One funding are based on criteria of need. Under these criteria, Merseyside has been identified as a region in need of assistance.[1] This highlights a major difficulty in terms of establishing concerted development action in the region: lacking any traditional regional identity, borders or boundaries, with no common institutions or local government - the only communality in Merseyside is that the EU has identified it as a region in decline (Interview 22). In terms of understanding the organization of the regional policy network then, in Merseyside, there is a clear policy domain - but the actions of established policy structures and agencies operating within the domain are not integrated across it.

Network membership

In Merseyside, the number of organizations involved in some aspect of regional regeneration and local development is in excess of one hundred.[2] This proliferation of development policy actors resulted mainly from central government's massive restructuring of local government throughout the 1980s (see Chapter 2). In Merseyside, however, the dissolution of the Metropolitan County of Merseyside further contributed to a fragmentation of sub-national government - a tendency that has increased in recent years rather than given way to more collaborative endeavours (Interview 15). Moreover, the organization of a national competition to obtain funding for local development initiatives under the SRB (detailed in Chapter 2) tends to stymie collaboration between competing local areas and often inadvertently fosters the creation of duplicate arrangements (Interview 15). Consequently, the Merseyside network exhibits a large and fragmented membership. Its members are defined according to a notional boundary within which they all operate, but across which they do not cooperate. This section examines the network's membership by dividing it into categories that represent the major regional policy interests: the Government Office for Merseyside; the local authorities; local business; regional quangos; the voluntary sector; and Area-based Partnership organizations.

The Government Office for Merseyside

On the one hand, the Government Office for Merseyside (GOM), as the regional representative of central government has both the resources and the capacity to direct policy in the region. This it does, in a limited way, in relation to its monitoring and evaluation of regional programmes and agencies (Interview 19). GOM's ability to manage integrated development in the region is, however, constrained by its limited authority (Interview 11). Whilst GOM is able to represent the Departments of Environment, Education, Transport, Trade and Industry, other key ministry bases remain in London. One local authority official explained: 'The Home Office isn't here, the Department of Health isn't here. So when we talk about integrating regional regeneration programmes, which the government now wants us to do, we find it awfully difficult at a regional level to do that because we keep having to go down to Whitehall' (Interview 15). Other network members, particularly from the partnership groups, referred to the difficulties they encountered trying to plan and coordinate local development projects because the UK office responsible for allocating grant aid from the European Social Fund is based in London (Interviews 6, 11). The government's reluctance to take an active role in the Objective One programme means that it has voluntarily withdrawn from the opportunity of leading the network.

In relation to regional development, the Government Office for Merseyside has three major functions. As a deliverer of government services, GOM is responsible for administering regional selective assistance, mostly to private companies, through the Department of Trade and Industry. It delivers the Single Regeneration Budget to successful applicants and provides a number of small-scale innovation and R&D grants across the area (HMSO, 1995). It also acts as the contracting agency on behalf of central government for regional agencies such as the TECs (Interview 19). As a regional monitor, GOM evaluates the performance of regional bodies in receipt of government funding, such as the Merseyside Development Corporation, the Liverpool Housing Action Trust, and the Training and Enterprise Council (Interview 19). Lastly, GOM uses its experience in both these areas to influence central government policy for the region (Interview 19).

GOM acts as 'the eyes and ears of the government in the regions' providing feed-back to decision-makers in London and assembling the regional statistical information on which decisions are based (Interview 21). With the exception of SRB allocations, the government's regional selective assistance is levied according to the needs of the area. The representation of this need is the responsibility of GOM. Nevertheless, senior officials in GOM are always aware that their proposals must be in accordance with government policy and in this respect it is clear that GOM acts as an outpost of central government in Merseyside, not as a regional advocate (Interview 19). Despite GOM's limitations, interviewees pointed to the importance of maintaining a government office in Merseyside because it provides them with an opportunity to 'get close to government thinking' that they regard as helpful, particularly in relation to bidding for government funding and selective assistance (Interviews 3, 6, 15).

The local authorities

The changes in Merseyside are typical illustrations of the new institutional and organizational landscape that has grown in the stead of traditional local government structures as a result of Conservative government reforms throughout the 1980s. The changed role of local government, from being 'service providers' to 'enabling authorities', is as much an act of necessity as of invention. Partnership arrangements are now used to counteract the increasing fragmentation of service delivery agencies and to help bear costs (Interview 4).

In terms of developing partnerships, Liverpool City Council (LCC) is widely acknowledged as the lead local authority. The Central Policy Unit (CPU) of LCC is primarily responsible for the authority's development strategy and its

Economic Initiatives Unit widely recognised and respected across Merseyside (Interview 22). A senior official at the CPU suggested that the success of the LCC Economic Initiatives Unit might be because of the large number of ex-Metropolitan County Council workers working in LCC (Interview 15). 'Ex-Mets' are able to draw on personal connections and resource networks to develop new initiatives across the region and informal relations between 'ex-Met' officers provide a useful set of contacts (Interview 15). He suggested that the strategic role of the CPU was facilitated largely by informal networks: 'that's how things get done, because the structures aren't there'(Interview 15). For the most part then, links between the local authorities are voluntary and informal in nature. Another LCC senior official argued that the setting up of a 'plethora of different groups for different issues' was a stop-gap measure, which only served to highlight the need for some form of over-arching regional agency (Interview 18).

To a limited extent, Merseyside's designation as an EU Objective One region provided a focus for more cooperative action. The Merseyside Chief Executives Forum, which provides a link between senior council administrators, has been strengthened by its increasing significance as a forum that contributes joint inputs from Merseyside local authorities into the Objective One programme (Interview 18). Similarly, the 38 Pathways Area Partnerships created across the region by the Objective One programme contributed new opportunities for co-ordination between local authority areas (Interview 18). Both the demands of the programme and the delivery needs of the Objective One area meant that local authorities needed to come together in order to make the most of the designation, but 'if there hadn't been an Objective One, it's highly unlikely that would have happened anyway' (Interview 15).

Local business

Efforts to kick-start the regional economy through local business in Merseyside have long suffered from three big problems, relating to its structure, its politics, and its image. In relation to its structure, the regional economy has traditionally depended on a few large-scale employers such as Littlewoods, Barings, GEC, Ford, Tate and Lyle, United Biscuits, Cammell Laird shipyard, and the Mersey Docks and Harbour Company. As a result, Merseyside bore the brunt of the restructuring of British manufacturing throughout the 1970s and 1980s, with the loss of thousands of jobs in food manufacturing, cable making, engineering and motor manufacture and was also severely hit by recession in the 1980s. Small and medium sized firms, service industries and the professions are not well-developed in Merseyside (*Financial Times*, 3/4/97).

Regarding the politics of the region, Merseyside has a long history of labour militancy. The Thatcherite policies aimed at slashing the power of trades unions and encouraging a more aggressive management style, all but destroyed the potential for successful development partnerships with big business in an area well-known for its radical left-wing politics and highly politicized workers. The Docks-side development in Liverpool is a case in point. The Liverpool dockers' protests and picket line at Seaforth docks, which began in September 1995 and did not conclude until February 1997, probably hurt Merseyside more than it did the Mersey Docks and Harbour Company (*The Observer Review*, 5/9/97; *Financial Times*, 3/4/97).

Finally, in relation to Merseyside's image, the difficulty for many local entrepreneurs arises in trying to persuade investors that Merseyside is changing (*Financial Times*, 3/4/97:2). Some business leaders believe that the Seaforth Docks dispute actually had a positive effect on Merseyside's labour relations reputation - one that might serve to encourage future investment. They point to the fact that despite an eighteen month long protest, port business continued to be profitable and was largely unaffected by the dispute (Interview 14). Whereas ten years earlier, hundreds of Merseyside trade unionists would probably have blockaded the port in support of the striking dockers, this did not occur in the Seaforth strike (*Financial Times*, 3/4/97:3).

The port may be thriving, but across the rest of the region private sector investment in development is patchy. Where larger companies exist, their relations with the local community are often more inclined to paternalism than partnership. Both Barings and Rowntree were frequently praised for their support of local charities. Vauxhall sponsors a successful CBED (Community Based Economic Development) enabling body, the Vauxhall Neighbourhood Council in north Liverpool (CBEDs are discussed in more detail below). In Knowsley, GEC provided an area of seven acres for another CBED group to set up offices for a number of small community businesses, managed workspace, access to IT and a community workshop. Still, when GEC entered into negotiations to sell the site, the CBED's future was not guaranteed (Interview 2). The irony is, that as larger companies down-size the need for small and medium sized business is greater than ever.

The importance of attracting industry and business into the Merseyside region as key primers in regeneration initiatives has been acknowledged in the Objective One programme for Merseyside that, with the exception of the 'Pathways to Integration' initiative, concentrates all of its attention directly on 'investing in industry and services on Merseyside' (CEC, 1994c:28). Under the first 'action for industry' driver, members of the business community in Merseyside have joined together with the local authorities to form the Mersey Partnership as part of the 'Merseyside Image Campaign' (Interview 18). With a budgetary contribution of approximately 47% from the EU, Mersey Partnership also receives contributions from the five local authorities, and grants from Merseyside Development Corporation and the Merseyside TEC (Interview 18). Significant contributions are also made by ten large companies in the area, with smaller contributions from thirty nine 'ordinary members' representing local business interests (*Financial Times*, 3/4/97). Mersey Partnership was the first forum to establish a united approach to image-building and investment marketing in the region that, in addition to the DTI's creation of Business Links, signals the advent of more concerted action between regional interests to develop small and medium-sized business.[3] 'After a very slow start, things are beginning to happen. Since 1992 [when] there were a lot of people talking, but not much evidence of anything being done, the best you could say is that the decline appears to have stopped' (*Financial Times*, 3/4/97).

Since 1994, the Objective One spending programme has introduced a strong project-based core with development grants for new buildings and the preparation of three key sites for inward investment in Merseyside: Speke/Garston, in Liverpool; Parkside in St Helens; and the Cammell Laird site in Birkenhead (*Financial Times*, 3/4/97). Some argue that involvement in the Objective One programme has helped to create a more strategic approach to business development and investment, evidenced for example by the Mersey Partnership (Interview 12). Other SMEs have criticised the programme because under EU rules they cannot apply for Objective One funds directly as they are reserved for restructuring industry rather than subsidizing individual businesses (Interviews 6, 11; *Financial Times*, 14/7/97). This apparent gap in support could, presumably, be ameliorated by increasing the linkages between the different 'drivers for change'. If, for example, apprentices or vocational trainees supported by ESF schemes could be matched with small businesses in need of subsidized labour, there might be a greater synergy between support measures. As yet, however, this is not provided for in the Merseyside network.

Quangos

The role of Merseyside Training and Enterprise Council (TEC) is two-fold, both operational and supervisory. In the former, it acts as a regional training agency, both managing the provision of training in the area, and carrying out some training programmes itself. In its supervisory capacity, it sets the standards for training courses in the area, and subsequently monitors and evaluates their provision. In this respect, the TEC has had a rough ride: providing training and being empowered to judge that provided by others, puts the TEC in the position of 'gamekeeper and poacher' at the same time (Interview 22). Community groups running their own training programmes and self-help initiatives often perceive the TEC as unfair and unwelcome competition and in some cases this has led to resentment. Since its creation, the TEC has understood that however it performs its job, some people believe it has no right to do it. Although this attitude was most prevalent in the TEC's early days, one TEC manager suggested that 'it is a tension that is constantly being resolved' (Interview 22).

Housing Action Trusts (HATs), on the other hand, were acknowledged as one of the successes in relation to development in Merseyside (HMSO, 1994). The local authorities, although sceptical of capital stock transfers, recognised that the introduction of housing associations provided a means by which to kick-start area regeneration that they could no longer afford (Interview 4). When Liverpool City Council transferred its tower blocks to HAT management, in one move it confronted the political and financial realities of government policy and rid itself of its most troublesome properties (Interview 4). A senior HAT executive suggested that 'The difference between HATs and conventional estates renewable programmes, is that HATs have powers and money to carry out community and economic development' (Interview 20). Wirral, for example, designated five Housing Renewal Areas, which - although they do not have extra resources - used their authority to encourage a multi-agency approach. The combination of HATs with Safer Cities initiatives in the Wirral helped to maintain and improve properties in the area (HMSO, 1994:118).

The same collaboration was not enjoyed by the Merseyside Development Corporation. Set up in March 1981, as one of the first government created Urban Development Corporations (UDC), its brief was to act as a 'lead agency' in regional regeneration, providing inspiration to the region, in the form of a 'key regional development project' (Interview 14). Referring to MDC's involvement in the docklands and adjacent areas of North Liverpool, a member of the Central Policy Unit in Liverpool City Council suggested that, 'in effect, that area was sliced away from the locality in 1981, instead of being perceived as being part of the area, and that's still the case' (Interview 15).

In the years after the introduction of Objective One programme in 1994, relations between LCC and MDC began to improve. A senior official from LCC referred to the belated recognition that both bodies shared certain priorities and could benefit from more communication (Interview 18). Consultation began informally at first, through links with the Liverpool (council) Officer Partnership Group, and their mutual involvement in other regional forums, such as the Merseyside Tourism and Conference Bureau (MTCB) (Interview 18). Relations were later more formally cemented in their joint participation in the creation of EU sponsored Mersey Partnership. A senior executive from MDC suggested that since then 'the main forum for consideration of Merseyside regional economic policy has been through the mechanism of the Objective One programme, which has drawn in a wide ranging membership from the public, voluntary and private sectors in formulating and operating the European funding programme (Interview 14). MDC was an active participant in the programme until its wound down operations, at the end of its life-span in March 1997.

As MDC was winding down strategy, another regional agency was just being born. Of the four agencies here, English Partnerships is probably closest to central government. Although it operates on a regional basis, it is funded directly by the SRB and monitored from London (Interview 24). English Partnerships is involved in three significant development initiatives across Merseyside. It acts as the 'lead agency' in the Speke/Garston area near Liverpool airport, developing a '21st century business park' and has been heavily involved in investment in the Parkside colliery site in St Helens and the Cammell Laird shipyard in Birkenhead (Interview 24). In some areas, where an SRB bid has been successful, this has led to a high level of cooperation between members of a local partnership arrangement. In Speke/Garston, for example, English Partnerships helped to lever in additional SRB funding, which was then used by other partnership members as matching funding to draw down Objective One assistance (Interview 11). The terms of reference for English Partnerships, however, mean that most of its assistance is directed towards the redevelopment of vacant, derelict or brown-field sites and because of this it could be argued that some areas of Merseyside have benefited disproportionately from English Partnerships investment.

The voluntary sector

There are five Voluntary Service associations in Merseyside, one in each of the five local authority areas. Although the voluntary sector has a strong presence throughout Merseyside, the Liverpool Council for Voluntary Services (LCVS) is the oldest and traditionally the most powerful, probably because it benefited from a larger and better resourced city council (Interview 13). Throughout the 1980s, the voluntary sector expanded and developed its role, filling the gaps created by the Conservative government policy of decreasing public service provision wherever possible. In response to the growth of voluntary sector agents and agencies operating in the communities of Merseyside, the other local authority areas recently began to nominate Community Development Officers amongst their staff. Sefton Council for Voluntary Service (SCVS) in particular is working towards a more formal structuring of its cooperation with the council (Interview 8). There were at one stage plans for a full-time, funded manager, employed by the SCVS, whose task would be the development of organizational links between the voluntary sector and the Sefton local authority. As yet, these have not come to fruition. Nevertheless, members of SCVS were hopeful that attitudes towards the voluntary sector were changing, and that the local authority were beginning to appreciate the value of their work (Interview 8).

Others, however, suggested that the voluntary sector's capacity for involvement in regional development is still not fully recognised (Interview 10). A representative of another 'self help' community organization noted that she and her organization were adept at operating 'on the ground level': as a regional body, the agency works across Merseyside and is specifically involved with seven area partnerships (Interview 17). 'We're plugged in, we know everybody, we've got the informal links, but we but we don't seem to be plugging up into anything above us' (Interview 17). Whilst the voluntary sector is often consulted about its own operations, it is rarely sought for its insight into development issues because it represents an informed and experienced opinion (Interview 10). In reference to the increasing appeal of 'bottom-up' development strategies, the director of one Merseyside voluntary agency argued that; 'People are paying lip-service, and some people are very genuine. For others it's just a buzz-word and they are keen to use it. But I think it will take something fairly major to make this inclusion real' (Interview 10).

Partnership groups

In Merseyside, there are two significant types of partnership groups, which illustrate perfectly the divergence between the UK government and the European Union over approaches to development: the 30 SRB bidding partnerships, representing those who won the competition for government regeneration funding; and the 38 Pathways to Integration Partnerships, representing those areas designated as most in need of assistance by the European Union's Objective One programme. Across Merseyside, Liverpool City Council (LCC) has done more than any other single body in the region to integrate UK and European development approaches, partially because within the region, Liverpool presents the area of greatest need, and also because LCC is the largest local authority with more resources to carry out such a strategy. Through its sponsorship of the 11 Pathways Partnerships in Liverpool, LCC has attempted to enhance their development potential by promoting community based economic development (CBED) in the Pathways Areas (Interview 15).

CBED operate according to the principle that local people know their own needs and abilities best and, given the appropriate support, are best placed to direct their own development (Interview 7). They begin by setting up an 'enabling body', owned by the local community and often in partnership with businesses and public sector agencies. The enabling body provides technical support and know-how for the development of community projects and businesses. It is intended to play an active part in getting projects off the ground, often putting together a package of financial aid to newly developed CBED groups (Interview 11). CBEDs are funded from a mixture of sources in the public and private sectors, and most usually launched on the back of a grant package that might include support from a government agency, a charitable trust, the local authority, or European grants (Interview 11).

Although the experiences of the Liverpool Area Partnerships have been mixed, the lessons that can be drawn from them are illustrative of the strengths and weaknesses of partnership arrangements across the region. Strong partnerships are usually well-funded. There is an agreement about their aims, objectives and strategy. Members of strong partnerships trust and respect each other, allowing them to cooperate and communicate effectively with each other. In this respect, a past experience of working together and a level of basic skills, further augments the partnership's ability to deliver. Added to this, some areas are more pre-disposed to successful development partnerships than others, with a mix of potential that can act as a pull factor for investment and development programmes in the area. These advantages may include: good site potential, in terms of location, infrastructure, property or land; a mixed population, in terms of ages, skills and experience; private sector interest in the area - perhaps a large company willing to invest, or a group of local businesses willing to get involved; and a tradition of community involvement in the area, providing ready-made social infrastructure for meeting, planning and working with the community (Interview 15).

The Speke/Garston Area Partnership is illustrative of these sorts of advantages. Close to the airport and the city, with road and rail connections to the rest of the North West region, the Speke/Garson area has large swathes of undeveloped land and a ready labour supply in the nearby urban conurbations. Partially because of its scope for a very physical approach to development and urban regeneration, the area has received substantial investment from English Partnerships. The area partnership's successful SRB bid, valued at around £17 million, led to the creation of the Speke/Garston Development Company (Interview 11). By bringing together all the key agents involved in regeneration in the area, the Speke/Garston Development Company has been able to devise a comprehensive and strategic approach to the areas development (Interview 24).

Speke/Garston area also boasts a successful CBED initiative. SMART, the Saint Mary's Area Regeneration Trust, evolved over a period of about ten years and at one stage - before CBED initiatives were officially recognised - it was operating from someone's kitchen (Interview 11). It is now a recognised CBED enabling body that receives funding from a combination of sources including: the European Union, in the form of ESF and ERDF grants; central government grants from the SRB allowance; Liverpool City Council; charitable trusts; and a small amount of self-generated revenue (Interview 11). The SMART executive board comprises a range of people who 'work, live, and are involved in the community' (Interview 11). Out of 21 voting members, 16 represent key organizations in the area, ranging from schools, tenants' groups, disability projects and local businesses, to representatives from GOM, Business Links, Mersey Travel, Mersey Partnership, English Partnerships and the City Council. It regards the co-opting of these interests as one of the most significant developments in its organization and a key element in its success.

Other partnerships have not been so lucky. Some are disadvantaged in terms of their geography, which limits their potential for development. They may for example be based primarily on an outer housing estate, with no private sector partners, or very few. The Netherley, Stanley and Queen's partnerships are good examples of these types of problems (Interview 4). Other partnerships are disadvantaged if there is no tradition of collectivism or community activity, or if that tradition is not as strong as it is in other areas. Building the necessary partnership skills can be very difficult in disadvantaged areas. Often when local people get involved in a partnership bid that is unsuccessful, they get disillusioned and fall away from community involvement (Interview 3). Subsequently, new people get involved with no previous experience. The result for the partnership is often a high turn-over of people and a low-level of skills and experience (Interview 10).

In some instances, the problems with creating partnerships have been further exacerbated by the pathways structure. One CBED enabling body manager suggested that 'basically a template was laid down across the area' (Interview 3). In some cases this took no account of strong community divisions that already existed. The North Liverpool Area Partnership, covering Everton and Vauxhall, for example, combines the city's Orange Order as well as a large Catholic population. Although sectarian difficulties are for the most part a thing of the past, the two community groups operate quite separately and independently of each other (Interview 3). Despite being a funded partnership, the agencies operating in the area still refer to problems in planning and communication (Interview 20). The CBED manager in the area explained how the partnership's development worker 'really just became the pawn that was battered from both sides' (Interview 3). The communities of Dingle and Toxteth present similar problems: the former perceived for the most part as white, working class, catholic Irish and the latter as one of Britain's oldest African-Caribbean communities (Interviews 7, 9). In this case, when the pathways boundaries were drawn, it was decided to separate the two groups. Organizations such as the TEC, Business Links, and the police, dealing with essentially the same problems across both communities, must each refer to duplicate community groups and forums in an area a little over three square miles.

The experience of other partnership groups across the region falls some way between the two extremes above, but in all cases lack of trust and/or communication between partnership members were cited as the chief problems (Interviews 2, 3, 6). Partnerships with little experience of working together often lack the communicative skills necessary to make them effective (Interview 9). One CBED enabling body manager spoke of the very poor links between members of his Area Partnership and the desire by some to use it as a platform for political control (Interview 3). Another stated that; 'Our partnership is about empire-building and in my opinion is to the detriment of its client group. We are working in spite of our partnership rather than because of it and I intend within the next two years to be totally autonomous. If I can get my training arm up and running [to provide revenue], I can ditch the Partnership and still deliver to the community' (Interview 2). A local authority officer with the Central Policy Unit of LCC argued that such 'dysfunctional partnerships' are ineffective and often provide a further barrier to effective development action (Interview 15).

In many cases, the difficulties described above are the consequence of attempting to define partnerships from the 'top-down' instead of supporting 'bottom up' partnerships centred around real community groupings. If a partnership has been 'drawn up from the outside', it has to over-come many more hurdles than a natural partnership. It must bring together groups with, at best, no common experience, and at worst, a history of antagonism. This necessitates a good deal of capacity-building within the community to create both the will and the where-with-all to build an effective partnership. As yet, this is not provided for in the Merseyside network.

Network resources

In Merseyside, the political wrangles between the UK and the EU over financial contributions to the EU have had a severe impact on the funding of development in the region. The UK government has traditionally taken the view that because the UK is a net contributor to the EU, money coming from Europe is 'its own money anyway' (Interview 21). In the words of one GOM official; 'It's getting some of our contribution back, so it's all treated as public money' (Interview 19). This British attitude to the use of EU funds directly contravenes *additionality* principle of EU financial assistance and has had severe consequences for the funding of regional regeneration in Merseyside. The EU's requirement of 'matching funding' in order to receive Objective One aid means that although the entire region of Merseyside is eligible for European Structural Funds assistance, the reluctance of UK government to match EU assistance has prevented many from taking advantage of Objective One funding. A senior GOM official explained the connection between UK regeneration funding and EU funding like this: 'It's a question of, if you've got some SRB money, then that's very useful because you can seek to make it go that much further with European money' (Interview 19). The problem with this, of course, is that not every area in Merseyside has SRB funding.

In relation to the ability of EU Objective One funding to promote *regional* development strategies and initiatives, the 'bottom line' is that European money is just as difficult to get as central government funding. A senior manager at Merseyside TEC highlighted the way in which the disbursement of EU regional assistance has been subsumed into a more generalized competition for resources, suggesting that 'all of the funding opportunities to make a difference within local partnerships, have been within the context of the previous government and the belief that you must compete for everything' (Interview 22). As a result, the additional funding provided by the Objective One programme is not available for all of the region to which it was designated and the competition for traditional non-EU sources of funding is all the more intense.

Across the policy network, the strong competition for limited sources of finance, impacts upon the distribution of all other resources in the network such as: information - about alternative sources of funding or innovative interpretations of 'matching funding'; knowledge - about practical problem solving or issues of best practice; and experience - in terms of skills learnt or experience gained. To share any of these, would be to lose a potential advantage in a bid for scarce resources. As a consequence, the development of partnerships is dogged by repeated slow learning curves and competitive attitudes between potential partners that stifle cooperation. The result is that the policy network as a whole, suffers from limited distribution of skills and a lack of development capacity (Interview 22).

Network dynamics

The EU's emphasis on planned, regionally-oriented, socially inclusive actions for development represents a significant divergence of opinion from the UK central government over what constitutes appropriate development action. In terms of understanding network dynamics, it demonstrates the fact that there is no real consensus between the two main development sponsors - the EU and the UK - over basic values and broad preferences of policy. As a consequence, despite the EU's intention to support concerted development action across Merseyside, the irony is that the introduction of 'European style' policy approaches has actually contributed to network instability. This has occurred for three main reasons.

First, the desire of the EU to inculcate community involvement in development policy represents a new and unfamiliar form of policy-making for many actors involved. The introduction of European-style policy approaches have required network members to organize themselves in new ways: at best, these are unfamiliar and necessitate new learning curves; at worst, they are unwelcome and have not been fully accepted by all members of the network. Second, even if such policy-making practices were to be achieved, there is still no clear agreement about either the desired policy outcomes, or even the precise area in which they should be realised. The resulting multiplication and fragmentation of agencies involved in regional development further inhibits concentrated development activity by network members. Third, the need to compete for funding between network members stymies the development of cooperative and/or coordinated development initiatives. Taken together, these developments have led to a network in which there are no clear leaders and very few organizational structures through which integrated development can be achieved. As a consequence, the capacity of network members to deliver coordinated development action is limited.

Since the organization of the network does not clearly specify the desired relationships between development actors, or their roles in relation to each other, most actors define their competencies and responsibilities according to experience and clearly the dominant ethos of value for money and competition for resources promotes a particular interactive dynamic between network members. Network members are included in policy measures because they have the most to offer (and conversely, the most to gain) in terms of policy delivery. They are not necessarily included because they are members of the constituency the policy is most likely to affect. This impacts upon their attitudes towards involvement with regeneration partnerships. Larger agencies, for example, are often reticent to act as a lead agency in any partnership initiative, preferring instead to be the 'funder of the last resort' (Interview 19). As a result, development strategies may be slow in getting off the ground and when they do, the agencies involved may prefer tried and tested policy responses, rather than new or innovative development strategies that require an element of risk-taking that cannot guarantee the agency's ability to reach agreed delivery targets or outputs. Smaller bodies, such as CBED organizations and local businesses often feel frustrated by the dual demands of working within a partnership and being obliged to 'stand on their own two feet'. They cite the problems of conforming to the partnership's need for accountability and desire for involvement in decision-making, juxtaposed with its lack of financial support or sharing of commercial responsibility. As a result, they too often regard themselves as 'reluctant partners'.

As a consequence, the primary motivation to join any partnership initiative is best summed up as 'rational self-interest'. One community worker described a group in his local partnership, where he had personal experience with one of the 48 member groups: 'That group has already gone along and said, "Where's our money?" because they're in the partnership. And that's what they do. I know that if th[is] group have gone along and done this, so have the other 47, and if they split the money up and just doled it out, it would achieve nothing' (Interview 6). The manager of another CBED enabling body stated: 'I feel that government bodies will try and take advantage of us if they can, it is the nature of such bodies... Our intention is to become independent. There is no alternative (Interview 2). A representative of Liverpool City Council, pointed to its status as the largest authority in the region, saying that: 'Certainly … there is not enough interaction between ourselves and other local authorities and I wonder whether part of the reason for that is because of the competitive basis we have to operate on' (Interview 4).

In a few instances, self-interest has led to increased cooperation between network members. Merseyside TEC for example, used SRB funding to set up a partnership with Liverpool City Council and Employment Services (a national government agency), to establish the 'Employment Links Service' (ELS).[4] In addition to its primary function of enhancing employment prospects for individuals in targeted communities, the ELS was intended to act as a 'pump-priming' project, designed to enable the partners to find different ways of working together that did not necessarily need on-going funding (Interview 23).

These examples serve to illustrate that the quality of relations between network members - in terms of the frequency and duration of their meetings, or the degree of trust, co-operation or respect between actors - is largely conditioned by the network environment and actors' perception of self-interest. Successful partnerships can and do emerge, but this network does not foster them.

Concluding remarks: characterizing the network and the policy process

Table 5 provides a summary of the main themes raised in this chapter and illustrates how the Merseyside network resembles very closely the ideal type *issue network* defined in the Marsh and Rhodes (1996) typology of networks.

The section dealing with network formation demonstrated that the 'region' of Merseyside has been created entirely by outside agents: determined by its Objective One status according to the EU; and as an area under the remit of the Government Office for Merseyside according to the UK central government.

Table 5: Characterizing the Merseyside policy network

Dimension	**Network features**
Formation	Merseyside presents neither a well-established nor a particularly well-integrated policy domain, within which the Objective One programme introduces new and unfamiliar forms of policy-making for many of the actors involved.
Membership	Large and fragmented, encompassing a wide range of interests between whom interaction fluctuates in frequency and intensity.
Resources	Few members have access to resources, which are limited and subject to intense competition.
Dynamics	Very limited consensus. Conflict is ever present.
Power	Unequal powers, reflecting unequal resources and unequal access. This is a zero-sum game.

Neither body, however, is responsible for strategic organization of policy across the region. The result is a large and fragmented network typical of the ideal type issue network (discussed in Chapter 1). Given the wide range of pre-existing policy fora and development interests throughout the region, this lack of structure contributes to network instability. The region is too large to sustain personalized relations between regional policy actors as is the case in Ireland, and yet there is no overall political or institutional organization of regional policy to determine the relative competencies of various development interests as there is in Germany.

In relation to network membership, the proliferation of network members, combined with an absence of regional policy structures, tends to stymie coordinated development action. At best different groups operate in different areas - sometimes co-ordinating their work, more often not. At worst different groups operate in the same area (of expertise or geography) either in competition with each other, or in wasteful duplication of functions. This attitude is further reinforced by the system of resource allocation for regional development in Merseyside.

The lack of consensus over policy aims and objectives between the UK and EU further supports the view that this network is best understood as an ideal type issue network. The UK government's reticence to offer 'matching funding' for EU aid has prevented many from taking advantage of Merseyside's Objective One designation. This contributes to network instability by encouraging the 'competition culture' between network members. Since the UK government will not provide the matching funding necessary to satisfy the EU Structural Funding principle of additionality, the competition for funding (that could be presented as a match to gain EU support) between development interests is all the more intense. This competition culture means that network members are not readily inclined to share information, knowledge or experience with each other for fear of developing the strength of their competition. It also underlines the fact that the distribution of resources between network actors remains central to any explanation of the network.

Finally, this chapter examined network dynamics and illustrated the extreme instability of the Merseyside network engendered by its 'competition culture'. Competition is encouraged by the networks (lack of) structure, which does not clearly determine uniform territories for action so that often different regional actors and agencies carry out similar tasks in the same area. The resulting proliferation of network members increases the demand for scarce resources and heightens competition. This points to a paradox at the heart of UK development policy. That is, the increasing fragmentation of local government, combined with the substantial cutbacks in public funding throughout the last decade, has meant that virtually no development project can get off the ground without some form of partnership arrangement between different funding bodies; however, the need of all network members to compete for scarce network resources promotes competition that inhibits the development of partnership arrangements. Since EU Objective One funding is not strategically managed or regulated, it further contributes to the network's competitive dynamic. The unfortunate irony of EU support to Merseyside is that competition for the necessary matching funding for EU aid further inhibits the development of cooperative, partnership arrangements that the EU is seeking to foster.

The evidence from this chapter suggests that the particular features of this network do not support the integration of alternative sets of policy actors that would be conducive to increasing EU involvement in the policy process and the development of European integration. The general disintegration of traditional sub-national government institutions in Britain has not been paralleled by the development of new institutional structures that facilitate the involvement of the EU in regional policy processes. Moreover, the proliferation of new organizations and agencies responsible for development action has led to a breakdown in consensus over policy aims and objectives that frustrates the development of 'elite activation' regarding EU involvement in policy. With both weak institutional development and limited elite consensus over policy, support for European integration is highly dependent on government attitudes and approaches that are supportive of EU involvement in policy. There was little evidence of either in this case study. As a consequence, the potential for either political or functional spillover in favour of integration is severely limited. Taken together, all of these features have a significant and detrimental impact on the integrative capacity of this network. This aspect of network organization is given more detailed analysis in the concluding chapter, which gives a comparative examination of change in policy networks in relation to the process of European integration.

Notes

1. The European Commission's *Single Programming Document* (SPD) notes that across Merseyside GDP per head of population, relative to the EU average, declined from 95% of the average in 1983, to 74% in 1989. By 1992, GDP was estimated to have fallen to 73% of the EU average. In addition, Merseyside exhibits: very high levels of unemployment, increasing in the 1990s to 70% above the EU average; high rates of long-term unemployment; declining economic activity rates; a high level of out-migration; a low level of small firm creation; poor records of employment performance; low levels of educational attainment and professional qualifications; and substantial amounts of derelict land (CEC, 1994c).
2. This includes: statutory services, relating to employment, urban policy and a variety of Task Forces; voluntary sector services; credit unions; unemployed resource centres; trade union groups associated with the voluntary sector; enterprise/business advice and consultancy groups; and a range of development trusts. A listing of all these groups may be found in the annual guide to statutory, voluntary, business and community organization in Merseyside, produced by Liverpool City Council and titled, *Let's take it from here.*
3. Business Links provides a point of entry for most services offered to small and medium enterprises by the DTI and other government departments, offering advice on regional selective assistance and sometimes assistance in grant applications.
4. Other main partners include the Liverpool Chamber of Commerce, Liverpool Council for Voluntary Service and Pathways Partnerships (source: Interview 23).

Chapter 7

Developing European Regions? Comparative Governance, Policy Networks and European Integration

Introduction

The comparative methodology provided by policy network analysis facilitates both a generalized comparison of alternative cross-national policy processes as well as a specific evaluation of the level of integration in policy networks. In the terms outlined at the start of this study, this enables an assessment of both horizontal and vertical dimensions of policy change. Regarding horizontal aspects of policy change, this comparison enables us to evaluate what the alleged trend towards 'new governance' involves in each state and the extent to which governments have lost their 'control capacity' over the provision of regional policy. Regarding the vertical aspects of policy change, the application of Lindberg's integration hypotheses as positive integration indicators for policy networks enables us to relate the differences found between cross-national networks to different levels of European integration. Both of these issues are considered here. Finally, the connections between different network forms, policy processes and levels of integration are also considered through a comparative evaluation of the alternative policy network configurations.

Regional policy change and the alleged move towards governance

The introduction to this study highlighted increasing use of the term 'governance' as a way of characterizing changing patterns of government in west European states. The 'new governance' is a short-hand way of referring to both the decreasing intervention of central government in public policy and the increasing involvement of a range of new policy actors. These developments are reflected in changes at the supranational level where 'government overload' and 'state inadequacy' have led many states to respond by 'drawing on resources from transnational cooperation as instruments of domestic policy' (Wallace, 1996:15). They are also reflected at national and sub-national levels by 'the supplanting of centralized, monolithic government, by an increasingly differentiated political system' and the growth of 'autonomous, inter-organizational networks between public, private and voluntary groups' (Rhodes, 1996:658). Policy change has not, however, been uniform across states. This section provides a cross-national comparison of regional policy processes in order to understand how these developments have been worked out in Germany, Ireland and Britain. Focusing in particular on: the role of central government; the role of sub-national government institutions and elected representatives; the role of quangos or alternative sorts of regional development agencies such as para-public institutions in Germany or state-sponsored bodies in Ireland; business involvement in development strategies; community participation and activism in local development initiatives; this section illustrates the enduring importance of central government, acting either directly or indirectly, to condition the process of policy change.

Central governments' role in regional development

In all three states, central governments play a crucial role determining the parameters of development policy action by defining the problems and issues that development policy is intended to address. Defining the 'development problem' differently in each of these states leads not only to different policy making structures, delivery mechanisms and funding regimes, but also to a range of other differences in approach related to alternative policy priorities, policy areas (both spatially and subject-related), and differential degrees of involvement from other policy actors. For example, in Germany regional development is about ensuring the same economic and development opportunities exist across the state, reflected in the federal policies of fiscal equalization and also in the concerted development planning that seeks to ensure uniform standards of development potential across the country. This conception of development views the promotion of regional development as a federal government 'obligation' and as a result, the parameters of development policy have been firmly fixed both by the federal system and by the *Rechtsstaat* concept that clearly sets out regional policy aims, the respective competencies of different levels of government, and the terms of involvement for a range of defined interests.

In Ireland, development is as much concerned with developing local communities and tackling social exclusion as it is with economic targets and because of this the tendency has been to concentrate policy initiatives at the local, as opposed to regional, levels of administration. As a result, development policy places emphasis on 'bottom-up' approaches to development that stress the importance of endogenous growth and local empowerment. The appropriate role for central government has been determined by a gradually emerging consensus about development that represents the outcome of a series of negotiations: at supranational level, between Irish governments and the European Commission over the deployment of EU assistance from the Structural and Cohesion Funds as well as a range of Community Initiatives; at national level, between the Social Partners in the form of a series of national concordats; and at sub-national level, in the promotion of a range of partnership projects between public, private, community and statutory bodies designed to support local development initiatives.

In Britain, development policy is concerned with creating the conditions necessary for economic growth. This is illustrated by a variety of policy actions designed to create incentives for investment and to attract private sector interests and industry into under-developed areas with a view to encouraging economic growth. British development policy is the least concerned with establishing particular geographical areas for policy action, or securing the involvement of a wide range of interests, reflecting the view that government's role is to set the right conditions for development, though the responsibility for achieving it lies elsewhere.

Whilst all three governments are in a commanding position to exert their influence over regional development, they have a variable capacity to affect regional policy processes depending on institutional configurations of national politics. In Germany, the federal system provides the strongest guarantee for a lasting central government role in regional policy, but at the same time constrains its room for manoeuvre: any radical overhaul of policy would require a major constitutional upheaval between the federation and the states. Thus whilst the German central government undoubtedly plays a more substantive role in the organization and administration of regional policy compared to its Irish and British counterparts, the Federal system ensures that this influence is equally balanced and constitutionally guaranteed in the federal governments of the German *Länder*. This institutionalized pluralism acts as a stabilizing influence on policy that prevents a major overhaul of the regional policy process. In Ireland, the practical constraints provided by coalition and the institution of programmatic government with the Social Partners means that although there is no constitutional protection for regional policy, the government's freedom of action is circumscribed by the need to develop consensus around policy change. Only in Britain does the political system ensure that a government with a large enough parliamentary majority is free to effect regional policy change entirely as it chooses, evidenced in the Thatcherite reorganization of local government throughout the 1980s and the Blair government's execution of devolution in 1999. This would suggest that British - and to a lesser extent Irish - central governments are in a better position than the German Federal government to affect substantive changes to regional policy processes.

Representative organizations of sub-national government

The powers and responsibilities accorded to sub-national government are variable in each of the states. Of the three states, the highest level of institutional autonomy for sub-national government is provided by the German system of co-operative federalism (see Chapter 2). However, the extreme juridification of the public policy process, as well as the highly bureaucratized proceduralism required to sustain it, leads to a highly formal and structured policy process. Sub-national government negotiates regional policy with a range of formally recognized and legally incorporated regional policy interests in accordance with formalized policy making procedures. The result is that the policy process is relatively bureaucratic and exclusive in its organization. Since this system is not easily subject to change, although sub-national government may influence policy outcomes over time according to changing policy aims and objectives, its capacity to affect or change the policy process is limited.

The formal powers of local government are least well developed in Ireland where the highly centralized government system, the evolution of the managerial system of local government and the ever-increasing number of alternative sub-national fora and agencies, have contributed to the diminishing significance of local government throughout the last few decades (see Chapter 2). Here, the stark choice between increasing irrelevance and a reinvention of its role, led Irish local government to embrace new ways of supporting regional development through cooperative relations with a range of development agencies empowered to deliver services and carry out tasks that local government could no longer manage single-handedly. This was made possible by a reappraisal of development policy approaches at national level and the significant involvement of the EU in a variety of development projects at local level, both of which encouraged 'bottom-up' development strategies involving new forms of partnerships in policy formulation and implementation. The consequence has been the creation of a complex sub-national organizational mosaic, co-ordinated by a national Operational Programme for Local Urban and Rural Development (OPLURD) and agreed by all the affected policy interests (see Chapter 3). Under the OPLURD programme, Irish local authorities have been able to increase their influence over local development by strategic use of their formal and informal local connections in the establishment of partnership projects and initiatives. As a result, despite the limited formal powers accorded to local government, Irish local authorities are in a good position to wield influence over policy and in doing so have ensured that they retain some capacity to influence the policy process.

In Britain, the highly centralized system of government combined with radical reforms to the functions and structure of local government throughout the 1980s meant that even though British local authorities started off with greater powers and responsibilities than their Irish counterparts, they found themselves in a position of declining influence and responsibility in relation to both the formulation and implementation of development strategies (see Chapters 2 and 3). The case study in Chapter 6 identified how the fragmentation of policy delivery mechanisms for regeneration initiatives at sub-national level has led to duplication of functions by many policy actors and agencies, a lack of strategic or integrated development action, and the proliferation of development interests competing against one another for scarce resources. In this environment British local government has lost a great deal of its traditional influence over the operation of regional policy.

The experience of Irish and British local governments demonstrate the alternative possibilities that 'the move towards governance' might mean in different states. In the regional policy of both states, the decreasing intervention of central government has been paralleled by the increasing involvement of a range of new policy actors. In Ireland this move represents central government's voluntary sharing of policy authority with a diverse range of policy actors at European, national and sub-national levels of government. In Britain, however, it represents central government's desire to remove local government from many areas of policy responsibility and increase private sector involvement, allowing central government to garner more policy authority at the expense of all other policy interests. The irony of this comparison is that the role of Irish local authorities appears to have changed from traditional conceptions of local government as a 'service provider' to a new role as 'enabling authority' in the manner that was much more clearly envisaged and desired by British reforms to local government throughout the 1980s. It would appear that through their neglect of sub-national government, Irish central governments have contributed far more positively to the changing role of local authorities than massive radical reforms executed in Britain.

The relative success that Irish local authorities have had in maintaining influence over local development compared to their British counterparts arises for two main reasons. First, the relationship between central government and local government has not been openly antagonistic as it has in Britain. Irish local government may not have enjoyed central government support, but neither has it suffered outright opposition to its involvement in regional development. Second, the changed role of Irish local authorities has evolved gradually over time: more recently, it has been coaxed by the establishment of OPLURD and government initiatives designed to support policy coordination and cooperation at local level; but overall, the incremental nature of the change has given local government time to adjust to new ways of working with new partners in policy. This was not the case in Britain where successive radical changes to local government organization throughout the 1980s disrupted many old ways of working before new policy partnerships or practices had a chance to develop. Attempts to change the role of local authorities in Britain and the evolution of a new role for local authorities in Ireland both illustrate common trends towards a new, though not exclusive, role for local government in development action. This trend appears to favour local authorities acting as 'development coordinators' - a role that German sub-national government has been adept at playing for some time.

Sub-national boards, bodies and quangos

The deployment of quasi-governmental agencies in development policy action represents one of the key changes in policy delivery associated with the so-called 'move towards governance'. Generally speaking, there are two main views about them: either they are non-elected, non-democratic and non-accountable instruments of central government; or they are specially constituted bodies responding to a particular policy need, which because of their unique terms of reference, may be freer and more focused in their approach to policy delivery than other more traditional public institutions. Encompassing a range of different sorts of bodies, from the *Thüringer Aufbaubank* (TAB) or Thuringian Bank for Reconstruction in Germany, to the range of state-sponsored bodies responsible for different aspects of development in Limerick and the variety of new agencies, such as English Partnerships or the Training and Enterprise Councils (TECs) in Merseyside, these sorts of bodies have been described as 'quasi-governmental agencies that fall in the 'twilight zone' between the public sector and private sector, and between central government and local government' (Cope and Atkinson, 1994:27). The evidence from this research suggests that the way in that they tend to be viewed in different states is a function of the overall policy environment.

In both Germany and Ireland, the inclusion of quasi-governmental agencies into the policy process is a function of the negotiated policy environment. In Germany this is achieved by extensive policy planning that ensures functional and territorial divisions of responsibility between different levels of government. Within this system of planning German para-public institutions are primarily associated with policy implementation as opposed to formulation. This has not been the case in Ireland where the co-option of state-sponsored bodies into partnership initiatives at local level has given them a role in the formulation of policy (in relation to their own specific areas of competence) as well as practical implementation. This incorporation of state sponsored bodies into the policy process has been facilitated by central government approaches designed to promote strategic planning of multi-agencied approaches to local development.

In Britain by contrast, the 'competitive culture' engendered by the continuous need of development policy actors to compete with each other for scarce resources, does not always support the successful insertion of quangos in the policy process. Where the competition for funding has been temporarily resolved, by a successful SRB bid for example, the case study in Chapter 6 illustrated that there are often good relations between quangos and other development policy actors. This begs the question: is it the access to resources that supports good relations, or is it the absence of competition? A comparison with the other two case studies suggests that the absence of competition is the more significant of the two. This is because in Germany, regardless of the level of resources apportioned to a particular territorial or functional policy areas, development action is planned to prevent competition between different actors and agencies working in the same areas of specialism or competence (see Chapter 4). In Ireland, development funding is not allocated as it is in the German budgetary model (illustrated in Chapter 4), but the terms of competition for resources are conditioned by the central government, which demands partnership approaches and multi-agencied responses to development. In this environment, even though policy actors compete for resources, it is in their own self interest to develop cooperative or friendly relations with other potential partners or co-sponsors (illustrated in Chapter 5).

The above examples suggest that the inclusion of quangos in development policy action is best achieved when they are incorporated into the policy process in a manner that is non-threatening to other policy actors: this can be achieved by extensive planning to determine respective policy actors competencies; or the creation of a consensus about the nature of policy aims and the appropriate ends to achieve them. In the absence of either of these features, the Merseyside case study in Chapter 5 showed how the introduction of new quangos into development action may be met with suspicion or resentment on behalf of the other policy actors. The challenge of 'new governance' therefore is not necessarily about the introduction of quangos into development policy action, but the manner in which they are introduced into policy processes and the level of understanding shared by policy actors about respective roles and competencies.

Business involvement in development

In attempting to compare the role of business in development action across each of the states, the most important distinction appears to be the extent to which business constitutes either a proactive or reactive force in development strategies. In other words, does development policy seek to *attract* business or to *involve* business in regional development strategies. Both Germany and Ireland have gone furthest in involving business in development policy through the extensive planning systems of the federal system and the negotiation of a national Operational Programme for Local Urban and Rural Development (OPLURD) with agreed Social Partners in Ireland (see Chapter 3). The case studies highlighted how in both Germany and Ireland, business interests are represented in the negotiation of development policy: for example in their representation on regional planning and advisory boards in Thüringen, or in the County Strategy Group and activities of the Enterprise Boards in Limerick (see Chapters 4 and 5 respectively).

In Britain, although both Conservative and Labour governments have sought the increased involvement and support of the private sector in a range of development initiatives, they have not sought to formally incorporate business interests into the regional policy process. This is less a reflection of the perceived importance of business for development and more a reflection of the perceived unimportance of planning. The British emphasis on deregulation and privatization meant that even as central government sought increasing participation of the private sector in economic development, it was less able to control it (see Chapter 3).

Clearly, all three states agree on the importance of attracting business into areas for development. Where they disagree, however, is in the measures they deem appropriate to achieve this. Whilst German and Irish approaches emphasise the interconnections between the development of business and other policy areas such as education, training, the environment and tourism for example, British policy approaches are much less coordinated. As a result, German and Irish approaches to business and development illustrate a greater inclination towards policy *dirigisme*, whereas British policy approaches are distinctly more *laissez-faire*.

Community and voluntary participation in policy

In Britain, there is a great deal of voluntary activity that remains relatively ignored in development policy formulation and implementation. In Germany, there is much less voluntary activity and it is not generally regarded as part of development policy practice at all. In Ireland, by contrast, widespread voluntary activity has led to the inclusion and incorporation of a range of community interests in local development policy formulation and implementation. Irish approaches to development policy have regarded community groups and voluntary bodies as 'additional policy resources' and evidence from the Irish case study suggests that the formal inclusion of community and voluntary participation in development policy represents a means of deriving 'added value' in terms of local knowledge, experience, community networks and support structures. These have often been utilised by local partnership development companies as a resource in their own right and also as a means of levering in EU funding by costing their voluntary contribution in terms of its financial value for 'matching funding'.

More generally, the incorporation of community and voluntary participation in Irish development policy is reflective of an alternative approach to development that is as much concerned with the development of human resources as it is with economic investment and growth. The Irish government has formally recognized and decided to promote the groundswell of local initiatives aimed at socio-economic improvement. The result has been the creation of a cadre of non-governmental actors who have facilitated the process of 'bottom-up' development, albeit a process of state-sponsored bottom-up development. This would suggest that increasing community and voluntary participation in policy is not just about finding cost-effective ways to carry out development action. It also represents a complete re-conception of the 'development problem'.

The significance of central governments in 'defining the development problem' has already been highlighted in the start of this section. More fundamentally, however, it points to the continuing significance of central government influence over policy change and develops our understanding of horizontal policy change associated with the alleged growth of 'new governance' in European states. The introduction to this study outlined Rhodes' (1996) propositions that changes in government have led to the development of 'governance as self-organizing policy networks' whereby 'the state becomes a collection of inter-organizational networks made up of governmental and societal actors with no sovereign actor able to steer or regulate'. Rhodes' (1996:659) assertions, however, that the consequence of developing ever more complex policy networks is a loss of the state's 'control capacity' over policy is not borne out in the regional policy processes of the three states.

In Germany, the range of actors involved in regional policy is pre-determined by federal and state constitutions and the policy procedures of the federal system. As a result, the range of regional policy interests has changed very little throughout the post-war period. Unification added new actors to the policy process, but not new interests: apart from a reconfiguration of development interests associated with 'rich' and 'poor' *Länder*, the range of policy interests remained the same. The relative fixity of federal institutions and the organization of regional policy making in the German system of 'cooperative federalism' means that in this policy area at least, the 'control capacity' of the federal government has not been diminished.

Ireland, by contrast, has seen a massive growth in the number and range of development policy actors and interests involved in the regional policy process, particularly since the mid-1980s. Lacking the formal policy structures provided by the institutions and conventions of cooperative federalism in Germany, Irish central governments have proceeded on an *ad hoc* basis to create a welter of state-sponsored bodies and boards designed to tackle different aspects of development. Moreover, the government has been happy to support the introduction of more new actors through its formal support and inclusion of community groups and area partnerships in the OPLURD framework. Central government's complicity in creating new policy interests, however, makes a nonsense of the idea that it has 'lost' its control capacity: the willingness of Irish governments to share and/or devolve policy authority to new sets of actors and to foster new sets of relations between them, is not regarded as a diminution of government control but rather as a positive redefinition of its role. Moreover, the key role played by Irish governments in the coordination and organization of this complex collection of interests means that its influence over regional policy is more important than ever.

In Britain, the deliberate fragmentation of sub-national government and regional policy institutions by central government throughout the 1980s, resulted in a massive growth of regional policy actors and interests. Moreover, the increasing complexity of the policy arena was matched by an increase in central government's control capacity. The long-standing aversion of British governments to strategic planning and policy programming, however, means that British governments have not used their position to develop any strategic organization of regional policy. Thus whilst Rhodes' assertion that the state has become 'a collection of inter-organizational networks made up of governmental and non-governmental actors' may be true for British regional policy, the British government has not lost its control capacity: rather through its 'hands off' approach to regional development, it has decided not to exercise it.

The evidence above indicates that state executives are able to retain significant influence over policy outcomes either indirectly, by determining the parameters of policy action, or directly as a policy actor in their own right. However, the level of policy authority or to use Rhodes' term, their 'control capacity', is considerably attenuated by the institutional configurations of domestic politics. Furthermore, there is no direct correlation between the degree of 'control capacity' exercised by central governments and the complexity of the policy arena: in Britain, increasing the actors and interests in regional policy has led to a centralization of policy authority, but no significant exercise of central government influence; in Ireland, increasing the actors and interests in regional policy has led to a decentralization of policy authority, but an increasing significance of central government's influence over policy. In German regional policy, both the range of policy interests and the 'control capacity' of the Federal government have remained constant.

Thus it would appear that increasing the number of policy actors and interests is not synonymous with decreasing central government control capacity. This proposition is born out in the next section dealing with policy change in relation to the process of European integration. It shows that the 'control capacity' of governments is intimately bound up with both government approaches to policy as well as institutional structuring of the policy arena, so that our understanding of policy change must necessarily consider the relations between the two. If, in the face of continuing horizontal shifts in the configuration of policy processes, we are to attempt a clearer understanding of the impact of European integration upon policy change, then more attention needs to be given to alternative conceptions of governance and the variable 'control capacity' of governments in different policy environments.

A comparative evaluation of the research hypotheses

According to the multi-level governance literature, European integration is a 'multi-level polity creating process' whereby policy authority is no longer vested entirely in central government institutions, but shared between policy actors at a variety of levels. Since the multi-level governance literature assumes that the integration process involves policy actors from different levels becoming intermingled in the policy process, we should be able to see evidence of this process at all levels of analysis. However, since the multi-level governance literature assumes that state executives are probably still the most important pieces in the policy puzzle, this research conducted a comparative study of regional policy in Germany, Ireland and Britain in order to assess the extent to which the polity-creating described by multi-level governance literature as evidence of integration is apparent in one policy area across three states.

In order to evaluate the extent of this alleged 'multi-level polity creating process', or in short the level of integration, Lindberg's (1963) neofunctionalist integration hypotheses were used to verify the process of integration in regional policy change in selected policy networks. Lindberg suggested that the process of integration would be manifest in four main ways: first, there would be institutional development of a kind that facilitated the European Union's direct involvement in policy; second, there would be what Lindberg termed 'elite activation', referring to the changing behaviour of key policy makers in favour of integration; third, the government would provide continuing support for integrationist measures; and fourth, functional and political spillover would lead to the creation of 'inherently expansive tasks', which would cement the level of integration achieved and create pressure for further integrationist action (Lindberg, 1963:6).

Hypothesis one

Hypothesis one proposes that if integration is taking place, there will be some form of institutional development that facilitates the European Union's direct involvement in policy. The results of this research suggest that the capacity of the European Union to influence regional policy is heavily dependent on the openness of the domestic institutional environment.

In Germany, for example, the roots of German sub-national government run deep. It could be argued that as a consequence of Allied occupation of Germany after the second world war, its origins predate the establishment of both the Federal Republic and the European Community (see Chapter 2). One consequence of this longevity, is that the institutions of the German *Länder* are firmly rooted in the wider political and institutional policy architecture of the federal system: this brings institutional stability and contributes to the political status of *Länder* institutions. In addition, strong constitutional guarantees and elaborate provisions for power-sharing in the system of 'co-operative federalism' ensure that the German *Länder* enjoy a level of autonomy far in advance of the sub-national institutions or either Ireland or Britain (see Chapter 2). It could be argued, however, that this level of institutional autonomy affords only minimal scope for the European Union to significantly affect the institutional architecture of regional policy delivery. Although the European Union *is* directly involved in policy because of the substantial aid it provides to the new *Länder* as Objective One regions, it has had little or no influence over the structures and institutions of sub-national government. This is because Structural Funds assistance has been delivered entirely through pre-existing Federal government institutions and policy mechanisms and has not effected any institutional change in its own right: it did contribute to policy change in the new *Länder*, but only insofar as it helped to promote the process of unification, which itself was guided and managed by pre-existing institutions and organizations of the Federal government. In this case,

EU Objective One assistance supports, rather than undermines, the policy authority of the federal government.

In Ireland, the development of sub-national institutions and organizations has proceeded in a haphazard fashion: many state sponsored bodies were created to effect policy delivery as and when it occurred to central government that they were needed. As a consequence, the mosaic of sub-national government has been described by some as an 'administrative jungle', one in which the relatively small-scale county unit remains the most meaningful area for development action (see Chapter 3). Together, the government's pragmatic approach to the development of sub-national institutions and the necessarily small-scale of most Irish development projects (based as they are on personal rather than formally structured relations) made Irish regional policy institutions especially susceptible to EU influence.

At national level, the government's pragmatism facilitated the creation of an independent body set up to administer and oversee the disbursement of EU Structural Funds: Area Development Management Ltd represents a new organization designed specifically to facilitate the European Union's direct involvement in policy. In addition to this, the creation of OPLURD represents the creation of a new policy architecture designed specifically to incorporate EU programmes and initiatives into a national policy framework.

At sub-national level, the growing trends towards 'participatory democracy' and partnership approaches to development in Ireland have coincided with EU emphasis on 'bottom-up' approaches to development and the creation of locally constituted development partnerships. Whilst it could be argued that this approach to regional policy has developed in response to the declining ability of local authorities to exercise their traditional competencies in this area, the new partnership approaches to local development have raised the profile of local authorities in an environment where continuing cuts in finances were leading them to become increasingly irrelevant. As a consequence Irish local authorities grasped the opportunity provided by EU pilot programmes and Community Initiatives to become key players in EU sponsored development projects. Operating amidst a wide range of other development interests in a variety of initiatives and projects under the auspices of the OPLURD programme, local authorities were able to buttress their status as elected, rather than self-selected, representatives in development action. The instigation of the Devolution Committee and government promises to reform local government are evidence of a newly emerging consensus about the important role played by local government in development action. It could therefore be said that in Ireland, the European Union has had a significant impact upon the institutions and organization of development policy delivery at both national and sub-national levels of government.

Of all three states, Britain has witnessed the greatest fragmentation of sub-national government structures and institutions through a series of local government reforms that took place throughout the 1980s (see Chapter 2). Merseyside, however, has been affected more than most. Chapter 6 illustrated that the 'region' of Merseyside was a short-lived construction of local government reform in the mid 1970s that was only recently resurrected by the EU designation of the area as a region eligible for Structural Funds assistance under Objective One criteria. As such it does not have a well-established regional identity and the sub-national institutions that operate across its area are not well-integrated. Despite the desire of the European Union to promote regionally-oriented, community-based and strategically planned development, the large and disparate membership of the Merseyside network militates against integrated development action in the region. Evidence from the Merseyside case suggests that participation in Objective One assisted projects by a range of development interests does encourage new forms of integrated development action, illustrated by the development of Mersey Partnership, the Pathways to Integration initiatives and some of the more successful regeneration partnerships. Compared to the Irish case, however, these initiatives represent a much more limited form of institutional development to facilitate the European Union involvement in policy, first because they are not spread uniformly across Merseyside and second, because they are not matched by any new institutional development at national level.

Hypothesis two

Hypothesis two concerning 'elite activation' proposes that if integration is taking place it will be manifest in the changing attitudes and behaviour of key network members *in favour of further integration*. These may be reflected in their own positive opinions about EU involvement in the policy process, or in the strategic development of either their own or their organization's interaction with the EU. If integration is occurring, then an increase in both of these developments can be expected to lead to a positive consensus regarding EU involvement in regional policy.

In Germany, the dissolution of democratic centralism in the former Democratic Republic and the complete transfer of institutional competencies from the Federal Republic into the new *Länder* of east Germany necessarily makes the experience of 'elite activation' in favour of integration a very uneven one. In the 'old' *Länder*, it has been suggested that 'in some ways the Federal Republic and European integration are like twins: neither can remember an existence independent of the other' (Bulmer and Paterson, 1987:15). The unification process effectively incorporated the new *Länder* into a complex system of interdependency associated with the institutions of 'co-operative federalism' that could easily be regarded as the instigation of 'multi-level governance'. Absorption into the Federal Republic ensured that the institutions created in the new *Länder* were automatically EU oriented, reflected for example in Thüringen's creation of a Ministry for Justice and European Affairs.

In the new *Länder*, however, the central role played by the Federal government in setting the terms and conditions of unification together with the complete reorganization of policy structures and competencies required by incorporation into the federal system meant that elite activation was largely *Bund*-centred. Chapter 3 detailed the commitment of east German officials to the new forms of institutional organization and integration with the west through the process of institutional transfer and *Verwaltungshilfe* from west to east Germany. This view was supported by the Thüringen case study in Chapter 4, which illustrated widespread support for federal policy practice and procedures despite their relatively recent establishment in the new *Länder*. Although policy institutions provided at *Land* level do help to create a consensus over policy that further supports unification, they also guarantee a level of institutional autonomy that insulates the new *Länder* from EU influence. Since EU Structural Funds assistance is mediated almost entirely through federal policy structures, its capacity to alter the behaviour of key policy makers and politicians is minimal. In this sense, attitudes towards the European Union are conditioned for the most part by political and institutional structures of the Federal Republic: 'elite activation' in the new *Länder* may be broadly in favour of European integration since this is an implicit part of unification with the Federal Republic, but this attitude does not significantly alter their strategic behaviour.

In Ireland changing attitudes towards regional development have promoted and supported elite activation in favour of European integration, creating a 'virtuous circle' where EU Structural Funds assistance has promoted and supported changing attitudes towards regional development. The instigation of 'partnership' approaches to policy-making at both national and sub-national levels is reflected in: national concordats between the government and recognized Social Partners; the stipulation that no development assistance will be given to organizations who do not operate the 'partnership principle'; the strong emphasis on multi-agencied strategic approaches to development; and the promotion of co-operation through the County Strategy Groups and area-based responses to development needs. Moreover, the setting up of a national Operational Programme to incorporate European, national and local development policy aims and objectives, illustrates how Irish development policy both promotes and supports the EU Structural Fund principles of planning, partnership, additionality, compatibility, concentration and coordination. The sychronicity of European and Irish regional policy aims has enabled the Irish to gain substantial support from EU Structural and Cohesion Funds as well as EU pilot programmes and Community Initiatives, thereby mixing positive opinions about the EU with strategic orientations towards the EU in equal measure.

Chapter 3 illustrated how the operation of a variety of EU programmes, initiatives and pilot schemes, as well as the introduction of new guiding principles for implementing Structural Funds projects that were carried out under the first National Development Plan, helped contribute to a changed approach to development in Ireland. The development of Irish regions has become a more inclusive process, involving partnerships between statutory and voluntary bodies, state agencies and private interests, local activists and local representatives. In sum, it marks a shift from what was an exclusive, 'top-down' and economically-oriented notion of regional development, to one that is more inclusive, organized from the 'bottom-up', and stresses the importance of human, rather than solely economic needs. This new approach to development has proved to be a success. As a co-sponsor and co-promoter of this success, the European Union is recognized as an important partner in Irish development action and its positive influence over policy change has led to a widespread consensus about the value of EU involvement in policy as well the strategic development of many projects designed to take maximum advantage of EU support.

In Britain, 'elite activation' in favour of European integration has been constrained by the lack of accommodation of EU regional policy in British regional regeneration initiatives. The clash of policy styles between national and EU regional policy approaches means that although the Objective One programme for Merseyside has placed an increased emphasis on area-based community development initiatives, evidenced in the Pathways to Integration Partnerships and a rise in CBED initiatives around the Liverpool area, this occurs in the wider context of British approaches to regional regeneration, which are not area-based and rely on competitive tender rather than strategic planning as a means of distributing resources. The UK government's reticence to offer matching funding for EU aid means that the region's eligibility for EU Objective One funding has contributed even further to competition between network members to gain access to these resources. Increasing competition inhibits the cooperative partnership arrangements that the EU is seeking to foster. Moreover, the Objective One programme introduces new and unfamiliar forms of policy-making for many of the actors involved, which contributes to network instability as policy actors attempt to find new ways of working together in a policy environment that does not support them. Again this does not support the creation of consensus over policy.

The case study in Chapter 6 highlighted the impact that the UK 'competition culture' has upon network dynamics. On the whole, attitudes towards development remain primarily determined by the need to compete for scarce resources with other policy actors and this encourages the fragmentation of policy delivery. The increased competition that availability of EU funding promotes only exacerbates this problem. The result is weak and impermanent relations between different sets of network members that vary in intensity on a project to project basis. Such extreme network instability does not support policy consensus and views about the involvement of the EU in regional development tend to vary according to the level of experience individuals and organizations have with EU initiatives. Since on the whole this is not widespread, there has not been any large-scale change of attitude or behaviour towards EU involvement in policy. This in turn has not led to any significant change of emphasis in British approaches to regeneration. Since traditional British regional policy approaches are incompatible with EU policy principles, the two sets of regional policy interventions have remained largely separate and the capacity or opportunity of the European Union to influence attitudes or behaviour towards European integration is limited.

Hypothesis three

Hypothesis three proposes that if integration is taking place, it will be manifest in government support for continuing integrationist measures, which according to Lindberg's hypotheses relate to institutional development facilitating, elite activation favouring, and government approaches supporting EU involvement in policy. The level of government 'enthusiasm' for policy integration may be gauged by examining not only whether the government enables EU involvement in policy or not, but also the degree to which they attempt to facilitate and support it. If governments are non-enthusiastic, they may give only minimal support in order to avoid the charge of obstruction or presiding over policy failure. If governments are enthusiastic, however, they may wish to develop the organization of policy in such a way that it actively supports further integration.

In Germany the federal government supports EU involvement in regional policy insofar as the regional policy architecture of the federal system satisfies EU policy principles of planning, partnership, additionality, compatibility, coordination and concentration. However, the Federal government still retains primary responsibility for development. This is reflected in the agreement between the Federal government and the European Union over Germany's reduced take-up of its entitlement to EU Structural Funding and also in the fact that what EU aid does come into east Germany is funnelled almost entirely through Federal government policy mechanisms and arrangements (detailed in Chapter 3). Even with the massive constitutional overhaul that unification entailed, no new policy institutions were created to enable the EU to participate directly in regional policy processes. The EU is involved through its provision of additional policy resources in the new *Länder* under Objective One criteria, though it has no direct influence over the formulation or implementation of regional development policy. As a consequence, the federal government has facilitated EU involvement in policy without giving the EU any additional influence over the policy process.

In Ireland, the formal incorporation of EU Structurally Funded programmes on a limited basis in the first National Development Plan (NDP) of 1988 and much more comprehensively in the 1994 NDP illustrates increasing government support for integrationist measures. OPLURD not only incorporates EU programmes and initiatives into a national policy framework, it also gives the EU a direct role in Irish regional policy administration through the establishment of ADM - an independent agency to disburse Structural Funds aid through a contractual arrangement with the European Commission. Added to this, through its incorporation of a range of different development interests from statutory and voluntary bodies, state agencies and private interests, local activists and public representatives, OPLURD provides a mechanism to negotiate consensus over policy action in a way that supports the 'bottom-up' area based approaches to development favoured by the EU (see Chapters 3 and 5).

OPLURD represents Irish governments willingness to set up new policy institutions that facilitate the incorporation of the EU into policy and to help create a consensus over policy between the range of newly incorporated partners in development action. This change of policy approach represents a significant shift in central government attitudes to regional policy, albeit one that was already emerging in other areas of Irish public policy. The willingness of successive Irish governments to relinquish their unique role in policy-making, for the inclusion of agreed 'social partners' demonstrates a changing attitude towards government, one that acknowledges the importance of inclusivity and partnership and that is readily supportive of EU involvement in the policy process. Irish governments have been explicit in their acknowledgement of the influence that EU involvement in development policy has had, crediting the European Union for helping to introduce new development strategies in both the first and second National Development Plans (see Chapter 3) and for developing EU policy principles of planning, partnership, additionality, compatibility, concentration and coordination. In their acceptance and promotion of this alternative view of development, Irish governments have embraced the ideals of programmatic government negotiated through 'partnership' and, given its success, it is hard to see how this system could be reversed even without the legal protection or constitutional guarantees provided by the German federal system of government.

In Britain, central government has accepted EU involvement in development policy only grudgingly, a point that was illustrated most clearly in Chapter 6, which pointed out that Merseyside almost lost its Structural Funding support because of the government's reluctance to tender a bid in accordance with EU rules. More generally, the operation of British regional policy is, to greater or lesser degrees, at odds with all of the Structural Funding policy principles. Whereas the EU seeks to promote *regionally*-oriented, community-based and strategically planned development initiatives, this study suggested that British policy approaches conform to an 'overarching view that has no concept of the region other than as a *container for programmes* of various kinds operated under the auspices of national government' and that British governments seem to have a 'natural antipathy towards strategic planning and thinking' (Chapters 3 and 6). The Merseyside case study identified a similar and equally significant clash of policy styles in relation to EU and UK approaches to funding development: whereas the EU has designated Merseyside as a region in 'need' of regional aid according to a range of Objective One assistance criteria, the UK government's allocation of resources to the region is based on competitive bids and tenders by regional interests, pitting often equally 'needy' groups against others in open competition for limited funding. The EU's requirement of 'matching funding' in order to receive Objective One funding means that although the entire region of Merseyside is eligible for European Structural Funds assistance, the reluctance of UK government to match EU assistance has prevented many from taking advantage of Objective One funding. Finally, whereas the EU places equal emphasis on development initiatives to build up social capital and to promote economic growth, British approaches to regional development focus much more concretely on the latter.

The significant difference between EU and British policy approaches has ensured that there is very little compatibility between British government and EU regional policy interventions. The British government has not sought to make any substantive changes to its own policy emphasis and neither has it attempted to coordinate its own regional interventions with those of the EU. The separateness of EU and British policy approaches contributes to a lack of consensus about the need for regional policy change. Without a strong consensus in favour of change, and with no desire for change on its own behalf, the British government has not introduced any policy innovations to accommodate EU involvement in policy. Central government acceded to partnership strategies because they were cheap, not because they offered mechanisms to develop communities' capacity for development. According to the terms of this hypothesis then, Britain's 'half-hearted' approach to EU involvement in policy is only barely avoiding the charge of obstruction or presiding over policy failure.

Hypothesis four

Hypothesis four proposes that if integration is taking place, it should - as a consequence of both functional and political spillover - lead to the creation of 'inherently expansive tasks' that will both cement the level of integration achieved and push for further integration where possible (where according to these hypotheses integration means institutional development facilitating, elite activation favouring, and government approaches supporting EU involvement in policy). Spillover refers to the idea that for the process of integration to move forward 'a given action, related to a specific goal, creates a situation in which the original goal can be assured only by taking further actions, which in turn create a further condition and a need for more action, and so forth' (Lindberg, 1963:6). In many ways, this hypothesis represents a composite of the previous three. For example, the logic of functional spillover suggests that if an initial form of institutional development that facilitates the involvement of the EU in the policy process proves successful, it should create greater pressure for similar developments in other aspects of the policy process. Alternatively, according to the logic of political spillover, if there is a convergence of elite attitudes in favour of integration and government support for it, this should lead to an increase in political activities that support policy integration.

In Germany, the capacity for functional spillover is limited by the relative rigidity of policy structures and institutions associated with the federal system. Examination of the first hypothesis illustrated how the institutional autonomy granted to German *Länder* by this system ensures EU involvement in Germany regional policy is effectively mediated through the institutions of the federal policy process and has not led to any great pressure for new institutional development. Regarding the potential for political spillover, examination of the second hypothesis showed how 'elite activation' is largely conditioned by the federal system. Even in the new *Länder*, which as Objective One regions receive the highest concentration of EU assistance, the unique conditions created by unification meant that 'elite activation' was focused entirely on changing attitudes and behaviour in favour of further integration at the *national* as opposed to European level of government. Hypothesis three demonstrated how the central role played both by the Federal government in setting the terms of unification, and the federal system in setting the terms of regional policy organization, has effectively circumscribed the process of policy change in the new *Länder* by channelling political activities through distinct federal policy mechanisms and arrangements. It could be argued that German pressure for the establishment of the EU's Committee of the Regions is one integrative outcome of this process but this is a study beyond the scope of this research. The regional policy process uncovered by this study points to only a limited capacity for functional and political spillover in the organization of German regional policy.

In Ireland, the capacity for functional spillover is greater than in Germany because the system of government and regional policy administration is not legally or constitutionally fixed. Chapter 3 illustrated how the Community Support Framework for Structural Funds assistance incorporated into the first National Development Plan (NDP) laid the foundations for the establishment of a more comprehensive policy architecture in the second. The Operational Programme for Rural Development (OPRD) in the first NDP established a framework for the subsequent more elaborate arrangements of OPLURD in the second NDP and pointed to the utility of increasing the compatibility, coordination and concentration of Irish and EU sponsored regional interventions. Since, however, OPLURD arrangements govern the period 1994-99 only, this points to the possibility that such institutional developments that support EU involvement in policy are not permanent so that the potential for functional spillover to may be more limited than it first appears.

The process of political spillover may be more deeply rooted in the Irish regional policy because it is supported by developments elsewhere in Irish politics. The advent of 'partnership government' reflects a change of attitude towards public policy that supports the inclusion of the 'Social Partners' in the policy process. In relation to regional policy in particular, this new approach to policy supports the incorporation of a variety of new actors in the policy process: the EU is widely acknowledged by them and the government as being an important partner in the policy process. This new consensus over regional development has led to a range of new vested interests in the policy process, most of whom are supportive of EU involvement in Irish regional policy, thus embedding it and the other new actors into the policy process.

In Britain the organization of regional policy militates against both functional and political spillover. In relation to functional spillover, the fragmentation of sub-national government structures and regional policy institutions prevents the development of technical pressures for integration. This is because the minimal impact that EU Structural Funds assistance has had upon the institutions of policy delivery has not led to any significant pressure for new institutional developments to facilitate EU involvement in policy. In relation to political spillover, the overall lack of coordination between development interests, the distinct clash of policy approaches that characterize British and EU regional interventions and only minimal government support for EU involvement in policy, combine to prevent the development of a strong consensus in favour of further integration.

A comparative evaluation of the four hypotheses above enables us to make an indicative assessment of the extent to which the 'polity creating process' referred to as the advent of multi-level governance is present in the regional policy processes in each of the states. By defining European integration as the process of 'multi-level governance building' we are implicitly accepting that European integration represents a continuum of change where the end-point is not yet determined. Envisaged in this way, the placing of states in relation to each other along this continuum is just as important as their location in relation to its beginning or end.

In Germany we can see that although there has been no new institutional development to facilitate EU involvement in policy, the present institutional arrangements of the federal system are able to effectively incorporate EU involvement in policy, albeit it with little or no policy influence. The primacy of federal institutions in the regional policy process means that despite EU involvement in the development of the new *Länder* through Objective One assistance, elite activation in favour of integration was primarily *Bund* oriented. Since German regional policy structures and processes are compatible with EU policy principles, the federal government is implicitly supportive of EU involvement in policy and this removes the need for any substantive change in policy approach as an expression of explicit support. As result, the limited potential for functional and political spillover may be because EU and German regional policy processes are already compatible.

In Ireland, there has been significant institutional development to facilitate EU involvement in regional policy through the institution of the OPLURD programme, which gives the EU a direct influence over the formulation and administration of regional policy. This level of influence has been facilitated by elite activation in favour of EU involvement in policy and concrete government action to support it. Lacking any constitutional grounding, legal guarantees, or long-term government commitments, the Irish regional policy process is more susceptible to change than its German counterpart. This is reflected in a greater capacity for functional and political spillover, though of the two political spillover is the more significant since the need for consensus is uppermost in the Irish political system. At present this consensus is strongly supportive of EU involvement in policy and the likelihood is that this will continue for the foreseeable future.

In Britain, the fragmentation of sub-national government means that institutional development is weak. There has been no new institutional development that supports EU involvement in regional policy and those policy structures that already exist do not facilitate it. The previous Conservative government was openly hostile to EU involvement in regional policy. The new Labour government is more open to the EU in general, but has made no specific efforts to encourage EU regional policy interventions. Not surprisingly, elite activation in favour of EU involvement in policy is patchy, reflecting low levels of functional and political spillover potential in the current regional policy set up.

By adopting the propositions of the multi-level governance literature as a working definition of European integration and by providing a set of hypotheses to verify whether or not this process is taking place, this research has gone some way towards clarifying our understanding of what precisely constitutes European integration and how it relates to the process of policy change in states. As well as providing an indication of relative levels of European integration in the regional policy processes of the three states, this evaluation also illustrates how progress towards integration is manifest in different ways in different states. For example, whilst the policy networks examined in Germany and Ireland could be said to be more integrated than the British network, the relative importance of different integration indicators is different in each state.

In Germany, the strong institutional framework provided by the federal system helps to create political consensus over development policy. At national level, the federal system of fiscal equalization mitigates against a lack of political consensus over the level of regional support given to the new *Länder* (see Chapter 3). At sub-national level, the Thüringen case study in Chapter 4 demonstrated how the institutional organization of development policy is structured in such a way as to sustain the current policy consensus. In Ireland, although institutional development is weak, the convergence of attitudes about development policy and of the expectations for it is all but complete. Policy consensus between the government and the Social Partners at national level is reflected in an agreed approach to development policy at local level. The Limerick case study illustrated the degree to which policy goals and expectations have converged. In Ireland then, continuing commitment to the 'partnership principle' supports a policy consensus in the same way that the institutions of the federal system do.

In Britain, institutional development is weak and there is little evidence of a political consensus that supports integration either. As a result, low levels of integration are both structurally and politically determined. Structurally, weak institutional development has occurred at national level through central government reorganization of local government (see Chapter 2), and at sub-national level through the creation of 'competition culture' in regional policy networks that stymies co-operation or consolidation in regional policy delivery (see Chapters 3 and 6). Politically, the fragmented state of sub-national institutions is accompanied by a lack of government support for continued integration and no real convergence of elite attitudes towards integrative policy measures.

The relative significance of different integration indicators in the three states is well illustrated above. The lower level of European integration found in the British case is both structurally and politically determined. Whereas the higher levels of European integration in the German and Irish cases, can be *either* structurally *or* politically determined, as evidenced by the German and Irish cases respectively. In both cases, the key to promoting integration is the creation of a consensus around the basic values and aims of policy. This work shows that the development of consensus is most closely associated with the incidence of ideal type *policy communities*, however, the evidence is that policy communities may be constructed in different ways in different states.

Alternative network types and their potential for integration

Clearly, the evidence from this work suggests that policy communities have, under the terms and conditions of their establishment, a greater propensity towards higher levels of horizontal and vertical integration between policy actors whereas issue networks by their very nature present a non-integrated policy network. This is because the members of a policy community can deliver their membership into agreements, guarantee their compliance, develop a lasting consensus over policy aims and ambitions and are generally supportive of negotiated policy outcomes. By contrast, however, the closer a policy network is to the ideal type issue network, the less likely are the chances of its supporting integration. This is because the membership of an issue network is large and unwieldy where contacts between members fluctuate in intensity and frequency and are usually conditioned by the need to compete for scarce resources thus inhibiting co-operative or integrative action amongst network members. In this sense, there seems to be a straight-forward correlation between Marsh and Rhodes' (1992) typology of networks and the extent of integration we can expect to find in alternative network types. Marsh and Rhodes' (1992) so-called 'continuum of ideal type networks' is, however, less straightforward than it first appears. This is because the dimensions of difference between ideal type networks are not uni-linear. In other words, ideal type networks do not range simply from very integrated policy communities to non-integrated issue networks. There may also be dimensions of difference between alternative forms of ideal types. This point is best illustrated by a comparison of the Thüringen and

Limerick case studies - both policy communities, but quite differently constructed. An overview of the main aspects of network organization discussed in the Thüringen and Limerick case studies reveals why this is so.

In relation to network formation, both the Thüringen and Limerick networks evidence a high degree of stability. In Thüringen this is provided by federal and state constitutional and legal guarantees supporting the structures and institutions of regional development policy in the Federal Republic. Added to this, the conventions of 'co-operative federalism', such as juridical proceduralism and the *gegenstrom* principle in inter-organizational bargaining support network stability by according policy actors a recognized status in the policy process and structuring relations so as to remove potential sources of conflict over respective policy competencies. In Limerick, this stability is provided by the OPLURD framework, which is negotiated in a national concordat between the Social Partners and government, setting out a strategic five year plan for development policy. Within this plan, the institution of Strategic Policy Committees and City/County Development Boards copper-fastens the importance of the county unit for development action and gives formal recognition to the range of local development interests and actors. Thus in Thüringen network stability is institutionally guaranteed, whereas the absence of such formal policy structures in Limerick means that central government is more significant in promoting network stability.

In relation to network membership, both the Thüringen and Limerick networks are based upon a small number of well-qualified and experienced policy actors, which facilitates good working relations and the negotiation of consensus. The Thüringen policy community, though much larger than Limerick, is functionally and territorially co-ordinated with a strong emphasis on the importance of public officials and proceduralism. As a consequence, its membership is formed predominantly by formal structural arrangements, such as the legal, constitutional and institutional provisions of the federal system in Germany. The result is a policy community where the membership is structured according to a hierarchy of 'insider' and 'outsider' groups and as a result the core membership is relatively 'exclusive'. The Limerick policy community is smaller and its membership is determined entirely by functional and personal relations in a personalized and relatively informal policy process. This policy community is for the most part informally structured and dependent upon personal ties and functional contacts. The local and personalized tradition of Irish politicking means that most of policy actors are highly experienced in working with each other. The incorporation of community groups and partnerships into development policy has been assisted by the government making partnership exercises a condition for its support. The result is a policy community that is highly inclusive and can in fact be very egalitarian. Thus, in Thüringen the membership is formally structured comprising of experienced bureaucrats, public representatives and the leaders of representative organizations who negotiate on their behalf. In Limerick, the membership is informally structured, comprising of experienced bureaucrats, community groups and development interests working together in a variety of local development partnerships.

In relation to network resources, both the Thüringen and Limerick networks have adequate resources. Although these are disbursed differently in each state, the distribution of resources is such that policy community members see themselves in a positive sum game, so that even if the benefits of the policy process do not accrue equally between them, they are still better off than they would otherwise be. This belief helps prevent a break-down in network relations that could result in the kind of damaging competition between network members that stymies cooperation and coordination in the policy process. This atmosphere is further supported by the production of longer-term strategic development plans that enable network members to negotiate spending priorities and objectives. In Thüringen, these are provided for in the Land Development Programme, or *Landesentwicklungsprogramms* (LEP), and in the four regional spatial plans, or *regionalen Raumordnungspläne* (RROP), produced by the regional planning boards (*regionalen Planungsgemeinschaften* (RPG)). In Limerick strategic plans are demanded by each of the sub-programmes under the OPLURD framework. Again, the former is constitutionally guaranteed by the Thüringen state planning law, or *das Thüringer Landesplanungsgesetz (ThPlG)*, whilst the latter is co-ordinated by central government through the OPLURD framework.

Finally, in relation to network dynamics, both the Thüringen and Limerick policy communities are characterized by a high degree of policy consensus. This is supported at sub-national level by aspects of network formation, membership and resources described above. It is also supported at national level through overarching planning systems for regional policy. In Germany this is provided for through the institutions and organization of 'cooperative federalism' and in Ireland by government programmes negotiated in national concordats between the government and Social Partners. Despite the evidence of strong policy communities in both cases, we can see that in Germany the formal structures of the federal system play a pre-dominant role in structuring the Thüringen policy community, whereas in Ireland central government partnership approaches to government have played the pre-dominant role in structuring the Limerick policy community. Both cases highlight the significance of alternative policy architectures in different states, in terms of their impact upon the structuring and organization of policy networks and their capacity to support policy integration. They also illustrate the relative paucity of integrative features in the Merseyside issue network.

Without the institutions of 'cooperative federalism' pertaining in Germany, or the 'government by partnership' that exists in Ireland, there is precious little to structure the Merseyside network. The Merseyside network has no overarching set of regional policy institutions, nor is it guided by central government approaches that support strategic development action. Its membership is too large to rely on personal ties and contacts, like the Limerick network, yet not sufficiently organized or co-ordinated to deliver representative interests to negotiate policy as the Thüringen network does. It could be argued that a comparison between Thüringen and Merseyside shows that the larger the network, the greater the need for formal structuring to maintain integrative capacity. Without such formal policy structures, the government's *laissez faire* approach to policy funding has substantially contributed to the instability of the Merseyside network. A comparison between Limerick and Merseyside shows that even where the resourcing of policy is not allocated (as it is in Germany), the way in which central governments structure the conditions of competition for funding affects the extent to which competition is 'healthy' or 'damaging' to network dynamics. The Merseyside case study highlighted how network dynamics are fundamentally conditioned by the need to compete for scarce resources. This 'competition culture' stymies collective action and prevents the growth of a policy consensus between actors that might possibly attenuate the lack of institutional or governmental support for the network.

The results of this research illustrates how the structuring of policy communities may be due to variable mixes of personal, political or institutional conditions and, presumably, this might also be the case with ideal type issue networks. This variety in network types has significant implications for the use of network analysis: first, it confirms their comparative utility; and second it dispenses with arguments about which network scholars or what kinds of network analysis are more useful. The cross-national comparisons presented in this work suggest that although networks may well be constructed differently in different states, they are nevertheless useful organizing concepts for comparison. Therefore arguments over the deployment of network analysis need to move on. The debate should not be about *how* networks might be constructed differently but *why* networks might be constructed differently.

This study has shown how the institutional and political contexts of different state systems condition the development of alternative network formations: different sorts of policy communities and networks have a differential capacity to sustain consensus between policy actors and promote policy integration between different levels of government. This points to the need to develop our understanding of the links between moves towards 'new governance' that constitute the horizontal dimensions of policy change and moves towards 'multi-level governance' that constitute the vertical dimensions of policy change in a manner which can acknowledge and explain the increased variety of alternative network configurations suggested by this research.

The study has shown that integration is not a uniform phenomenon. Not only can we point to greater or lesser degrees of integration in the same policy areas in different states, but we can also point to the manifestation of integration in different ways in different states (arising as a consequence of different mixes of institutional, political and policy-related variables in the development policy networks in different state systems). In relation to the correlation between certain network types and increased capacity for integration: although policy communities have been identified as being more supportive of integration than issue networks, they nevertheless do not guarantee that the influence of the European Union will be significant. Integration is about a coincidence of consensus between policy actors from different levels of government and as such should be regarded as a positive-sum phenomenon.

In states that support integrated (development) policy communities, such as Germany and Ireland, the increasing incidence of European Union sponsored development action is not matched by commensurate decreasing of central government sponsored development action. Quite the reverse: the two are often mutually supportive and because of this, policy integration should not be understood as a zero-sum power relationship between different levels of governance. That is to say, that the increased involvement of the EU in regional development policy is not necessarily sustained by decreasing the 'control capacity' or policy authority of central governments. In this respect, the literature on state autonomy and different conceptions of state capacity might well be a fruitful basis for further theorising of integration through the use of networks (see for example: Evans, 1995; Bourdieu, 1994; Bourdieu and Wacquant, 1992). In sum: this research has identified a comparative methodology to identify the differing levels of policy integration in selected case studies where the level of EU involvement in policy is significant; future research should be concerned with explaining why these differences occur.

Bibliography

ADM (Area Development Management Ltd) (1995) *Annual Report*, Dublin: ADM

Adshead, M. (1996) 'Agricultural networks in Ireland and the EU', *West European Politics*, 19/3/583-608

Adshead, M. and Quinn, B. (1998) 'The move from government to governance: Irish development policy's paradigm shift', *Policy and Politics*, 26/2/.209-225

Alter, K.J. (1996) 'The European Court's political power', *West European Politics*, 19/3/458-487

Armstrong, K. and Bulmer, S. (1998) *The governance of the single European market*, Manchester: Manchester University Press

Atkinson, R. and Moon, G. (1994) 'The City Challenge Initiative: an overview and preliminary assessment', *Regional Studies*, 28/8/94-97

Bache, I. (1998): *The politics of European Union regional policy. Multi-level governance or flexible gatekeeping?*, Sheffield: Sheffield Academic Press

Balfour, M. (1992) *Germany. The tides of power*, London: Routledge

Bannon, M. (1991) 'The contribution of the management system to local and national development', in Barrington, T.J. (ed.) *City and County Management 1929-1990: a retrospective*, Dublin: IPA, pp.44-45

Barlow, M. (1995) 'Greater Manchester: conurbation complexity and local government structure', *Political Geography*, 14/4/379-400

Barrington, T.J. (1980) *The Irish Administrative System*, Dublin: Institute for Public Administration (IPA)

Barrington, T.J. (1987) 'Ireland the interplay of territory and function', in Rhodes, R.A.W. and Wright, V. (eds) *Tensions in the territorial politics of Western Europe*, London: Frank Cass

Berking, H. and Neckel, S. (1991) 'Aussenseiter als Politiker: Rekrutierung und Identitaten neuer lokaler Eliten in einer ostdeutschen Gemeinde', *Soziale Welt*, 42/3

Bomberg, E. (1994) 'Policy networks on the periphery: EU environmental policy and Scotland', *Regional Politics and Policy*, 4/45-61

Bomberg, E. (1998) 'Policy networks in the EU: explaining EU environmental policy', in Marsh, D. (ed.) *Policy networks in comparative perspective*, Milton Keynes: OUP

Bourdieu, P. (1994) 'Re-thinking the state: genesis and structure of the bureaucratic field', *Sociological Theory*, 12/1/1-18

Bourdieu, P. and Wacquant, L. (1992) 'The logic of fields', in Bourdieu and Wacquant (eds) *An invitation to reflexive sociology*, Chicago: University of Chicago Press, pp.115-140

Breuel, B. (1994) 'Treuhandanstalt: Bilanz und Perspektiven', *Politik und Zeitgeschichte*, 44/43-44/14-20

Bromage, A.W. (1954) 'Irish councilmen at work', *Administration*, 2/1/93-111
Bruinvels, P. and Rodrigues, D. (1989) *Investing in Enterprise - a comprehensive guide to inner city regeneration and urban renewal*, Oxford: Basil Blackwell
Buchanan, T. (1969) *Regional studies in Ireland*, Dublin: An Foras Forbatha
Bulmer, S. (1983) 'Domestic politics and European Community policy-making', *Journal of Common Market Studies*, 21/349-363
Bulmer, S. (1989) 'Territorial government', in Smith, G., Paterson, W.E. and Merkl, P. (eds) *Developments in west German politics*, London: Macmillan, pp.40-59
Bulmer, S. (1994a) 'The governance of the European Union: a new institutionalist approach', *Journal of Public Policy*, 13/351-380
Bulmer, S. (1994b) 'Institutions and policy change in the European Communities', *Public Administration*, 72/423-444
Bulmer, S. and Paterson, W. (1987) *The Federal Republic of Germany and the European Community*, London: Allen and Unwin
Bulpitt, J. (1983) *Territory and power in the United Kingdom*, Manchester: Manchester University Press
Bundesministerium der Finanzen (1990) *Bundeshaushalts-ordnung*, Bundesministerium der Finanzen: Bonn
Bundesministerium für Verkehr (1993) *Ergänzende Information zum Bundesverkehrswegeplan 1992*, Bonn: Bundesministerium für Verkehr
CAAS Ltd (1997) *Independent appraisal report on the co-ordination of local development for the county city and council strategy group*, Dublin: CAAS Ltd
Cameron, D.R. (1992) 'The 1992 initiative: causes and consequences', in Sbragia, A. (ed.) *Euro-politics: institutions and policy-making in the 'new' European Community*, Washington, DC: Brookings Institution, pp.23-74
Cawson, A. (1992) 'Interests, groups and public policy-making: the case of the European consumer electronics industry', in Greenwood, J., Gröte, J.R. and Ronit, K. (eds) *Organized interests and the European Community*, London: Sage, pp.99-118
Chubb, B. (1992) *The government and politics of Ireland*, 3rd edn, London: Longman
Coakley, J. and Gallagher, M. (eds) (1993) *Politics in the Republic of Ireland*, Dublin: Folens/PSAI Press
Cochrane, A. (1990) 'The changing state of local government: restructuring for the 1990s', *Public Administration*, 69/3/281-302
Coleman, W.D. (1990) 'State traditions and comprehensive business associations: a comparative analysis', *Political Studies*, 38/June/231-252
Collins, N. and Walsh, J. (1995) 'Member states and their regions: Ireland', in Sweeney, G.P. (ed.) *Regional and local development*, Dublin: DIT, pp.1-236
CEC (Commission of the European Communities) (1975) Council Regulation EEC No.724/75 of 18:03:75, in *Official Journal of the European Communities*, No. L 73, 21:03:75, Brussels: CEC
CEC (1988) Article 4 Council Regulation EEC No. 2052/88 of 24:03:88 in, *Official Journal of the European Communities*, No. L 185; 15:07:88, Brussels: CEC
CEC (1991a) *Generaldirektion für Regionalpolitik: info background*, Europäische Unternehmens- und Innovationszentrum, Brussels
CEC (1991b) *Community Support Framework 1991-1993 for the areas of eastern Berlin, Mecklenburg-Vorpommern, Brandenburg, Sachsen-Anhalt, Thüringen and Sachsen in the Federal Republic of Germany*, Brussels: CEC
CEC (1993a) *Generaldirektion für Regionalpolitik: info background.* Länderprofil

Deutschland, Brussels: CEC

CEC (1993b) *Agreement on the implementation of the Global Grant under Decision C(92) 2145 of September 1992*, Luxembourg: Office for official publications of the European Communities

CEC (1994a) *Guide to Community Initiatives 1994-1999*, Brussels: CEC

CEC (1994b) *Community Support Framework 1994 -1999, for the areas of Eastern Berlin, Mecklenburg-Vorpommern, Brandenburg, Sachsen-Anhalt, Thüringen and Sachsen*, Brussels: CEC

CEC (1994c) *United Kingdom, Merseyside 2000, Single Programming Document for Merseyside 1994-1999*, Brussels: Directorate General for Regional Policies, CEC

CEC (1994d) *Generaldirektion für Regionalpolitik: Europäischer Funds für regionale Entwicklung. Europäischer Sozialfonds. Operationelles Programm für Thüringen*, Brussels: CEC

CEC (1994e) *Generaldirektion für Regionalpolitik: Gemeinschaftliches Förderkonzept Deutschland für die Entwicklung und strukturelle Anpassung der Regionen mit Entwicklungsrückstand (Zeille) 1994 -1999*, Brussels: CEC

CEC (1997) Commission of the European Communities *European Union regional policy and cohesion*, Luxembourg: Office for official publications of the European Communities

Cope, S. and Atkinson, R. (1994) 'The structures of governance in Britain', in Savage, S.P., Atkinson, R. and Robins, L. (eds), *Public policy in Britain*, Basingstoke: Macmillan

Coyle, C. (1990) 'Irish local bureaucracies in national and European Communities' policy process', Paper delivered to the ECPR workshop on local and regional bureaucracies in European states, University of Limerick

Coyle, C. (1994) 'Irish local administration in the national and European policy process', *Research in Urban Policy*, 5/21-41

Coyle, C. (1994) 'Irish local bureaucracies in national and European Community policy process', Paper delivered to the ECPR workshop on local and regional bureaucracies in European states, University of Limerick, 17-18th September

Daugbjerg, C. (1997) 'Policy networks and agricultural policy reforms: explaining deregulation in Sweden and re-regulation in the European Community', *Governance*, 10/2:123-141

Daugbjerg, C. (1999) 'Reforming the CAP: policy networks and broader institutional structures', *Journal of Common Market Studies*, 37/3:407-428

Davies, H. (1993) 'Free markets and centralised power: a British paradox', in Bennett, Robert J. (ed.) *Local government in the new Europe*, London: Belhaven Press

Dawson, N. and Parkinson, M. (1991) 'Merseyside Development Corporation 1981- 1989', in Keith, M. and Rogers, A. (eds) *Hollow Promises*, London: Mansell

DCC (Docklands Consultative Committee) (1985) *Four year review of the LDDC*, London: DCC

Deakin, N. and Edwards, J. (1993) *The enterprise culture and the inner city*, London: Routledge

Deutsch, K.W. (1954) *Political community at the international level - problems of measurement in international relations*, New York: Double Day

Deutsch, K.W. (1957) *Political community and the North Atlantic area: international organization in the light of historical experience*, New Jersey: Princeton University Press

Deutscher Bundespost Telekom (1994) *Telekom 2000 - Schrittmacher beim Aufbau Ost*, Bonn: Deutscher Bundespost Telekom

Deutscher Gewerkschaftsbund (1994) *Geschäftsbericht DGB-Landesbezirk Thüringen*, 23 Mai 1992 - 22 Jan 1994

Devlin, L.S. (1969) *Report of the public services organisation review group, 1966-69*, Dublin: Stationery Office

Dooney, S. and O'Toole, J. (1992) *Irish Government Today*, Dublin: Gill and Macmillan

Dowding, K. (1994) 'Policy networks: don't stretch a good idea too far', in Dunleavy, P. and Stanyer, J. (eds) *Contemporary Political Studies 1994*, vol.1, Belfast: Political Studies Association of the UK, pp.59-78

Drerup, D. (1997) 'German policy perspectives', in Bachtler, J. and Turok, I. (eds) *The coherence of EU regional policy. Contrasting perspectives on the Structural Funds*, London: Jessica Kingsley Publishers with the Regional Studies Association, pp.337-345

DTER (Department of Transport, Environment and the Regions) (24:09:1998) *Regeneration programmes - the way forward*, http://www.local.detr.gov.uk/regenera.htm

Dyson, K. (1992) 'Theories of regulation and the case of Germany: a model of regulatory change', in Dyson, K. (ed.) *The politics of German regulation*, Aldershot: Dartmouth

Eckey, H.F. (1991) 'Komponenten einer Newordnung der Raumordnungspolitik angesichts veränderter Rahmenbedingungen. Folgerungen aus dem Raumordnungsbericht 1991', in *Informationen zur Raumentwicklung*, 11/12/703-714

Eising, R. and Kohler-Koch, B. (eds) (1999) *Transformation of Governance in the European Union*, London: Routledge

EURES (Institute for regional studies in Europe) (1995) 'Regional development in Europe in theory and practice: Germany', in Sweeney, G.P. (ed) *Regional and local development*, Dublin: Dublin Institute of Technology, pp.1-162

Evans, P. (1995) 'The state as problem and as solution', in Haggard, S. and Kaufmann, R. (eds) *The politics of economic adjustment*, Princeton, NJ: Princeton University Press, pp.139-181

Falkner, G. (1999) 'European social policy. Towards multi-level and multi-actor governance', in Eising and Kohler-Koch (eds) *Transformation of Governance in the European Union*, London: Routledge

Farrell, B. (1983) 'Ireland - from friends and neighbours to clients and partisans: some dimensions of parliamentary representation under PR STV', in Bogdanor, V. (ed.) *Coalition government in western Europe*, London: Heinemann

Farrell, B. (ed.) (1988) *De Valera's constitution and ours*, Dublin: Gill and Macmillan

FÁS (1996) *Mid-west rolling regional development plan 1996-1999*, Unpublished FÁS

Finlay, F. (1998) *Snakes and ladders*, Dublin: New Island Books

Fitzmaurice, J. (1988) 'An analysis of the EC's cooperation procedure', *Journal of Common Market Studies*, 16/389-400

Flowerdew, R., Francis, B. and Lucas, S. (1994) 'The Standard Spending Assessment as a measure of spending needs in non-metropolitan districts', *Environment and Planning C: Government and Policy*, 12/1-13

Ford, G. and Lake, G. (1991) 'Evolution of European science and technology policy', *Science and Public Policy*, 18/38-50

Fuchs, G. (1994) 'Policy-making in a system of Multi-Level Governance. The Commission of the European Community and the restructuring of the telecommunications sector', *Journal of European Public Policy*, 01/01:177-194

Gemeinde- und Städtebundes Thüringen (1996), *Geschäftsbericht 1995/96*, Erfurt: Gemeinde- und Städtebundes Thüringen

Geyer, R. (1996) 'EU social policy in the 1990s: does Maastricht matter?', *Journal of European Integration*, 20/1/5-33

Gibson, J. (1992) 'British local government finance under the Conservatives', *Local Government Studies*, 18/4/55-78

GLC (Greater London Council) (1984) *London's Docklands*, London: GLC

Goetz, K.H. (1993) 'Rebuilding public administration in the new German *Länder*: transfer and differentiation', *West European Politics*, 16/4/447-469

Goetz, K.H. (1995) 'Administrative reconstruction in the new Länder: the federal dimension', paper presented at the workshop 'State and civil society in the new German Länder', LSE, 8-9th December

Goldsmith, M.J. and Page, E.C. (eds) (1987) *Central and local government relations. A comparative analysis of West European unitary states*

Government of Ireland (1930) *Dublin City Management Act*, Dublin: DSO

Government of Ireland (1934) *Limerick City Management Act*

Government of Ireland (1939) *Waterford City Management Act*

Government of Ireland (1952) *Finance (Excise Duties Vehicles) Act*

Government of Ireland (1963) *Local Government (Planning and Development) Act*

Government of Ireland (1971) *White Paper: Local Government Reorganisation*

Government of Ireland (1973) *Local Government Discussion Document*

Government of Ireland (1985) *Local Government Reform*

Government of Ireland (1991a) *Programme for Economic and Social Progress*

Government of Ireland (1991b) *Local government reorganisation and reform*

Government of Ireland (1993) *National Development Plan 1994-1999*

Government of Ireland (1994) *Government of renewal - 1994 programme for government*

Government of Ireland (1995) *Operational programme: local urban and rural development 1994-99*

Government of Ireland (1996a) *Better local government. A programme for change*

Government of Ireland (1996b) *Devolution Committee interim report*

Grabher, G. (1997) 'Adaptation at the cost of adaptability? Restructuring the eastern German regional economy', in Grabher, G. and Stark, D. (eds) *Restructuring networks in post-socialism. Legacies, linkages and localities*, New York: Oxford University Press, pp.107-134

Grahl, J. and Teague, P. (1989) 'The cost of a neo-Liberal Europe', *New Left Review*, 114/33-49

Gray, C. (1994) *Government beyond the centre. Sub-national politics in Britain*, London: Macmillan

Groom, A.J.R. (1994) 'Neo-functionalism: a case of mistaken identity', in Nelson, Brent F. and Stubb, Alexander C.G. (eds) *The European Union. Readings on the theory and practice of European integration*, London: Lynne Rienner, pp.111-123

Gunlicks, A.B. (ed.) *Local government reform and reorganisation: an international perspective*, London: Kennikat Press

Haas, E.B. (1958a) 'The challenge of regionalism', *International Organization*, 12/440-58

Haas, E.B. (1958b) *The uniting of Europe - political, social and economic forces, 1950-1957*, London: Stevens and sons

Haas, E.B. (1964) *Beyond the nation state - functionalism and international organization*, Stanford, California: Stanford University Press

Haase, T., McKeown, K. and Rourke, S. (1996) *Local development strategies for disadvantaged areas. Evaluation of the Global Grant, 1992-1995*, a report prepared for Area Development Management Ltd, Dublin: Kieran McKeown Ltd, Social and economic research consultants

Hahne, U. (1985) 'Regionalentwicklung durch Aktivierung intra-regionaler Potentiale. Zu den Chancen endogener Entwickslungsstrategien', *Schriften des Instituts für Regional forschung der Universität Kiel*, Band 8, München

Harding, A. (1991) 'The rise of urban growth coalitions, UK style?', *Environment and Planning: C*, 9/295-317

Hederman O'Brien, M. (1989) 'Whatever happened to rates? A study of Irish tax policy on domestic dwellings', *Administration*, 37/4/334-351

Heritier, A. (1993) 'Policy-Netzwerkanalyse als Untersuchungsinstrument im europaischen Kontext: Folgerungen aus einer empirischen Studie regulativer Politik', in Heritier, A. (ed.) *Policy-Analyse, Kritik und Neuorientierung*, Opladen: Westdeutscher Verlag, pp.432-447

Heseltine, M. (1980) 'Co-operation between business and local government', Speech to the London Chamber of Commerce, Guildhall, London

Hesse, J.J. (ed.) (1978) *Politikverflechtung im foderativen Staat*, Baden- Baden: Nomos

Hesse, J.J. (1987) 'The Federal Republic of Germany: from co-operative federalism to joint policy-making', in Rhodes, R.A.W. and Wright, V. (eds) *Tensions in the territorial politics of Western Europe*, London: Cass, pp.70-87

Hix, S. (1994) 'The study of the European Community: the challenge to comparative politics', *West European Politics*, 17/1/1-30

Hix, S. (1996) 'CP, IR and the EU! A rejoinder to Hurrell and Menon', *West European Politics*, 19/4

HMSO (1983a) Government Paper, Cmnd 9063 *Streamlining the cities: government proposals for reorganising local government in Greater London and the Metropolitan counties*, London: HMSO

HMSO (1983b) Department of the Environment, Cmnd 9008 *Rates*

HMSO (1986) Department of the Environment, Cmnd 9741 Green Paper, *Paying for local government*

HMSO (1988) Department of the Environment, *Action for Cities*

HMSO (1991) Department of the Environment, *City Challenge - round one winners*

HMSO (1994) Department of the Environment, *Assessing the impact of urban policy*

HMSO (1995) Central Office of Information, *Urban regeneration*

HMSO (1995) Department of Trade and Industry, *Investing in the assisted areas. A guide to regional selective assistance*

HMSO (1997) Department of the Environment, Transport and the Regions, *Single Regeneration Budget Challenge Fund Round 4 supplementary guidelines*

Hochberg, A. (1996) 'A critical appraisal of EU regional policy for the new *Länder* of the Federal Republic of Germany', Institute for German Studies Discussion paper series 96/7, University of Birmingham

Hoffmann, G. (1992) 'Die staatliche Mittelstanz in den neuen Bundesländern', *Die Öffentliche Verwaltung*, 45/16,/689-96

Hoffmann, G. (1993) 'Die Bezirksregierung Dessau - Aufbau und Arbeit einer Mittelbehörde in Sachsen-Anhalt', *Die Neue Verwaltung*, 1/6-9

Holland, S. (1980) *Uncommon market*, London: Macmillan

Hooghe, L. (ed.) (1996) *Cohesion policy and European integration: building multi-level governance*, Oxford: Oxford University Press

Hooghe, L. and Keating, M. (1994) 'The politics of EU regional policy', *Journal of European*

Public Policy, 1/367-393

Hooghe, L. and Marks, G. (1996) 'Territorial restructuring in the European Union: regional pressures', in Cassese, S. and Wright, V. (eds) *La restructuration de l'Etat dans les pays d'Europe occidentale*, Paris: Editions La Découverte, Collection 'Recherches'

Horgan, J.J. (1926) 'Local government developments at home and abroad', *Studies*, 15

House of Commons (1926) *Local Government (County Boroughs and Adjustments) Act*

House of Commons (1929) *Local Government Act*

House of Commons (1972) *Local Government Act*

Ionescu, G. (ed.) (1974) *Between sovereignty and integration*, London: Croom Helm

Ionescu, G. (1975) *Centripetal Politics: government and the new centres of power*, London: Hart-Davis Macgibbon

IPA (Institute of Public Administration) (1971) *More Local Government*, Dublin: IPA

IPA (1997) *Annual Directory*, Dublin: IPA

Jeffery, C. (1994) 'German federalism', in Dunleavy, P. and Stanyer, J. (eds) *Contemporary Political Studies 1994*, vol.2, Belfast: Political Studies Association of the UK, pp.765-778

Kearney, B., Boyle, G.E. and Walsh, J.A. (1995) *EU LEADER I initiative in Ireland*, Dublin: Department of Agriculture, Food and Forestry

Keating, M. and Midwinter, A. (1994) 'The politics of central-local grants in Britain and France', *Environment and Planning C: Government and Policy*, 12/177-194

Keohane, R.O. and Hoffman, S. (1990) 'Community politics and institutional change', in Wallace, W. (ed.) *The dynamics of European Integration*, London: Pinter, pp.271-292

Kickert, W. (1993) 'Autopoiesis and the science of (public) administration: essence, sense and nonsense', *Organization Studies*, 14/261-278

King, D. (1993) 'Government beyond Whitehall: local government and urban politics', in Budge, I. and Mckay, D. (eds) *Developments in British Politics 4*, London: Macmillan, pp.194-218

King, D. (1993) 'Government beyond Whitehall: local government and urban politics', in Dunleavy, P., Gamble, A., Holliday, I. and Peele, G. (eds) *Developments in British politics 4*, London: Macmillan, pp.194-218

KMPG (1991) *Report on the financing of local government*, Dublin: DSO

Kohler-Koch, B. (1996) 'Catching up with change. The transformation of governance in the European Union', *Journal of Common Market Studies*, 3/3/359-380

Kohler-Koch, B. (1997) 'Organized interests in European integration. The evolution of a new type of governance?', in Wallace, H. and Young, A. (eds) *Participation and policy-making in the European Union*, Oxford: Oxford University Press, 42-68

Kohler-Koch, B. (1999) 'The evolution and transformation of European governance', in Eising, R. and Kohler-Koch, B. (eds) *Transformation of Governance in the European Union*, London: Routledge

Komito, L. (1989) 'Voters, politicians and clientelism: a Dublin survey', *Administration*, 37/2/171-196

Komito, L. (1992) 'Brokerage or friendship? Politics and networks in Ireland', *Economic and Social Review*, 23/2/129-145

Kruse, H. (1990) 'Reform durch regionalisierung', *Eine politische Antwort auf die Umstrukturierung der Wirtschaft*, Frankfurt/New York: Campus Publishers

Laffin, M. (1986) *Professionalism and policy*, Aldershot: Gower

Lange, P. (1992) 'The Maastricht social protocol: why did they do it?, *Politics and Society*,

21/5-36

Lawless, P. and Brown, F. (1986) *Urban Growth and change in Britain*, London: Harper and Row

Le Galés, P. and Lequesne, C. (eds) (1998) *Regions in Europe*, London: Routledge

Leach, R. (1994) 'Restructuring local government', *Local Government Studies*, 20/3/345-360

Leach, S. (1993) *Local government review: a crisis of credibility*, London: European Policy Review Forum

Leach, S. (1994a) 'The local government review: a critical appraisal', *Public Money and Management*, 14/1/11-16

Leach, S. (1994b) 'The local government review: from policy drift to policy fiasco', *Regional Studies*, 28/4/537-543

Lee, J.J. (ed.) (1979) *Ireland 1945-70*, Dublin: Gill and Macmillan

Lee, J.J. (1989) *Ireland 1912-1985*, Cambridge: Cambridge University Press

Lehmbruch, G. (1994) 'The process of regime change in East Germany: an institutionalist scenario for German unification', *Journal of European Public Policy*, 1/1/115-43

Lehmbruch, G. (1994) 'Transformation einer real-sozialisitschen Verwaltung in eine klassisch-europäische Verwaltung', in Seibel, W., Mäding, H. and Benz, W. (eds) *Verwaltungsreform und Verwaltungspolitik im Prozeß der deutschen Einigung*, Baden-Baden: Nomos

Limerick City Enterprise Board (1996) *Annual Report*, Limerick: CEB

Limerick County Enterprise Board (1996) *Annual Report*, Limerick: CEB

Lindberg, L. (1963) *The political dynamics of European economic integration*, Stanford, Calif.: Stanford University Press

Lindberg, L.N. (1965) 'Decision-making and integration in the European Community', *International Organization*, 19/56-80

Lindberg, L.N. (1966) 'The European Community as a political system - notes toward the construction of a model', *Journal of Common Market Studies*, 5/4/344-387

Lindberg, L.N. and Scheingold, S.A. (1970) *Europe's would-be polity- patterns of change in the European Community*, New Jersey: Prentice Hall

Liverpool City Council (1997) *Community Based Economic Development*, Liverpool: LCC

LLA (Local Authority Associations) (1994) *Briefing by the Local Authority Associations in England and Wales on the additionality of European funding*, London: LAA

Lloyd, P. and Meegan, R. (1996) 'Contested governance: European exposure in the English regions', *European Regional and Planning Studies*, 4/1

London Docklands Consultative Committee (DCC) (1985) *Four year review of the LDDC*, London: DCC

Lörler, S. (1993) 'Probleme einer zweistufigen Landesverwaltung in einem Flächenstaat', *Die Öffentliche Verwaltung*, 46/6/244-48

Marks, G., Hooghe, L. and Blank, K. (1996) 'European integration from the 1980s: state-centric *v.* multi-level governance', *Journal of Common Market Studies*, 34/3/341-378

Marks, G., Nielsen, F., Ray, L. and Salk, J. (1996) 'Competencies, cracks and conflicts: regional mobilization in the European Union', in Marks, G., Scharpf, F.W., Schmitter, P. and Streeck, W. (eds) *Governance in the European Union*, London: Sage, pp.40-63

Marsh, D. and Rhodes, R.A.W. (1992) *Policy networks in British government*, Oxford: Clarendon Press

McAleavey, P. (1992) 'The politics of European regional development policy: the European Commission's RECHAR initiative and the concept of additionality', University of

Strathclyde papers on government and politics, No. 88, Department of Government: University of Strathclyde

McAleavey, P. (1993) 'The politics of European regional development policy: additionality in the Scottish coalfields', *Regional Policy and Politics*, 3/88-107

McManus, M. (1993) 'The Republic of Ireland', in Chandler, J.A. (ed.) *Local government in liberal democracies*, London: Routledge, pp.28-52

Meegan, R. (1990) 'Merseyside in crisis and in conflict', in Harloe, M., Pickvance, C. and Urry, J. (eds) *Place, policy and politics: do localities matter?*, London: Unwin Hyman Ltd, pp.87-107

Michie, R. and Fitzgerald, R. (1997) 'The evolution of the Structural Funds', in Bachtler, J. and Turok, I. (eds) *The coherence of EU regional policy. Contrasting perspectives on the Structural Funds*, London: Jessica Kingsley Publishers with the Regional Studies Association, pp. 14-28

Ministerium für Wirtschaft und Infrastrukur (1997) *Raumordnungs Bericht*, Erfurt: Ministerium für Wirtschaft und Infrastruktur

Moravcsik, A. (1991) 'Negotiating the Single European Act', in Keohane, R.O. and Hoffmann, S. (eds) *The new European Community*, Oxford: Westview Press, pp.85-132

Moravcsik, A. (1993) 'Preferences and power in the European Community: a liberal intergovernmentalist approach', *Journal of Common Market Studies*, 31/473-524

Moravcsik, A. (1998) *The choice for Europe. Social purpose and state power from Messina to Maastricht*, London: UCL Press

Morris, R (1990) *Central and Local control of education after the Education Reform Act 1988*, London: Longman

Müller, C.P. (1992) 'Trotz bedenken der Landräte', *Frankfurter Allegemeine Zeitung*, 30 October, p.11

NESC (National Economic and Social Committee) (1990) *A strategy for the nineties*, Dublin: NESC

NESC (1994) *New approaches to rural development*, Dublin: NESC

Nicoll, W. (1984) 'The Luxembourg Compromise', *Journal of Common Market Studies*, 23/1/35-43

North, R.C., Koch, H.E. and Zinnes, D.A. (1960) 'The integrative functions of conflict', *Journal of Conflict Resolution*, 4/355-374

O'Donnell, R. and Walsh, J. (1995) 'Ireland: region and state in the European Union', in Rhodes, M. (ed.) *The regions and the new Europe*, Manchester: Manchester University Press, pp.200-228

O'Malley, E. (1992) *The pilot programme for integrated rural development 1988- 90*, Paper No. 27, Broadsheet Series, Dublin: ESRI

Olson, M. (1996) 'The varieties of Eurosclerosis: the rise and decline of nations since 1982', in Crafts, N. and Tonilio, G. (eds) *Economic growth in Europe since 1945*, Cambridge: Cambridge University Press, pp.73-94

OECD (Organisation for Economic Co-operation and Development) (1991) *Economic survey: Germany*, Paris: OECD

OECD (1996) *Ireland: local partnerships and social innovation*, Paris: OECD

Ossenbühl, F. (Hg) (1990) *Föderalismus und Regionalismus in Europa*, Baden-Baden: Nomos

Osterland, M. (1993) 'The re-establishment of local government in the former GDR', *Local Government Policy Making*, 20/1/6-17

Parkinson, M. (1989) 'The Thatcher government's urban policy, 1979-1989: a review', Centre for urban studies, University of Liverpool, working paper No.6

Paterson, W. and Southern, D. (1991) *Governing Germany*, Oxford: Basil Blackwell

Peters, G. (1998) *Comparative politics. Theory and methods*, London: Macmillan

Peterson, J. (1991) 'Technology policy in Europe: explaining the framework programme and Eureka in theory and practice', *Journal of Common Market Studies*, 29/269-290

Peterson, J. (1994) 'Policy networks and governance in the European Union: the case of Research and Development policy', in *Contemporary Political Studies Volume I*, proceedings of the Annual Conference of the PSA, University of Wales, Swansea, 9-13 March

Peterson, J. (1995) 'Decision-making in the European Union: towards a framework for analysis', *Journal of European Public Policy*, 2/1/69-94

Petzold, S. (1993) 'Zur Bildung von Ämtern und Verwaltungsgemeinschaften in den neue Ländern - Ein Überblick', *Die Neue Verwaltung*, 2/20-23

Pierre, J. and Peters, G. (2000) *Governance, Politics and the State*, London: Macmillan

Pierson, P. (1996) 'The path to European integration. A historical institutionalist analysis', *Comparative Political Studies*, 29/2/123-163

Priewe, J. and Hickel, R. (1991) 'Eine Politik der De-industrialisierung durth die Treuhandanstalt?', in Priewe and Hickel (eds) *Der Preis der Einheit: Bilanz und Perspektiven der deutschen Vereinigung*, Frankfurt-am-Main: Fischer, pp.164-88

Putnam, R.D. (1988) 'Diplomacy and domestic politics: the logic of two-level games', *International Organization*, 42/427-460

Quinn, R. (1996) Address to the Regional Affairs Committee of the European Parliament by the Minister of Finance for Ireland, 7 May 1996

Rhodes, M., Heywood, P. and Wright, V. (1997) 'Towards a new Europe?', in Rhodes, M., Heywood, P. and Wright, V. (eds) *Developments in west European politics*, London: Macmillan Press, pp.1-15

Rhodes, R.A.W. (1981a) *Control and power in central-local government relations*, Aldershot: Gower

Rhodes, R.A.W. (1981b) 'The changing pattern of local government in England: reform or reorganisation?', in Gunlicks, A.B. (ed.) *Local government reform and reorganisation: an international perspective*, London: Kennikat Press, pp.93-111

Rhodes, R.A.W. (1986) *The national world of local government*, London: Allen and Unwin

Rhodes, R.A.W. (1988) *Beyond Westminster and Whitehall*, London: Unwin Hyman

Rhodes, R.A.W. and Marsh, D. (1992) 'New directions in the study of policy networks', *European Journal of Political Research*, 21/181-205

Rhodes, R.A.W. (1994) 'The hollowing out of the state', *Political Quarterly*, 65/138-151

Rhodes, R.A.W. (1995) *The new governance: governing without government*, London: RSA and ESRC

Rhodes, R.A.W. (1996) 'The new governance: governing without government', *Political Studies*, 44/4/652-667

Rhodes, R.A.W. (1997) *Understanding governance. Policy networks, governance, reflexivity and accountability*, Buckingham: Open University Press

Rhodes, R.A.W., Weller, P. and Bakvis, H. (eds) (1997) *The hollow crown: countervailing trends in core executives*, London: Macmillan

Richardson, J.J. and Jordan, G. (1979) *Governing under pressure. The policy process in a post-parliamentary democracy*, Oxford: Martin Robertson

Risse-Kappen, T. (1996) 'Exploring the nature of the beast: international relations theory and comparative policy analysis meet the European Union', *Journal of Common Market Studies*, 34/1:53-80

Roberts, P. (1993) 'Managing the strategic planning and development of the regions: lessons from the European perspective', *Regional Studies*, 27/8/759-768

Rosamund, B. (2000) *Theories of European integration*, London: Macmillan

Rosenau, J.N. and Czempiel, E.O. (eds) (1992) *Governance without government: order and change in world politics*, Cambridge: Cambridge University Press

RWI-*Mitteilungen* (1990) 1/2/1990

Sandholtz, W. and Stone Sweet, A. (1998) *European integration and supranational governance*, Oxford: Oxford University Press

Sandholtz, W. and Zysman, J. (1989) '1992: recasting the European bargain', *World Politics*, 42/01:95-128

Scharpf, F.W., Reissert, B. and Schnablel, F. (1976) *Politikverflechtung. Theorie und Empirie des kooperativen Foderalismus in der Bundesrepublik Deutschland*, Kronbert: Scriptor

Scheytt, O. (1993) 'Rechts- und Verwaltungshilfe in den neuen Bundesländern am Bespiel der Kommunalverwaltung', in Pitschas, R. (ed.) *Verwaltungsintegration in den neuen Bundesländern*, Berlin: Duncker und Humblot, pp.70-88

Schmidt, M.G. (1987) 'West Germany: the policy of the middle way', *Journal of Public Policy*, 7/2/135-177

Schmidt, M. (1992) 'Political consequences of German unification', *West European Politics*, 15/4/1-15

Shaw, K. (1993) 'The development of a new urban corporatism: the politics of urban regeneration in the north east of England', *Regional Studies*, 27/3/251 -259

Shaw, K., Fenwick, J. and Foreman, A. (1994) 'Compulsory Competitive Tendering for local government services: the experiences of local authorities in the North of England 1988-1992', *Public Administration*, 72/201-217

Silvia, S.J. (1997) 'German unification and emerging divisions within German employers' associations', *Comparative Politics*, 29/2/187-208

Singer, D.J. (1961) 'The level-of-analysis problem in international relations', in Knorr, K. and Verba, S. (eds) *The international system*, Princeton, New Jersey: Princeton University Press, pp.77-92

Sinnott, R. (1995) *Irish voters decide. Voting behaviour in elections and referendums since 1918*, Manchester: Manchester University Press

Smith, G. (1992) 'The nature of the unified German state', in Smith, G., Paterson, W., Merkl, P.H. and Padgett, S. (eds) *Developments in German politics*, London: Macmillan, pp.37-51

Smith, E. (1994), *The German economy*, London: Routledge

Stewart, J. and Davis, H. (1994) 'A new agenda for local governance', *Public Money and Management*, 14/4

Stewart, M. (1996) 'Urban Regeneration', in Leach, S., Davis, H. and Associates, *Enabling or disabling local government*, Buckingham: OUP, pp.144-57

Stoker, G. (1994) *Local governance in Britain*, Glasgow: Department of Government papers, University of Strathclyde

Stone Sweet, A. and Sandholtz, W. (1997) 'European integration and supranational governance', *Journal of European Public Policy*, 4/3

Sturm, R. (1992) 'Government at the centre', in Smith, G., Paterson, W.E., Merkl, P.H. and Padgett, S. (eds) *Developments in Germany politics*, London: Macmillan, pp.103-134

Sturm, R. (1992) 'The changing territorial balance', in Smith, G., Paterson, W.E., Merkl, P.H.

and Padgett, S. (eds) *Developments in German politics*, London: Macmillan, pp.119-134

Teasdale, A.L. (1993) 'The life and death of the Luxembourg Compromise', *Journal of Common Market Studies*, 31/4/567-579

Thomas, I.C. (1992) 'Additionality in the distribution of European regional development fund grants to local authorities', *Local Economy*, 6/4/292-310

Thompson, P. (1992) 'Public sector management in period of radical change: 1979-92', *Public Money and Management*, 12/3/33-41

ThLPlG (*Thüringer Landesplanungsgesetz*), 17 July 1991

ThVLep (Thüringer Verordnung über das Landesentwicklungsprogramm Thüringen), *Gesetz- und Verordnungsblatt für den Freistaat Thüringen*, 34, Dezember 1993

Timmins, G. (1998) 'Trade union responses to globalisation: the German case', paper presented to the Political Studies Association annual conference, Keele University, April 7-9

Tricker, R.I. (1984) *International corporate governance*, Englewood Cliffs, NJ: Prentice Hall

Wallace, H. (1993) 'European governance in turbulent times', *Journal of Common Market Studies*, 31/3/293-303

Wallace, H. (1996) 'The challenge of governance', in Wallace, H. and Wallace, W. (eds) *Policy-making in the European Union*, Oxford: Oxford University Press, pp.3-36

Walsh, J. (1992) 'The Republic of Ireland', in Townroe, P. and Martin, R. (eds) *Regional development in the 1990s: the British Isles in transition*, London: Jessica Kingsley Publishers

Walsh, J. (1993) *Models for local and regional development in Ireland*, Maynooth, Co. Kildare: St Patrick's College, Centre for Local and Regional Development

Walsh, J. (1995) 'Local Development theory and practice: recent experience in Ireland', paper presented to International seminar on marginal regions, St. Patrick's College Maynooth, July 23-25th

Wessels, W. (1992) 'Staat und (westeuropaische) Integration: Die Fusionthese', *Politische Vierteljahreschrift, Sonderheft Die Integration Europas*, pp.36-61

Williams, T. (1993) 'Local government role-reversal in the new contract culture', in Bennett, R.J. (ed.) *Local government in the new Europe*, London: Belhaven Press, pp.95-108

Wilks, S. and Wright, M. (1988) *Comparative government-industry relations*, Oxford: Clarendon

Wilson, D. and Game, C. (1998) *Local government in the United Kingdom*, London: Macmillan, 2nd edn

Wincott, D. (1993) 'The Treaty of Maastricht: an adequate "constitution" for the European Union?', *European Public Policy Institute (EPPI) Occasional Papers*, 93/6, University of Warwick

Wollmann, H. (1997) 'Between institutional transfer and legacies: local administrative transformation in Eastern Germany', in Grabher, G. and Stark, D. (eds) *Restructuring networks in post-socialism. Legacies, linkages and localities*, New York: Oxford University Press, pp.324-342

Yuill, D., Allen, K., Bachtler, J., Clement, K. and Wishlade, F (eds) (1995) *European Regional Incentives*, London: Bowker-Saur

Yuill, D., Bachtler, J. and Wishlade, F. (eds) (1996) *European Regional Incentives*, London: Bowker-Saur

Interviews (names have been withheld, since anonymity was a condition of all interviews)

Germany:

Interview 1: 01:04:97, IHK zu Erfurt, Friedrich-List-Straße 36, O-5010 Erfurt

Interview 2: 03:04:97, IHK zu Suhl, Auenstraße 27, 98529 Suhl

Interview 3: 08:04:97, Gemeinde- und Städtebund, Thüringen e.V. (Kommunalespitzenverbände), Richard-Breslau-Str.14, 99094 Erfurt

Interview 4: 09:04:97, PDS Fraktion, Thüringer Landtag, Arnstädter Str.51, 99096 Erfurt

Interview 5: 10:04:97, Technologie- und Gründerzentrum Ilmenau GmbH, Ehrenbergstraße 31, O-6300 Ilmenau 2

Interview 6: 10:04:97, Technologiezentrum Erfurt GmbH, Wilhelm-Wolff-Straße 6, O5080 Erfurt

Interview 7: 11:04:97, Entwicklungsgesellschaft, Südwest-Thüringen mbH, Am Bahnhof 3, 98529 Suhl

Interview 8: 11:04:97, Technologie- und Innovationspark Jena GmbH, Gerbergasse 18, O-6900 Jena

Interview 9: 14:04:97, Thüringer Ministerium für Wirtschaft und Infrastruktur, Abt. Wirtschaftspolitik, Johann-Sebastian-Bach-Str.1, 99096 Erfurt

Interview 10: 14:04:97, Bürgschaftsbank Thüringen (BBT), Arnstädter Str.28, 99096 Erfurt

Interview 11: 15:04:97, Thüringer Ministerium für Wirtschaft und Infrastruktur, Abt. Mittelstand und Wirtschaftsförderung, Johann-Sebastian-Bach-Strrr.1, 99096 Erfurt

Interview 12: 15:04:97, Thüringer Aufbaubank, Abt. Antragsbearbeitung GA, Am Bahnhof 3, 98529 Suhl

Interview 13: 16:04:97, IHK zu Gera, Feuerbachstraße 9, O-6500 Gera

Interview 14: 16:04:97, Thüringer Finanzministerium, Wilhelm-Wolf-Str.9, 99099 Erfurt

Interview 15: 17:04:97, Thüringer Landesregierung, Thüringer Staatskanzlei, Chef: StaSekr., Regierungsstr. 73, 99084 Erfurt

Interview 16: 17:04:97, Thüringer Innenministerium, Schillerstr.27, 99096 Erfurt

Interview 17: 21:04:97, Landratsamt, Ilm Kreis, Ritter Str. 14

Interview 18: 21:04:97, Thuringer Ministerium für Justiz und Europaangelegenheiten, Alfred-Hess Str. 8, 99094 Erfurt

Interview 19: 22:04:97, Thüringer Ministerium für Wissenschaft, Forschung und Kultur, Juri-Gagarin-Ring 158, 99084 Erfurt

Interview 20: 22:04:97, SPD Fraktion, Thüringer Landtag, Arnstädter Str.51, 99096 Erfurt

Interview 21: 24:04:97, CDU Fraktion, Thüringer Landtag, Arnstädter Str.51, 99096 Erfurt

Interview 22 and 23: 24:04:97, Forum WestThuringen e.V., EU- Modellprojekt zur Regionalentwicklung, Ev. Stift Reinhardsbrunn, 99894 Friedrichroda

Interview 24: 25:04:97, Thüringer Landkreistag e.V., Richard-Breslau-Str.13, 99094 Erfurt

Interview 25: 25:04:97, Thüringer Ministerium für Landwirtschaft, Naturschutz und Umwelt, Abt. Raumordnungsrecht, Europäische Raumordnung, Max-Reger-Str. 4-8, 99096 Erfurt

Interview 26: 28:04:97, Ministerium für Wirtschaft und Technik, Johann-Sebastian-Bach-Str.1, 99096 Erfurt

Interview 27: 28:04:97, Bund Umwelt und Naturstuck Deutschland (BUND), Landesverband Thuringen.

Ireland:

Interview 1: 22:08:96, EU Liaison Officer, Institute for Public Administration (IPA), University of Limerick, Limerick
Interview 2: 25:08:96, Chairperson, PAUL Partnership, University of Limerick, Limerick
Interview 3: 26:08:96, EU Liaison Officer, Shannon Development, Shannon, Co. Clare
Interview 4: 26:08:96, Senior Development Officer, Limerick Corporation, O'Connell Street, Limerick
Interview 5: 27:08:96, Chief Administrator, County Liaison Officer, Limerick County Council, O'Connell Street, Limerick
Interview 6: 27:08:96, Director, Centre for International Cooperation, Shannon Development, Shannon Airport, Co. Clare
Interview 7: 28:08:96, Strategic Planning Office, Shannon Development, Co. Clare
Interview 8: 29:08:96, Director, Mid-west Regional Authority, Main Street, Nenagh, Co. Tipperary
Interview 9: 30:08:96, Chief Executive Officer, Limerick County Enterprise Board, O'Connell Street, Limerick
Interview 10: 30:08:96, Assistant Chief Executive Officer, Limerick City Enterprise Board, O'Connell Street, Limerick
Interview 11: 01:09:96, Assistant Principal, Finance Division, Department of Finance, Dublin 1
Interview 12: 03:11:97, Community Development Officer, Ballyhoura Development Company Ltd, Kilfinane, Co. Limerick
Interviews 13, 14 and 15: 03:11:97, Local Development Liaison Team, (co-ordinators for County Strategy Groups), Department of Tourism, Recreation and Leisure, Interview A: Development Officer for south-west Ireland, Interview B: Development Officer for north-west Ireland, Interview C: Development Officer for border regions
Interview 16: 05:11:97, Principal Officer, Department of Enterprise and Employment, Oireachtas, Dublin 1
Interview 17: 10:11:97, Chief Executive, Area Development Management (ADM) Ltd, Dublin
Interview 18: 10:11:97, Development Consultant (Irish nominee to OECD local development monitoring committee), Liberty Hall, Eden Quay, Dublin 1
Interview 19: 10:11:97, Chief Executive, Irish Trade Union Trust, Liberty Hall, Eden Quay, Dublin 1
Interview 20: 12:11:97, Councillor, Limerick Corporation, Limerick
Interview 21: 13:11:97, Chair, Limerick County Strategy Group, Limerick
Interview 22: 13:11:97, Community Activist, Moyross Partners, Moyross, Limerick
Interview 23: 14:11:97, Community Development Officer, West Limerick Resources Ltd, Newcastlewest, Co. Limerick
Interview 24: 17:11:97, *FÁS* (The Training and Employment Authority), Mid-west Regional Headquarters, O'Connell Street, Limerick

Britain:

Interview 1: 11:10:96, Senior Academic, University of Liverpool (responsible for co-authoring the *Single Programming Document 1994-1999*), University of Liverpool
Interview 2: 10:07:97, General Manager, Croxteth Enterprise Training and Employment Centre Ltd (CENTEC), East Lancashire Road, Liverpool L10 5BE
Interview 3: 13:07:97, Managing director, Everton Development Trust, 98, Great Homer

Street, Liverpool L5 6LG

Interview 4: 15:07:97, Liverpool City Council Housing and Consumer Services, Directorate, Millenium House, 48-72 Victoria Street, Liverpool L1 6JN

Interview 5: 16:07:97, Senior Research and Information Officer, Merseyside Trade Union Community and Unemployed Resource Centre, 24, Hardman Street, Liverpool L1 9AX

Interview 6: 16:07:97, Director, Merseyside Skills Training Ltd, 40, Rodney Street, Liverpool L1 9AA

Interview 7: 17:07:97, Task Force Leader, Granby/Toxteth Task Force, 129b Lodge Lane, Toxteth, Liverpool L8 0QF

Interview 8: 21:07:97, Director, Merseyside Community Accounting Service, Fingerprint House, South Road, Liverpool 22

Interview 9: 21:07:97, Chair, Dingle 2000 Development Trust, 300 Park Road, Toxteth, Liverpool L8 4UE

Interview 10: 22:07:97, Director, Merseyside Development Foundation, Spinney House, Church Street, Liverpool L1 3AS

Interview 11: 23:07:97, Development Manager, Saint Mary's Area Regeneration Trust (SMART), 17, South Parade, Speke, Liverpool L24 2SE

Interview 12: 24:07:97, Director, Urban Strategy Associates, (responsible for co-authoring the *Single Programming Document 1994-1999*), Merseyside Network for Europe, Graphic House, 107, Duke Street, Liverpool L1 4JR

Interview 13: 24:07:97, Community Development and Equality Officer, Liverpool City Council Community Development and Equality Unit, Blackburn Chambers, Dale Street, Liverpool L69 2AJ

Written communication 14: 08:08:97, Assistant Director - Economic Development, Merseyside Development Corporation, Royal Liver Building, Pier Head, Liverpool

Interview 15: 13:08:97, Area Initiatives Co-ordinator, Central Policy Unit, Liverpool City Council, Millennium House, 48-72 Victoria Street, Liverpool L1 6JN

Interview 16: 13:08:97, Development and Environmental Services Directorate, Planning and Transportation Service, Liverpool City Council, Millennium House, Victoria Street, Liverpool, L1 6JF

Interview 17: 14:08:97, Programme Director, Mersey Common Purpose, c/o Royal Mail Liverpool, Copperas House, Liverpool L3 1AA

Interview 18: 14:08:97, Assistant Chief Executive, Central Policy Unit, Liverpool City Council, Municipal Buildings, Dale Street, Liverpool L69 2DH

Interview 19: 18:08:97, Government Office for Merseyside, Directorate for Regeneration, Transport and Planning, City Challenge, Task Force and Housing Team, Cunard Buildings, Water Street, Liverpool L3 1EG

Interview 20: 30:08:97, Director, Liverpool Housing Action Trust, Cunard Buildings, Water Street, Liverpool L3 1EG

Interview 21: 03:09:97, Government Office for Merseyside, Home Office Advisor, Cunard Buildings, Water Street, Liverpool L3 1EG

Interview 22: 11:09:97, Strategy and Policy Manager, Merseyside TEC Ltd, Dale Street, Liverpool

Interview 23: 11:09:97, Employment Links, 15/17 Seymour Street, Liverpool L3 5PE

Written communication 24: 27:03:98, English Partnerships, Dale Street, Liverpool

Index